P9-DFM-186

CONSULTATIVE SELLING™ ADVANCED SIXTH EDITION

Mack Hanan's Consultative Selling™ strategies are amplified in two complementary AMACOM books: *Competing on Value* by Mack Hanan and Peter Karp intensively examines the value basis for selling at high margins, and *Sales Shock!* by Mack Hanan explores the application of co-management strategy by consultatively trained sellers.

CONSULTATIVE SELLING™

Advanced Sixth Edition

The Hanan Formula for High-Margin Sales at High Levels

Mack Hanan

AMACOM
American Management Association
New York • Atlanta • Boston • Chicago • Kansas City • San Francisco • Washington, D.C.
Brussels • Mexico City • Tokyo • Toronto

Special discounts on bulk quantities of AMACOM books are available to corporations, professional associations, and other organizations. For details, contact Special Sales Department, AMACOM, an imprint of AMA Publications, a division of American Management Association, 1601 Broadway, New York, NY 10019. Tel.: 212-903-8316. Fax: 212-903-8083

Library of Congress Cataloging-in-Publication Data

Hanan, Mack.
Consultative selling : the Hanan formula for high-margin sales at high levels / Mack Hanan.—6th ed.
p. cm.
Includes bibliographical references and index.
ISBN 0-8144-0503-7
1. Selling. 2. Selling—Key accounts. I. Title.
HF5438.25.H345 1999
658.8'1 DC21 *99–17579*
CIP

Printing number

10 9 8 7 6 5 4 3

To my partners,
James Cribbin
and
Herman Heiser,

who set out with me to improve the profits of our clients, and who, along the way, enriched me with their knowledge, their skills in implementing it, and their discipline in refusing to settle for anything less than continuous improvement as our standard of performance

CONTENTS

Preface to the Advanced Sixth Edition

In my introduction to the first edition of this book in 1970, I wrote that "there is a whole new ball game in selling today." I gave the new ball game its name of Consultative Selling™. Some people found the name unpronounceable: was it con-sul′-ta-tive or con-sul-ta′-tive? Others found its strategies unconventional. Many more found the entire process unnecessary, saying that the old way of selling, which I called vending, was not "broke," and that it did not need fixing.

A few venturesome companies came forward and took a chance on Consultative Selling. Today, no company stands a chance without it.

Sales managers who used to ask, "Why do I have to sell in a way that improves my customers' profits?" have learned that it is the only way to have their own profits on sales improved in return.

Sales representatives who used to ask, "Why do I have to know my added value as a revenue-generator or cost-reducer for my customers?" have learned that the only way they can justify the costs they represent to their customers is to give them even more value.

Business managers who used to ask, "Why can't I continue to use a cost-plus pricing model?" have learned that cost-plus is discounted down to margin-minus by their customers and that the only way to get margins is to give new streams of cash flow whose value can be shared as a form of price.

Chief executives who used to ask me, "What do I need you

for?" have learned that they need me to equip their sales forces with an answer to that same question when it is asked by their own customers that will give them a compelling reason to buy.

In an era when customers control the way they want to be sold and, by doing so, have superseded their suppliers' pretensions of account control; when products and services, however new, are likely to enter their markets as instant commodities; when margins are the reward for improving a customer's profits rather than for improving your products or services; either you never leave home without new competitive advantages to bring to a customer or you stay in the car.

Today's account manager—no longer Arthur Miller's road warrior who is "out there with a suitcase and a smile"—carries improved profits, not products, in his bag. His is not the gift of gab but the greatest gift of all, being able to help a customer grow his business so the consultative seller's business can be grown by high-margin sales in return.

In 1970, creeping commoditization was already in hot pursuit of proprietary brands. Sales representatives were already sounding alike, on the way to becoming commodities themselves. Price lists were already bargaining chips. Customers were already looking for help from their suppliers to make their businesses more competitive, but not many of their suppliers were listening; they were preoccupied with protesting to customers why each supplier was better than the others. Venting had become nine-tenths of vending.

The pioneers who were the first to put their hands in mine had the market all to themselves for improving customer profits. Phil Smith partnered with Oscar Mayer around a value proposition that opened up the packaging of their new product portfolio to him in spite of duplicative competition with commodity processes and prices. Paula Brown partnered with United Technologies around a value proposition that opened up their telecommunications networks to her in spite of obsolescent technology and higher prices.

Bill Franklin and John Malone pushed and pulled their engineering-obsessed company into proposing business values instead of operating specifications. Tom Kearney missionizes Consultative Selling in one of the world's most formidable product-based corporations. Kevin Howell makes sales history by closing a $1.25 million agreement in the midst of a Consultative Selling training program where his account team and their customer manager are learning together how to partner in profit improvement. Danielle Buth goes on year after year being Salesperson of the Month by reducing her small-to-midsize manufacturing customers' costs and increasing their revenues a little more each time she walks in their doors.

The Smiths, Browns, Franklins, Malones, Kearneys, Howells, and Buths of the world of Consultative Selling keep their eyes on the eagle: their customers. They never see their competitors who keep their eyes on each other and mutter medieval mantras about "killing the competition." For every sign on the walls at Hewlett-Packard that read "Kill DEC," there was an equal and opposite sign at DEC that read "Kill H-P." Meanwhile, their customer mid-level operating managers, whose names they did not even know and whose problems and opportunities are enigmas wrapped in mysteries, were looking in vain for help to avoid being killed by their own competitors.

The power of Consultative Selling to compel customer awareness, positive attitude, and acceptance has been proven over and over again by companies as diverse in size, industry, and nationality as Asea Brown Boveri and Zytron.

Consultative Selling even works inadvertently when it is unwittingly practiced by accidental consultants.

Lew Platt is the very model of an accidental consultant. He has always been proud to tell customers about Hewlett-Packard, somewhat in the style of motion picture impresario Sam Goldwyn. When Goldwyn, who was the G in MGM, was asked how he was, he would say, "Enough about me. Let's talk about you. How did you like my last picture?"

Lew Platt talks about the challenges that face H-P and what H-P is doing about them because he thinks that it builds credibility with customers. Let's talk about you, he is apt to say. What do you think about the way H-P is reducing inventory? The way we're reducing receivables? The way we're reducing product design cycles? The way we're reducing manufacturing costs?

Platt envisions H-P as "a functional, generic commodity business" rather than as a vertical marketer adding value by customizing systems for individual customer needs. Platt prefers to leave that to H-P's value-added business partners, the third-party resellers that Platt calls VABs. He likes to say that when people challenge him with what twenty-five words he would use to describe H-P, he can do it in only two: measure and compute, without encumbering them further with a third word about their added value.

One day when Lew Platt was telling some customer people about H-P, he looked up to see that, as he put it, "Their eyes had glazed over." They were not being turned on by the standard H-P way of doing things. Platt made an intuitive decision. Instead of continuing to talk about H-P, he began to talk about what some of H-P's customers were doing to add value to their operations: Here's what one of them is doing to improve quality. Here's what another one is doing to increase productivity by managing assets better—lowering inventory levels, getting rid of unneeded factory floor space, and replacing people with automation. Here's what a third customer is doing to lower material costs. Here's how much they're being lowered.

It woke them up, Platt said.

Once they were awake, Platt could return to telling them about the standard H-P way of doing things—one of which was to talk about the challenges that faced H-P and what H-P was doing about them.

For a few moments Lew Platt, a vendor of information-based systems, had gone consultative. He would be the first to tell you that he had not meant to. Although he was startled by what he had done, he was, without knowing it, on safe ground. As far back as the 1960s, Tom Watson, Jr., was restructuring IBM so it could become its customers' profit-improving consultant. We make computers, Watson used to say. But we sell customer growth by applying them. In many cases, Watson was able to prove that IBM could grow its customers more cost-effectively than they were growing themselves. A dollar invested with IBM, he went around telling customers, can yield a greater rate of return than the same dollar invested in your own operations. Then he would set about to quantify it.

He was continually asked how long he thought he could go

on selling like that. His answer was, "Until our customers tell us that they have all the growth they need."

Tom Watson spent his time denying customers the right to remain stagnant or to be complacent in the face of decline. Others, the confirmed vendors, deny the need to change. They are, they claim, already adding value, calling high in their customer organizations and being prized for their knowledge of customer operations. But when they share common denominators, the truth comes out:

- "We call on a wide range of contacts within our customer base: purchasing agents, technical staffs, business managers, and others. We like to think that we have access to multiple contacts at multiple levels throughout our customers' organizations. But in a practical sense, we spend more time with the technical groups and end up selling to the purchasers."
- "Our customers are very well aware of our manufacturing costs and how they impact our product costs. We can justify price increases only if raw material costs increase or market conditions change. Regardless of any value-added services we try to associate with our products, our customers still know what the price of the product is, and that's all they will pay us for."
- "Our sales reps are making an average of 400 calls a year. That stretches them very thin. They know they're on a treadmill of discounting their values away, but they don't have the time to get off it and do anything else. If they try, our customers' purchasing agents do everything they can to discourage them, which includes threats to stop doing business."
- "The best return we have been able to get for our investment in value-added services is the right of first refusal, which doesn't cost our customers anything the way paying us a price premium would."

In one industry after another, value is no longer able to be recovered by price. As a result, price no longer reflects value. Any sales strategy that still relies on price is obsolescent, if not already obsolete, because it will never be able to earn back the value added by its products or services. Price has ceased to be a medium of exchange of one value for another; it has become a target for discounting back to its baseline of cost. As price is subject to devaluation, so is the worth of the technology that underlies the products and services and systems it represents.

If value is no longer to be found in the product, it must be looked for in the product's contribution to customer profits.

As a result, sales forces are being segmented into two groups. The old group, the *quals,* is still qualifying customers, trying to sell product and service qualities such as features and functions and believing that something called "total quality" can be charged for. The up and coming group, the *quants,* quantifies customer costs and revenues and sells the quantified values that come about from improving them. Only the quants are surviving because the only customers who can survive are quants themselves.

A qual seller is content, even proud, to use the term "solution selling" to describe a price-performance sale that contributes "40 percent less product loss and running a week with no out-of-spec product" for a bakery. He is comfortable speculating that these outcomes have meant "millions over a year period." A quant consultative seller calculates the savings in materials costs, energy, and labor, adds the incremental revenues gained by 40 percent more marketable product, and sells the total added value at a value-based price. The total added value, not the product and service system that has contributed to it, is the true "solution."

The 1970s and the 2000s are a world apart. Yet they are more similar than different in the ways that Consultative Selling works because price-performance selling and features-and-benefits selling are no more able to stand up against profit-improvement selling today than they were then. But one fact of life is very different. In the pre–globally competitive 1970s, you could still be a peacock because lots of other birds of a feather in your industry had the same high sales costs, low margins, and long selling cycles. Today, with their sales forces re-engineered to sell profits, not products, to "get to close" on the first call, and to sell at high margins to high-level customer decision makers, the survivors will use you as a feather duster.

PREFACE

If you want "best practices" in owning margins, you must use Mack Hanan's Consultative Selling™. Nothing else can sustain a competitive advantage for you in making profits from sales. The features and benefits of your products and services can no longer sustain margins. Your technology can no longer sustain margins. Your brand names can no longer sustain margins. Only the value of the outcomes that your products, services, or systems can add to customer operations has the power to sustain margins because your added values permit customers to sustain their own margins.

Mack Hanan's Consultative Selling™ is the delivery system for value. In return for improved customer outcomes, Consultative Selling delivers improved margins back to you.

- Instead of sitting across from a purchasing manager—or a manager of information services or telecommunications who has a purchasing role—consultative sellers sit side by side with a midlevel operating manager who runs a profit-centered line of business or a cost-centered business function.
- Instead of selling the added cost of a product, service, or system feature by feature and benefit by benefit on price and performance, consultative sellers sell the added value of an improved contribution to profits.
- Instead of asking for money, they offer money in the form of a return on their customer's investment.
- Instead of a spec sheet with line item prices, they specify the value they can add on a costs and benefits analysis of line item cost savings and revenue benefits.

- Instead of talking down their competitors, they talk up the enhanced competitive advantage a customer can seize over his own competitors.
- Instead of paying lip service to the concept of partnership, they create the new streams of cash flow that pay their entry fee into true customer partnerships.
- Instead of professing added value, they propose it in quantified, time-framed terms, measuring it milestone by milestone, selling it, being evaluated on it, and being paid for it.

No wonder Ann Gessen's internal memo to her manager at Metaphor Computer Systems is typical of every seller's first date with Consultative Selling:

> I presented my first Profit Improvement Proposal yesterday—a preliminary PIP to a senior VP of operations to get his feedback before formally presenting to him and the other senior managers next week. He went nuts! "This stuff is great. I can't believe it. Your company is finally doing something right by relating to me as a business manager. I came in here dreading that you were going to give me a standard price-performance pitch. What a relief!" At that moment, all I wanted to do was to kiss Mack Hanan.

If Ann Gessen had been a vendor instead of a consultative seller, her customer would never have been able to share the opportunity she represented to make his operation more competitive. Only his dread, not his profits, would have been realized. Ann would have presented him with a "discussion document" or a "concept presentation," two forms of confessions of ignorance about the relationship of her customer's business and her own. Or, even more demeaning, she would have tried to sell him a "study." Discounting is the name of the luxury tax she would have had to pay for the enjoyment of her ignorance.

Consultative Selling makes more money for you than vending because it generates new high-margin sales volume that vending would never have been able to bring in. These incremental flows of new cash dollars into your business have a greater net worth to you because they can be achieved at lower selling costs than vending.

By way of example, Figure P-1 shows the before-and-after Consultative Selling norms of an information technology product line according to five key performance indicators: average margin, length of sales cycle, average annual revenue per sales representative, average dollar value per sale, and revenue-to-investment ratio per sales representative.

Consultative Selling works equally well for public sector customers whose businesses are nonprofit or not-for-profit.

Vending ignorance ends and Consultative Selling wisdom begins when a sales representative puts his or her first Profit Improvement Proposal®—nicknamed PIP®—in front of a customer manager and they begin to sharpen up the PIP's problem or opportunity diagnosis, firm up its prescription for an optimal solution, and close the proposal by going upstairs for funds.

Consultative Selling's three strategies of positioning you as a value-adder, proposing the financial value you can add, and partnering with a customer manager to co-manage the realization of the value are designed to take you through the PIP cycle in minimal time with a maximum hit ratio. When you use PIPWARE® soft-

Figure P-1. Before/after norms for Consultative Selling.

Key Performance Indicator	*Before Consultative Selling*	*After Consultative Selling*
Average Margin	0.80	350.0
Sales Cycle	365 days	90 days
Average Annual Revenue per Sales Rep	$1.5M	$4.5M
Average $ Value per Sale	$300,000	$1.25M
Revenue: Investment Ratio per Sales Rep	5:1	100:1

ware*—the Profit Improvement Proposal on a Disc—the minimal time to complete a PIP is less than a minute. Each additional iteration takes another sixty seconds.

When you partner with a customer manager through the intermediary of a Profit Improvement Proposal in PIPWARE form, your proposal is no longer yours alone. On-line customer inputs make it "ours," a partnered business case in which the customer becomes preinvested in the joint creation of the solution as the first step to his or her investment in its funding. As a result, the hit ratio from PIPping is almost always one to one. Why not? With your help, a customer ends up proposing to himself.

Mosaix is a manager of customer telecommunications services. "For many years," its people say, "Mosaix won deals with superior technology. Our salespeople focused on selling product—great product, but product. We got into pricing wars. We claimed technological superiority. Competitors claimed feature superiority. Customers were confused. Our win rate declined to one win in ten bids."

Realization dawned: compete on value, by making positive contributions to reduce customer costs and improve revenues. Mosaix experimented with Consultative Selling. "The performance of our consultative sellers eclipsed the product sellers with eight high-margin wins out of every ten."

In addition to preserving margins and increasing the win rate, Consultative Selling proved to have another advantage for Mosaix. "It kept out competitors."

As Mosaix discovered, Consultative Selling restructures the entire vendor sales process:

- It redefines the product from representing a material or piece of equipment or a packaged good to represent *profits*.
- It removes price from representing the cost of products, services, or systems and repositions it as the *investment* required to realize an added value.

*Profit Improvement Proposal™, its acronym PIP™, and PIPWARE™ are registered trademarks of Mack Hanan. Evaluation copies of PIPWARE may be downloaded from the Internet Web site www.salestoolz.com.

- It redefines competition from representing a supplier's rivals to consisting of a customer's current *costs* or *sales revenue* targets.
- It repositions the supplier's core capability from creating improved products or services to creating *improved profits for customers.*
- It redefines the customer from a Box 3 techno-purchaser to a *Box 2 line of business or business function manager.*
- It redefines the seller from vendor to *consultant* and redefines the customer to a *client.*

Consultative Selling's critical success factor is its ability to free price from cost and competition by relating price to an investment. In this way, it can be compared to the value of new profits that are to be improved by the seller—in other words, it can be compared to its return instead of to its cost or performance.

By altering the unit of sale from a product to an improvement in profits, Consultative Selling changes the basis on which sales are made. All sales are the result of comparison. Vendor sales compare competitive products on the basis of their price and performance. Consultative sellers compare a customer's current operating performance with a future improvement. They differentiate themselves by selling the difference.

In this way, Consultative Selling enables account managers to pull off the "hat trick" of selling:

1. Compel customers to increase their use of the seller's products or services.
2. Obtain a higher margin for it.
3. Provide customers with a higher return than by discounting price.

At the same time, it prevents the "discounter's syndrome" shown in Figure P-2 from selling profitless volume.

Ever since the first consultative seller—inexpertly taught and excessively counseled by me—proposed the first PIP to the first customer manager to ever be partnered with a value proposition,

Figure P-2. Discounter's syndrome.

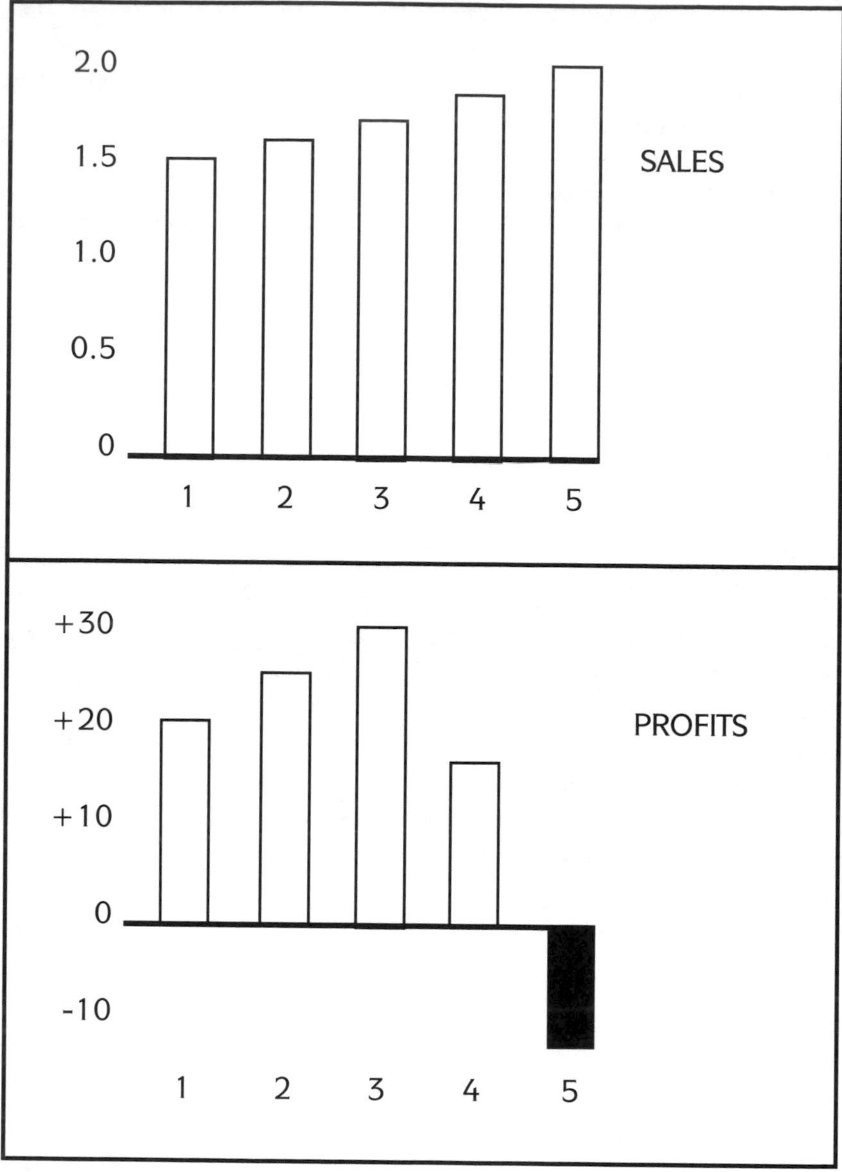

and unexpectedly closed it, two results have become commonplace. One is competitive. The other is cooperative.

- Consultative sellers overwhelmingly shut out vendors who are still cold-calling or reactively responding to requests for proposals, seeking coaches to get them around so-called technical buyers and other gatekeepers, asking for the right to conduct high-school grade "research" to learn a customer's needs, filling out blue sheets or green sheets or yellow sheets on customers' personal or professional proclivities, or chasing foxes. It is not surprising that vendors are downstairs trying to start up sales cycles while consultative sellers are upstairs closing them.
- Consultative sellers immediately capture customer managers who own the needs that compose their leads. Before they leave home, they know where they can add value, how much value they can add, how soon they can add it, and how sure their customers can be that they will realize it. Their positioning is based on owning their industry's standard of value for their applications. This is what gets them in the door upstairs and earns them the right to partner on the first call, which confers the right to propose a close at the same time.

In closing out their competitors and closing fast with their customers, consultative sellers have re-engineered the sales function.

- In support of Consultative Selling, their companies are reorganizing around their markets; building customer satisfaction into their products, services, and systems with concurrent customer inputs being made into R&D and manufacturing; and converting their sellers into customer co-managers whose selling has become the subset of their consulting.
- In parallel with Consultative Selling, their customers are re-engineering the way they buy, converting their purchasing managers into asset managers, demanding a return from them on the assets they acquire, and training them to present appropriations requests for funds in the form of business cases that are actually pro-forma Profit Improvement Proposals.

Initially conceived as a sales strategy, Consultative Selling has changed the terms and conditions of competition, the supplier relationships of customers, and the organization structures of the companies that practice it: not just in expected operations such as marketing support and customer input into R&D but also in the forms of virtual organizations with spun-out or outsourced sales forces and the two-tier sales force model with a top tier composed of consultative sellers dedicated to key account customers and a bottom tier of third-party resellers, telemarketers, and retailers.

Outsourcing, facility management and category management, networking, systems integration, and process re-engineering would all be impossible to propose, evaluate, or finance without Consultative Selling.

The consultative seller's added value lies in his or her ability to apply intellectual capital to an otherwise physical capital proposal and thereby add value to it. Physical capital is a commodity. Only the value added by intellectual capital is brandable, which means that it alone is capable of commanding margin. Intellectual capital is the intensely personal possession of each consultative seller. Ultimately, it is his or her differentiator. It allows one seller to prescribe a solution that returns $1.50 for each customer dollar invested while another seller can return only $1.00, with both of them using the same physical capital components.

As the contact point between suppliers and customers or providers and clients moves up the value chain from seller-buyer to co-manager–manager, consultative sellers alone, of all supplier people, possess the mindset and skillset necessary to oversee their mutual growth. They are their customers' and clients' natural growth partners. As a result, they are their own companies' natural developers of continuous new streams of profitable sales volume.

There are two ways to train and support a sales force to compete on the value they bring to customers.* The way that works is to train them in Mack Hanan's Consultative Selling. The other way, which does not work, is to do what Cap Gemini Sogeti did with its computer services sales force, once Europe's biggest.

*See Mack Hanan and Peter Karp, *Competing on Value* (New York: AMACOM, 1991).

Cap Gemini got off on the wrong foot by wanting its sales force to call high so as to reach out to its customers' chief executives and chief financial officers to discuss "broad management issues" that could be solved with computer systems. The company put its people through a training program that was misrepresented as "Consultative Selling." Cap's sales representatives were trained so ineffectively that they had to take their trainers along with them on sales calls. This compounded the problem since the trainers were also ineffectively trained. The salespeople ended up telling stories to their customers—first, trying to explain the trainers' presence by positioning them as consultants or assistant sales representatives; second, by winging it when it came to quantifying the value they claimed they could add to a customer's operations.

Customers responded with befuddlement and outrage. When pressured to put up their value or shut up, the Cap sales force made things even worse by vending their computer services—the thing they knew best but that CEOs and CFOs cared about least. Meanwhile, downstairs, their traditional data center customers had a fit over being bypassed. Upstairs and downstairs, it was lose-lose.

The Cap managers responsible for the fiasco tried to explain it by saying that "people resist change." With quotas to meet and very much aware of where their commissions came from, the Cap sales force showed less resistance to change than to ineffective training.

When you do it right, you get results like the AT&T consultative sellers who are trained to sell this way to a pharmaceuticals business manager: "If you keep running your order entry operation the way it is now, it is going to make a negative contribution to profits of about $8 million over the next five years from lost orders due to your failure to make same-day shipments. What if we can save a net $4.7 million of the $8 million in the next two years, with payback of your investment in year one? What if we can roll over some of that $4.7 million to go after the remaining $3.3 million? By funding its investment from a portion of your savings, you will not have to draw down your operating budget."

You may think that you are already doing this in your business, or at least something like it, some of the time if not all of the time, with some of your customers if not all of them. Unless you are trained in Mack Hanan's Consultative Selling, you are not.

As Consultative Selling advances into the next generation of business, consultative sellers are becoming the sole survivors of direct sales forces. Who needs vendors when all they do is discount price? Who can afford vendors when they add more to the cost of sales than they recover in margins? Who can justify vendors when customers publish requests for proposals on their Web sites or fax RFPs, circumventing human contact? And who will vendors call on as customers outsource and downsize their purchasing functions?

Figure P-3 shows the advance of Consultative Selling as vendor sales forces are retrained to sell consultatively or are replaced by third-party resellers, telemarketers, cataloguers, and Internetters. From now on, the rule is clear: Whenever a human being adds his or her cost of labor to the sales process, only Consultative Selling can add back the value to pay for it and still make a profit.

Consultative Selling was originated by Mack Hanan to be the ultimate expression of one-to-one marketing: one Profit Improvement Proposal for an improved profit contribution by one application to one operation of one customer manager by one sales representative. Each PIP is one of a kind. It is application-specific, operation-specific in a specific industry, and customer manager-specific in its enhancement of one of his key performance indicators. It is also sales rep–specific. It comes out of each rep's individual mindset. Except by chance, no one else is likely to diagnose a customer problem or opportunity in exactly the same way, prescribe exactly the same return on the same investment within the same time frame. As much as Consultative Selling is single-customer marketing, it is also single-rep selling.

Each consultative seller who is doing his job should be able to point to improvements in customer operations to which his specific PIPs have been contributing:

- Is cash flow increasing in volume or coming in faster in a customer's line of business that has been PIPped? How valuable is the increase? What is the value added by faster inflow?

Figure P-3. Advance of Consultative Selling.

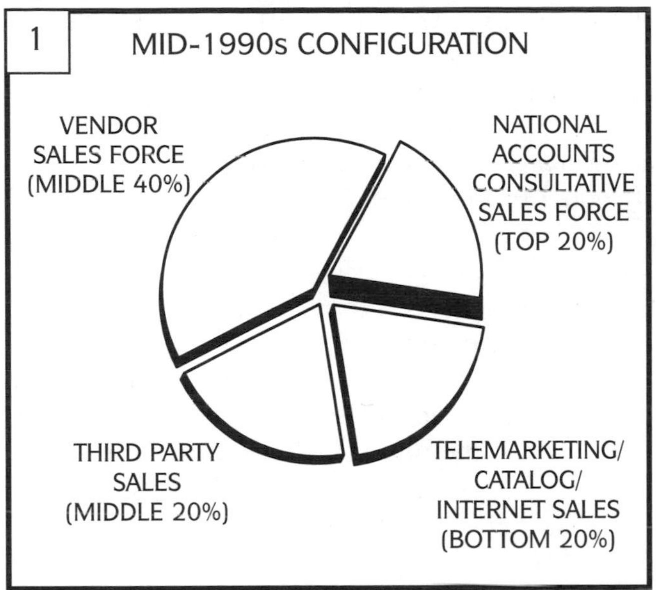

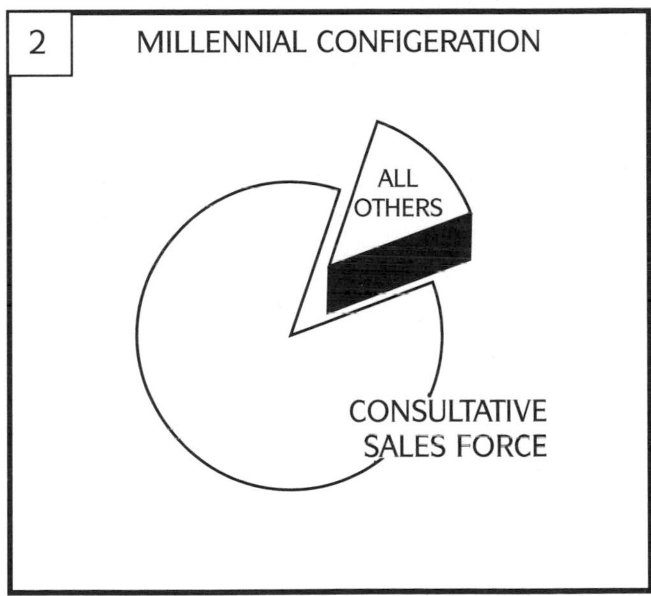

- Is working capital increasing? By how much? How soon after PIP implementation?
- Are receivables being collected faster? How valuable is the increase? By how much has the cost of collecting each dollar been reduced?
- Are same-day shipments increasing? By how many dollars' worth of goods? By how soon after PIP implementation?

In this way, Mack Hanan's Consultative Selling™ stands alone in contrast to the commoditization of products, services, and people in vendor selling. Suppliers and providers are branded by the differentiations of their PIPs. So are their customers. And so are their sales representatives and account managers, who become known by the contributions they make to the outcomes they affect.

Introduction

The Consultative Selling Mission

Consultative Selling is profit improvement selling. It is selling to high-level customer decision makers who are concerned with profit—indeed, who are responsible for it, measured by it, evaluated by it, and accountable for it. Consultative Selling is selling at high margins so that the profits you improve can be shared with you. High margins to high-level decision makers: This is the essence of Consultative Selling.

Since 1970, Consultative Selling has revolutionized key account sales. It has helped customer businesses grow and supplier businesses achieve new earnings along with them. Everywhere it is practiced, Consultative Selling replaces the traditional adversarial buyer-seller relationship with a win-win partnership in profit improvement. This is no mean feat. To accomplish it, Consultative Selling requires strategies that are totally divorced from vendor selling. It means that you stop selling products and services and start selling the impact they can make on customer businesses. Since this impact is primarily financial, selling consultatively means selling new profit dollars—not enhanced performance benefits or interactive systems, but the new profits they can add to each customer's bottom line.

Consultative Selling is selling a dollar advantage, not a product or process advantage. There is no way to compromise this mission. Anything less is vending.

Vending is discount selling, giving away value to make a sale. Discounting is taking on many forms that go far beyond price-cutting. Each of them represents another giveaway of margin that adds up to a hidden reduction in selling price:

- Multiyear contracts with built-in annual price cuts
- Zero inventory and just-in-time delivery
- Sharing in product development
- Free aftermarket services, such as training and maintenance
- Free upgrades
- Lease financing at below-market rates

Consultative Selling, on the other hand, is high-margin selling. Full margins are the proof of value. When they are discounted, that is proof that their value was not sold. The most frequent reasons are that it was not known or that it could not be proved.

Performance values put into a product or service are validated by the financial values a customer gets out of them. Performance values are important only insofar as they contribute to the value of a customer's operations—either they add the value of new or more profitable revenues or they help preserve that value by reducing or avoiding costs that would otherwise subtract from it.

Discounting denies that superior value has been put in. Or it denies that superior value can be taken out—or, if it can, that it can be documented. With each discounted sale, value is either denied or downgraded. It is obvious how this deprives the seller of a proper reward. Less apparent, perhaps, is how his customer is also deprived. Unless he can know in advance what value to expect, which means how much new profit he will earn and how soon he will earn it, he cannot plan to put it to work at once. He incurs opportunity cost even though he adds value, because he cannot maximize it. His own growth is impaired along with the growth of his supplier.

As long ago as the early 1970s, Bill Coors of the Adolph Coors Company said that "making the best beer we can make is no longer enough" of a value on which to base a premium price. Making the customer best in some way or other would be necessary to maintain the margins that were once easily justified by product quality alone. In 1977 a company named Vydcc was finding it increasingly difficult to cost-justify its high-quality, high-priced information systems when competing against the decreasing costs of competitive systems. Its managers realized too late that the justification of a premium price could no longer be attributed to hardware performance. "Future hardware will all look alike," they admitted after the fact. "The greatest values will be in training, software, and system support. You will be able to almost give away the hardware."

COMPARING CONSULTATIVE SELLING TO VENDING

Vendors sell price-performance benefits to purchasing agents. Consultative sales representatives sell up. They form partnerships with business function managers whose processes they improve. They also partner with line-of-business managers whose sales they improve. These are their first levels of partnership. At the second level, they partner with purchasing, forming a relationship that permits both partners to work with function managers and line managers in a triad of mutual interests. This is the consultative uniqueness. No vendor using allegedly "professional selling skills" can replicate it.

Vendors have many adversaries, both customers and competitors. Consultative sellers have partners. This relationship is bedrock. Consultative sales representative Richard Ricca puts it this way:

> Your unique Consultative Selling has helped me earn the President's Award twice. This is an unprecedented achievement in the history of my company. To quantify that, it represents thousands of bonus dollars plus a European vacation for two. I know I will take my wife. But my customer partner deserves it more.

Vendors bid in a crowd, reacting to requests for proposal. Consultative sellers take the initiative and seek out profit opportunities for their customers. When they propose, there are no crowds.

Vendors use their product catalogs as their sales database. Consultative sellers use databases of facts and figures about their customers' operations as their source of knowledge about what to sell, how, and to whom.

Vendors are only as good as their last price. Consultative sellers are as good as their last improvement in customer profit and the continuity they have built into it so that the next opportunity, and the next, are implicit to the customer.

Vendors spend their sales lives trying to be accepted as an alternative supplier of products. Consultative sellers gain acceptance as exclusive partners in creating new profits. Vendors can be terminated by a small difference in price. To dislodge a consultant requires proof of a significant difference in profits and a deteriorated partnership.

By definition, all vendors who sell similar products or services are alternatives to each other. Each is differentiated only by price. Using the same type of plea bargain to "earn the right to propose" above the purchasing level, vendors make commoditized sales pitches about the commodities they sell that end up, to no surprise, with commoditized discount schedules. Some vendors even attach their discount schedules to their bids just in case any doubt remains about their commodity status. No wonder they appear to be interchangeable, substitutable, and replicable, one for another. Whether or not there is actually an oversupply in their industries, they can often make it seem that way by the steady state of sameness they convey.

For these reasons, no vendor can compete with a properly trained consultative sales representative. Even retrofitted vendors cannot stay in the game if they have been given only the cosmetics of consultative positioning without a solid foundation in the economics of customer operations and the financial savvy to make a positive change in them.

When they try to pass as consultants, cosmeticized vendors

are blown away not by their competitors but by their customers. It may take the customer a while after a sale to find out whether a vendor's product works. But the customer knows even before the sale whether a consultant's proposed profit is really going to be forthcoming and whether his proposal is based on accurate knowledge or guesswork.

The differences between vending and Consultative Selling are significant. They are differences of 180 degrees. Their languages are different. Their mindsets are different. Their definitions of product, price, performance, customer—yes, even of selling—are different, as Figure I-1 shows. The main difference is in their ability to produce profits on sales.

Consultative Selling takes a position about the sales process. It says that there are two ways to sell. One is the way of the outsider, which is the way that most suppliers approach their customers. The outsider's gatekeeper into a customer's business is his purchasing function. At the gate, vendors who hope to sell high come face to face with gatekeepers who want to buy low. This is where sales cycles are born, costs of sale begin to accumulate, and margins are sacrificed to "move the iron." For every so-called coach, champion, or foxy politicizer who is cultivated at the gate, a supplier's cost of sale is being extended, his sales cycle stretched thin, and his eventual discount deepened. Meanwhile, consultative sellers beyond the gate are extending customer budgets, stretching customer cash flow, and deepening their eventual profits. In the same customer worlds, these two strategies go on every day.

What separates them? They live by different rules:

- Vendor suppliers sell computers because they make them. Consultative sellers may make computers, but they sell the value they add by reducing a customer's downtime.
- Vendor suppliers sell packaging because they make it. Consultative sellers may make packaging products, but they sell the value they add by increasing customer revenues and reducing shipping costs.
- Vendor suppliers sell wireless telephone systems because they make them. Consultative sellers may make wireless

Figure I-1. Consultative Selling vs. vending.

Consultative Selling	*Vending*
The seller supplies profit as his product.	The seller supplies product.
The seller offers a return on the customer's investment.	The seller charges a price.
The seller uses a Profit Improvement Proposal.	The seller uses an order form.
The seller quantifies the benefits from his customer's investment.	The seller attempts to justify his cost.
The seller attaches his investment to the customer's return.	The seller attaches his price to his product.
The seller helps his customer compete against the customer's competitors.	The seller competes against his own competitors.
The customer closes.	The seller tries to close.
The seller sells to a business manager.	The seller sells to a purchasing manager.
The seller features his customer's improved performance.	The seller features his product's performance.
The seller's product is improved customer profits.	The seller's product is equipment, a service, a process, or a system.
The seller sells to a dedicated industry and to dedicated customers within it.	The seller sells to a dedicated territory.

telephone systems, but they sell the value they add to it by allocating manufacturing labor more cost-effectively.

No matter what vendor suppliers make, they sell it.

No matter what consultative sellers make, they sell the value it adds.

The essential differences between Consultative Selling and vending are made clear where value meets price at the point of sale:

- Vendors sell to buyers who want to minimize the prices they pay for operating assets. This requires vendors to sell against their competitors. Consultative sellers sell to operating managers who want to maximize the value they add to their assets. This allows consultative sellers to sell by comparing current customer outcomes to future outcomes that they propose to competitively advantage.
- Buyers want to reduce two types of direct costs: their costs of acquisition and costs of ownership. Operating managers want to reduce the opportunity costs of delay in making their operations more competitive. This is why buyers can wait for a lower price while operating managers cannot wait for an added value.
- Buyers want to help reduce their suppliers' internal operating costs and share in the gains through reduced prices. Customer operating managers want to reduce their own internal costs and are willing to share in the gains from improved outcomes. This is why buyers try to control supplier operations while customer managers bring in consultative sellers to help control their own operations.

MAKING CONSULTATIVE CHOICES

Selling offers practitioners three choices. If they make the right ones, they can maximize the earning power of their products and services. Before that can happen, they must first realize that the choices are available to them and, second, that the answers that lead to nontraditional profits and revenues are, themselves, nontraditional answers.

1. *What do you want to be compared with?* All selling provokes comparison. The traditional comparison positions one supplier's product as better than another's. If you choose to make your customers compare your product features and benefits with those of a competitor, the customer will cancel out the similarities and devalue the differences by asking you to discount their worth. If the only difference is price, you will suffer fierce margin pressure.

On the other hand, you can choose another comparison. Instead of competing against the value of a rival supplier, you can compete against the current value that a customer is receiving from one of his businesses or business functions that you can affect. If it is a cost center, what is its current contribution to cost? If it is a profit center, what is its current contribution to profits? In either case, the customer's current performance is your competition. Can you give him a competitive advantage by helping him differentiate himself from his own competitors? This is what he tries to do in his own business. If you can help him, you can sell him.

When you choose to make a customer more competitive, you compete against his own rivals: his own costs that are unnecessarily high or his own revenues that are unnecessarily low.

2. *Where do you want to attach price?* Price is always "of something." The traditional object of price is a product or service. If you choose to attach your price to your product, the customer will compare it to the prices of competitive products. If your product is more similar than superior to them, or not sufficiently superior to make a difference, or is equal or inferior to its competitors, your price will be downgraded.

On the other hand, you can choose another attachment for price. Instead of inviting comparison with competitive prices, you can position your price as an investment and attach it to the customer's return. When the customer compares the return against the investment required to achieve it, the rate of return compares the productivity of investing with you against the rate of return from other incremental investments he or she is making all the time. The customer's investment performance is your competition. As long as you equal his or her hurdle rate for incremental investments, you represent an acceptable deal.

When you choose to make a customer more money, you become a supplier of funds instead of a disbursement. Your price, now no longer a cost but a returnable investment, can be directly compared against the return, and is therefore freed from comparison with competitive product prices. Instead of having your price reduced, the customer may increase the investment if it will disproportionately increase the return.

3. *Who do you want to make the decision?* There are two kinds of customer decision makers. One is a purchasing manager who buys a product's price-performance. The other is a business manager who operates a cost center or profit center and who does not buy at all. Instead, he sells proposals to add value to the business line or function he manages, requesting funds from top managers to improve his contribution to profits.

The traditional buyer is a cost-controller. If you choose to confront him as your decision maker, he will faithfully negotiate away your margins in order to lower "the cost of goods bought." That is his job. Your relationship will be win-lose and you will lose more than you win.

On the other hand, you can choose to partner with managers who will act as your "economic sellers" inside their businesses, promoting your proposals to improve their contributions to profits. They compete for access to funds against all other managers; if they do not get funds, their operations cannot grow, nor can they grow along with them. They will sell for you—actually, they will be selling for themselves, with your help—if you can add to the value of their proposals by allowing them to promise a greater return, a faster return, or a surer return.

If you make the three right choices, you will be in position to compare your value against a customer's current value, attach your price in the form of an investment to your value, and partner with a business manager who will sell your value. You will be selling like a consultant.

No vendor sales force can stand up to a competitor who sells consultatively. The computer industry discovered that when it tried to vend against IBM. A decade later, IBM made the same discovery when some of its business units, exhilarated by their technology, lapsed into vending. They had to discount by up to 50 percent until they could reaffirm their mission to sell improved profits instead of improved boxes. AT&T discovered the power of Consultative Selling when it was forced to become competitive against MCI and Sprint. R. J. Reynolds made the same discovery when Philip Morris trained its entire cigarette sales force in Consultative Selling and reversed Reynolds's historic role of category leader within a single year. At the other end of the size spectrum, the fledgling home health care industry discovered the power of Consultative Selling when Jim Sweeney used it to make his Home Health Care of America—later known as Caremark—the fastest growing business of the 1980s.

APPLYING THE CONSULTATIVE SELLING PROCESS

Figure I-2 shows the four-part Consultative Selling process:*

1. It starts with a value database on the values you normally add to customer operations. Your normal values-added—your "norms"—are derived from the value database.
2. By comparing customer revenues and costs against your norms, a lead database is automatically created. A lead opportunity exists wherever your norms offer a competitive advantage over a customer's current performance.
3. Proposable leads flow into closable proposals. The outcomes from each closed proposal are fed back into the value database to fertilize your norms.

*Fast-Value Calculator(TM), Fast-Lead Targeter(TM), Fast-Close Proposer(TM), and Fast-Penetration Planner(TM) are modules of Mack Hanan's Consultative Selling Expert-Xystem(TM).

Figure I-2. Consultative Selling work flow.

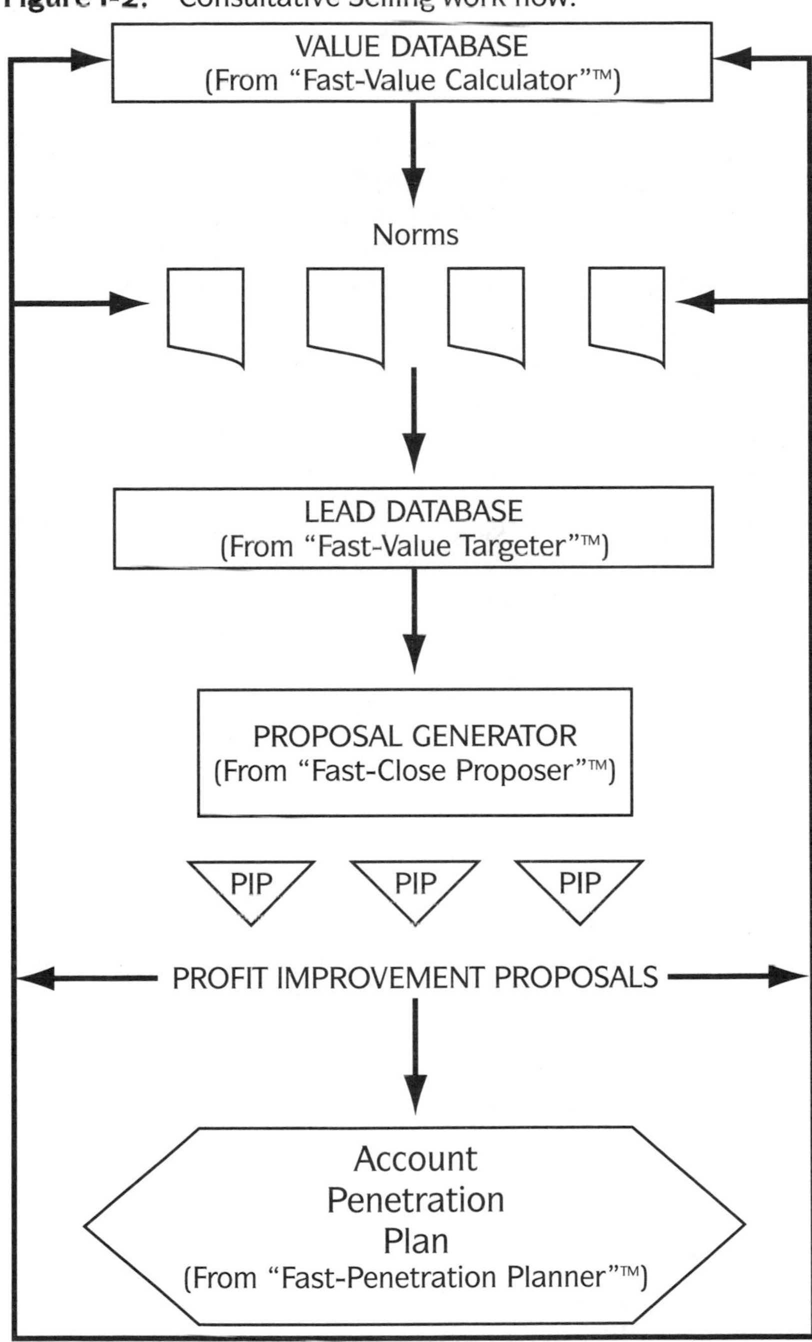

4. The process culminates with a partnered penetration plan that locks in your consultative partnership and locks out competition.

For many suppliers, such as manufacturers of components and subsystems to original equipment manufacturers (OEMs), Consultative Selling is their saving grace. Without it, they become vendors by default as they stand by helplessly and watch their products disappear—and their margins along with them—inside their OEM customers' equipment.

"We are such a small part of the end product," they lament. "The user never sees us. Unless something goes wrong, he never knows we're there." Or "There must be hundreds of suppliers they could buy from instead of us. If we try to raise our price, we're gone."

Honeywell Control Systems once said these same things. Then, applying Consultative Selling strategies, Honeywell has begun to quantify the added values they can bring. They have come up with a checklist of dollar-valuable benefits for their OEM customers, each one of which can form the basis for high-margin sales:

Revenue Improvers

1. Faster new product start-up time
2. Improved product yield
3. Improved quality
4. Assured production scheduling

Cost Savers

1. Reduced installation time
2. Reduced maintenance time
3. Reduced labor
4. Reduced process downtime

Honeywell has also prepared a checklist of added values that can be offered by OEMs to their own customers as a result of the contributions made by Honeywell's controls:

Revenue Improvers

1. Product uniformity
2. Same-day order fulfillment
3. Longer term warranty
4. Reduced downtime

Cost Savers

1. Reduced energy costs
2. Reduced manufacturing cycle costs
3. Reduced environmental penalties
4. Reduced costs of scrap and rework

Honeywell's controls still remain unseen unless there is trouble. But Honeywell's contributions to customer profits are now made immediately visible, before installation, on a PIPWARE cost-benefit analysis. By equipping its customers' sales forces with their own cost-benefit analyses and training them to sell consultatively, suppliers like Honeywell can help create cash flows that they would never otherwise be able to effect and can partner with their OEMs in sharing the benefits.

The same strategy can be employed with dealers, distributors, and third-party value-added resellers [VARs]. In this way, suppliers who are low on a value chain can extend their reach to end users to whom the value added is highest and whose gains are greatest.

CONDENSING THE SALES CYCLE

When you sell as a vendor, you invite the two-pronged costs of a drawn-out sales cycle. You incur the direct costs of selling over and over again until a sale is made or lost. Either way, you also incur opportunity cost. While you are waiting to close with one customer, you are delayed in starting up a new sales cycle with another. You pay this part of the price in lost opportunities or inflated costs for staff that could be smaller if it could be freed sooner to make the next sale.

Vendor sales cycles are unnecessarily prolonged because it is in the customer's interest to trade off time for the price cuts that inevitably accompany it. Consultative Selling makes time the customer's enemy. Delay works against the customer because it increases the opportunity cost of not improving profits day by day, week by week, and month by month. The longer the customer delays, the greater the cost. Once a revenue improvement or cost reduction is available, the customer must begin to flow it into operations or it is lost, either in whole or in part.

This internal pressure to improve profits provides customers with a strong incentive to close proposals. Each day's delay postpones payback of their investment and moves the eventual return on the investment at least one more day into the future. Because of the time value of money, each dollar they can obtain from working with you is worth more to them today than it will be worth tomorrow. If they have it today, they can invest it. By not having it until tomorrow, they sacrifice the value of both the principal and its interest.

By prolonging your sales cycle through vending, you sacrifice the contribution your own sales force can make to your profits. Assume that you currently have a twelve-month sales cycle, which is a common cycle in telecommunications and data processing system sales. Make the further assumption that each sales representative has an annual quota of $1.5 million and costs you $300,000 a year. If you can shorten the sales cycle by only one month through Consultative Selling, you can save $25,000 on the cost of each representative each year. The extra month of selling time will give you an incremental yearly gain of $125,000 in sales by each seller.

This adds up to a total improved contribution per representative of $150,000 a year. If ten representatives deliver the same incremental contribution, you will have achieved the equivalent contribution of one additional representative each year: $1.5 million that you will not have to spend a single dollar to realize. This virtual sales representative will be your most productive seller because he will generate only revenues, no costs.

Figure I-3 shows the Hewlett-Packard sales cycle, typical of

Figure I-3. Vendor sales cycle.

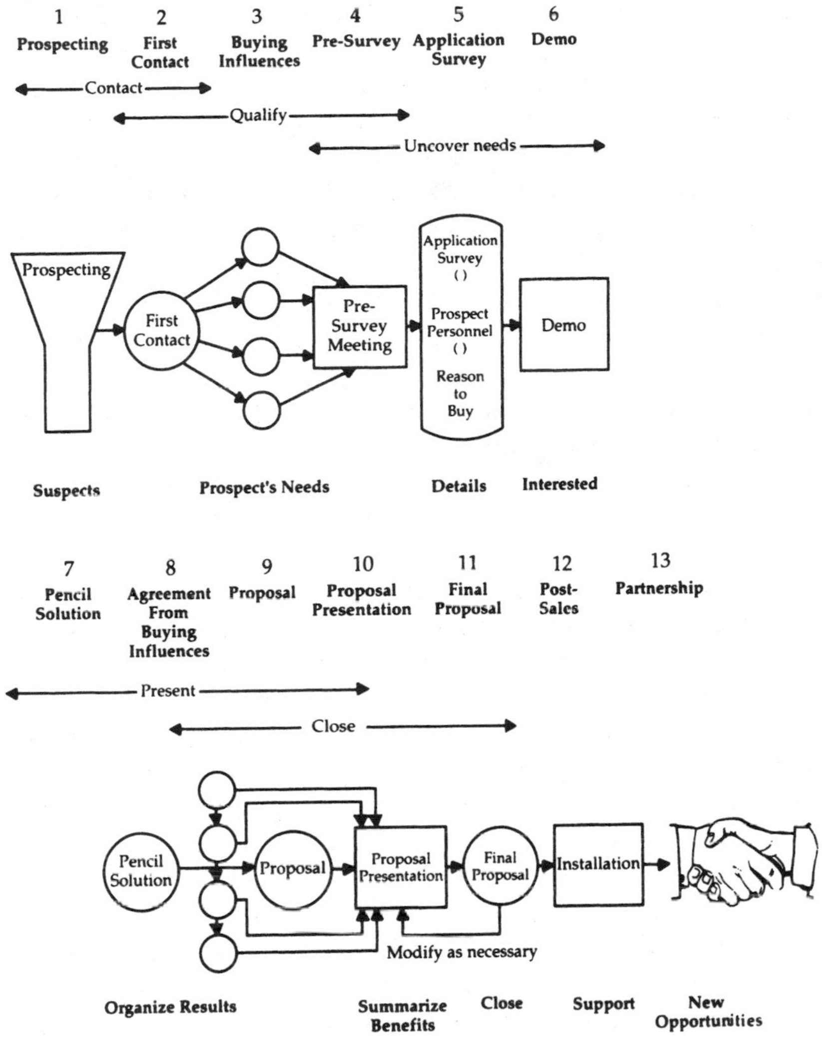

vendors. The close takes place, if at all, at the end of eleven successive steps.

The origin of the time costs and direct costs in the H-P type of sales cycle are shown in Figure I-4. Line A-B represents the increasing direct costs of sales from a prolonged sales. It also includes the opportunity costs of a delayed close that postpones the creation of a receivable. While these costs rise as the vendor sales

Figure I-4. Vendor sales cycle costs.

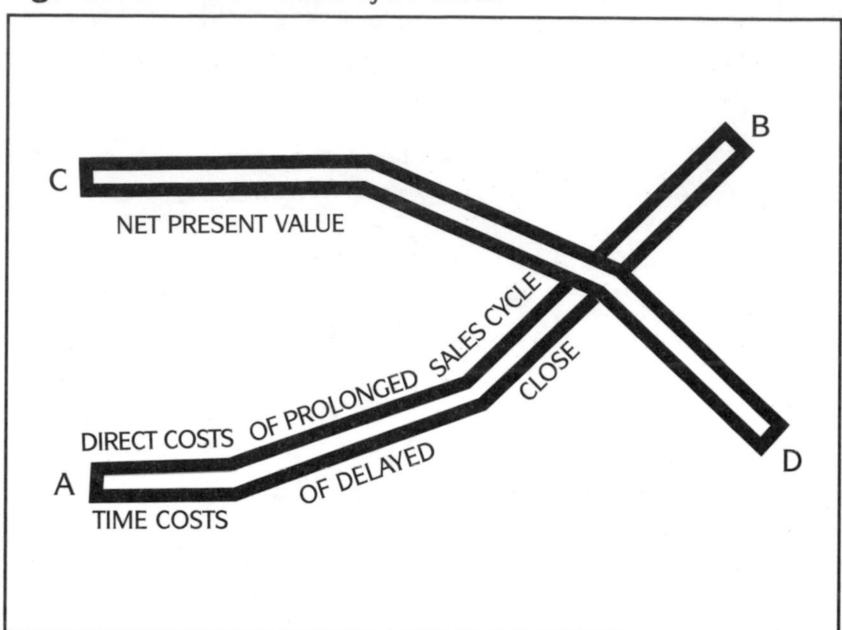

cycle goes on, line C-D shows how the net present value (NPV) of the vendor's technology decreases over time, making it worth less when the customer finally decides to buy. The customer is being cheated of the supplier's value as well, but he is able to compensate for some of his loss by paying a lower price.

Making Yourself the Number-One Asset

Management is "getting the most out of the least amount of assets." An asset is a cost, something that has been invested in with the expectation that it will produce a return that exceeds the investment. This is what every customer decision maker tries to decide every day: Which assets should I invest in to maximize my return? Consultative Selling is your best strategy to get your proposals on his list.

Customer managers are employers of assets. Their supervisors measure them on how profitably they employ their assets to produce sales. Some assets are in the form of cash. Other assets are in the form of cash yet to come, which is called receivables, and cash sunk, which is called inventory and plant and equipment. Inventory and equipment come from suppliers. Through Consultative Selling, you can find out how much of a return the customer is getting on the assets he has acquired from you in the past, and you can project how much he will be able to yield on new assets you are proposing.

The way the customer determines his return on the investments he makes when he buys from you is to divide the profits they contribute by the amount of the investment. This tells him whether he is going to come out with a net gain by doing business with you and, if he is, how much it is likely to be. It is up to you to tell him how you will make money for him. Will you help him increase his volume or his margins? Or will you help him reduce his operating costs? Or will you do both? If you can answer yes to any of these questions, you may be able to sell to him on the basis of your return instead of your cost.

Once you free yourself from being positioned as an added cost, the customer will be able to regard you as an adder of value—an asset whose investment pays back a profit. The price that you ask him to pay to invest in the assets you want to sell to him can now be freed from being attached to the asset itself and can become related to the customer's return. By relating your price to your value as a profit contributor instead of to the performance features of your asset or to the prices of your competitors' assets, your price will be seen as an investment in a profit-making asset.

The *V* word—*value*—is the key word in Consultative Selling. The consultative seller knows his value, sells his value, positions his value as his product, and prices its value. He takes pride in his value and is sure about his ability to deliver it to his customers. His value is not in providing a service. Instead, his service is providing his value.

In the same way that value has taken on enhanced meaning over Consultative Selling's first quarter-century—from meaning a low-priced bargain to high-margin benefits—the consultative seller is also undergoing continuous enhancement. He and she are increasingly becoming electronically enabled partners in customer profit improvement, always PIP-ready to propose at any time, from any place, without regard to proximity to customers in either space or time. Their space is cyberspace. Their time is real time. Both are without boundaries.

"Making calls" is a telesales* or digital function, unrelated to shoe leather. "Drive time" is disk drive time. "Feet on the street" are being replaced by PIPs on the fax or on the computer screen. With a laptop and a Consultative Selling ExpertXystem(TM) on a CD-ROM, a consultative seller in the Mack Hanan mode is a formidable market power.

PIPWARE permits each consultative seller to be a perpetual proposal machine, PIPping targets of opportunity as they arise as well as proposing according to plan. Databases containing norms for each application-specific solution can be accessed in microseconds, together with a data warehouse of PIP portfolios from which the norms are derived. Values that have not yet been included in the norm databases can be accessed by retrospective software, their norms calculated and leads targeted based on their deviation from the consultative seller's norms.

Mack Hanan's Consultative Selling makes "getting to close" predictable at a hit rate that is virtually one to one. There are two reasons why this is so: It compels buy-in on first proposal from customer managers who want to realize the full net present value (NPV) of a supplier's technology without incurring the opportunity cost of delay; and, just as it wins faster, it enables suppliers to lose faster and cut their losses as soon as they perceive, during first proposal, insufficient partnerability on the part of a customer. This saves them the ongoing costs of making one cut after another, only to end up with discounted margins that can make a sale, assuming it eventually takes place, profitless.

In these respects, not only is Mack Hanan's Consultative Selling the master quantifier of added values, it is also the unfailing qualifier of opportune and inopportune selling situations.

*The complete guide to applying Consultative Selling strategies to telesales is available in *Consultative TeleSelling(TM): The Hanan Formula for High-Margin Sales at High Levels by Telephone* by Mack Hanan (New York: The Greymatter Group Inc., 1999).

GRADUATING FROM VENDING INTO CONSULTING

Vending has "hit the wall." It has ceased being a viable way to sell at margin for four reasons:

1. Revenues no longer ensure profits. Volume sales that are profitless are not only commonplace, they have become the easiest sales to make.
2. Quality, so-called value-added services, and customer satisfaction cannot be charged extra for. They are standard entry fees into price competition, not ways of avoiding it. None of them can be priced. Nor can any of them be traded off against a price break.
3. Operating margin, often referred to as yield, has become the criterion of a "good sale" because it is the only reward that is bankable.
4. Technology cannot command margin anymore. It becomes replicated too easily and obsolescent too soon to provide a sustainable basis for differentiation.

Quality profits—which means profits that are enriched by the full, fat net present value of your technology—are obtainable only by the consistent turnover of quality Profit Improvement Proposals.

The essential differences between Consultative Selling and vending are made clear when value meets price at the point of sale.

Consultative sellers never hear the question, "What do you want to sell me?" They hear instead, "How will my operation look as a profit contributor after your solution is applied compared to how it looks today? How will it look against my major competitors? How will it look against your norms for best practices?" This is what value sounds like when it is put into play.

In this way, Mack Hanan's Consultative Selling stands alone in contrast to the commoditization of products, services, and people in vendor selling. Suppliers and providers are branded by the differentiation of their PIPs. So are their customers. And so are their sales representatives and account managers, who become known by the contributions they make to the outcomes that they affect.

The graduation to Consultative Selling from vending requires as much unlearning as new learning. Unlearning means no longer positioning a selling proposition to a hospital, for example, as "a reconfiguration of desktop terminals." Instead, it means repositioning the proposal as "an increased revenue inflow from faster, more accurate patient admissions." In Consultative Selling, the value proposition is always stated in customer terms: terms that specify and quantify the advantage to revenues or costs rather than descriptions of the operating specifications that can yield them. A proposition that is presented in the technical language of desktop terminals will be evaluated by a desktop terminal buyer. A consultative proposal, on the other hand, will be evaluated for its competitive advantage by the manager who benefits from being made more competitive.

The patient admissions manager looks at desktop terminals as enablers. What do they enable, he asks? Faster and greater cash flows, he answers. The IT buyer looks at the same terminals but asks a different question: How much do they cost per millions of transactions?

Your answer to the question, To whom do you propose?, is the key to what you sell and how you sell it. Do you sell products and services or do you sell their contributions to customer profits? Each answer will lead you to a different funder. Desktops come out of IT budgets. All computer vendors bid for their share. "We must get a bigger share of our customers' IT budgets," their mission statements say. "We deserve more of your business," their proposals say. Consultative proposals go into an operating manager's budget. "You deserve more revenues," they say. "What if we can help you improve the revenue contribution made by each patient you admit by this many dollars? What if we can help you admit this many more patients at this improved contribution?"

Fighting over a finite and often shrinking budget is vendor destiny. Vendors are budget depleters. Consultative sellers are budget extenders. They multiply a budget's funds by putting in more than they take out: by returning more than a customer manager invests with them. Customer managers fund consultative sellers in order to get greater yield out of the part of their budgets that they allocate to their PIPs. The effect on each customer manager is the equivalent of a larger budget than his or her top managers have appropriated. This positions consultative sellers as alternate funders, not alternate vendors.

PART I

CONSULTATIVE POSITIONING STRATEGIES

1

How to Become Consultative

In just three sentences you reveal whether you are a consultative sales representative.

In the first sentence, a consultant identifies a customer problem in financial terms—what the problem is costing the customer, or what the customer could be earning without the problem. If you mention your product or service at this point, you are vending and not consulting.

In the second sentence, a consultant quantifies a profit improvement solution to the problem. If you mention your product or service at this stage, you are vending and not consulting.

In the third sentence, a consultant takes a position as manager of a problem-solving project and accepts single-source responsibility for its performance. In the course of defining the project in terms of contribution to customer profit, you will be able to mention products and services for the first time.

If you are selling as a consultant, it is easy to predict what the fourth sentence must be. It will be a proposal of partnership with your customer's managers in applying your system to solve the customer's problem.

A consultant's problem-solving approach to selling requires helping customers improve their profits, not persuading them to purchase products and services. To solve a customer's problem, a consultant must first know the needs that underlie it. Only when a customer's needs are known can the expertise, hardware, and services that compose a system become useful components of their solutions. This is the difference between servicing a product and servicing a customer. It allows your relationships with customers to be consultative rather than the simple sell-and-bill relationship that characterizes traditional customer-supplier transactions at the vendor level.

The ideal positioning for a consultative seller is *customer profit improver.* You can achieve this position by affecting one of a customer's operating processes in two ways: reducing its contribution to cost or increasing its contribution to sales revenues. A consultative seller's primary identification with profit improvement rather than with products, equipment, services, or even systems themselves gives the sales approach an economic objective. It focuses attention on the ultimate end benefit of a sale, not its components or cost. This gives you the same profit-improvement positioning as your customer has. It also professionalizes your mission by expressing it in business management terms, not sales talk.

SELLING RETURN ON INVESTMENT

From a customer's point of view, a consultative sales representative is an integral part of every sale. Unlike product vendors, who are identified as a part of their own company and therefore do not go along with the sale of their product or service, consultative sellers are embedded in their systems and are "packaged" along with them. Although a piece of equipment may endure longer than the equipment vendor does, the consultative seller generally goes on making an important contribution to customer profit long after the original system has been installed. The seller's durability with a customer aptly defines the vital role a seller plays over and above the other elements of a consultative system.

A consultative sale is not the sale of products or equipment. Nor is it the gift of so-called "value-added services," which are actually cost-added services since their dollar value added to customer operations is almost always unknown and their cost is almost always unrecoverable by attempts to price them. A consultative sale is the sale of a positive return on the customer's investment: the economic impact of what is sold and not the components of the sale itself.

The most difficult challenge to consultative sellers is to stop selling products and start selling the added financial values that they can contribute to a customer's business. This requires more than merely substituting one vocabulary for another; it means substituting one mindset for another. Before this can be done, however, you must first undergo a desensitization to traditional product affiliations.

Most sales representatives metamorphose into consultants through a two-stage process. The first stage is to forsake performance benefit orientation for financial benefit orientation. This is akin to the classic features-versus-benefits conversion that all vendors undergo. It is the next order of magnitude. But in Consultative Selling, performance benefits are insufficient reasons for a customer to buy. Performance benefits describe what a product *is;* they are its operating specifications. Consultative Selling requires a seller to describe what a product *does;* these are its financial specifications. It is the end accomplishment of a product's performance benefits that must be sold.

The second stage in translating performance benefits to financial benefits is the calculation of their dollar values. These values, referred to as incremental profits, are the consultative seller's stock in trade.

Product desensitization starts with awareness that systems selling is a translated dialogue. All systems components, including the systems seller, must be translated into a customer value. Hanging out a laundry list of systems components is meaningless unless their individual contribution to the customer's incremental profit is quantified. Mentioning product, elaborating on the technological superiority of equipment, extolling its construction characteristics or other qualities—all are meaningless unless their incremental contribution to the system's capability for profit improvement is quantified.

Translating product performance benefits into incremental profit benefits is the way consultants must think. "What is the contribution to customer profit?" is their key question. They sensitize themselves to bottom-line thinking because they have learned that intermediate-line thinking fails to accomplish two key objectives. It fails to position their customers as clients, since a client is a bottom-line beneficiary. And it fails to position themselves as consultants, since a consultant is a supplier of bottom-line benefits.

Nothing will deposition a seller from a consultative stance faster or more certainly than lapsing back to preoccupation with product. It is the consultative seller's deadliest sin and an ever-present pitfall. At a customer's top tier, it can be fatal. The word *product* rather than *profit* lies poised from long habit on the tips of most vendors' tongues, ready to undo them. The best way to avoid slips of the tongue is to learn to use the new frame of reference in parallel with the old one and translate as you go. Whenever a product is mentioned, define it immediately in terms of its contribution to customer profit. This is what customers do; they listen for the numbers. Consultative sellers must become sensitive to this need and deliver the benefit that customers seek: quantification of the dollar values they will receive, not enumeration of the products or their performance specifications.

CONVERTING CUSTOMERS INTO CLIENTS

Preparation for Consultative Selling begins with identification of the customer accounts that are the best prospects for profit improvement. These accounts will be your principal source of profitable sales revenues. By concentrating on them, you will have your priority market segments pinpointed as major targets.

In every market, the familiar 80-20 rule will prevail: 80 percent of sales come from 20 percent of accounts. For consultative sellers, this means that only about 20 percent of all customers will contribute to profit heavily enough for them to become a consultative seller's clients. Yet these relatively few customers will contribute as much as 80 percent of your profitable sales.

The 80-20 proportion is a generality. In some markets, it will require somewhat more than 20 percent of all customers to supply 80 percent of your profitable volume; in others, far less than 20 percent may do it. In this way, the 80-20 rule averages out.

Since client accounts will be those in the 20 percent category, the core of every consultative business is obviously quite small. This is a sobering fact. Every key account is precious; to lose one is to lose lifeblood. You must become as important to every key customer as the customer is to you. Only when you become a customer's preferred profit improver can this happen. You must know more about the customer's processes than anyone else does. And you must be able to supply profit-improving strategies to those processes better than any other seller can.

Not all of your profitable sales volume will come from key accounts. If up to 80 percent of profit comes from 20 percent of accounts, then 20 percent of profit must come from the remaining 80 percent of accounts. This is good money; it need not be left on the table. But it will almost always be more expensive to earn because its sources are far less concentrated, their needs for individualized treatment may be considerably greater, and they may not offer the same opportunity for repeat, high-volume follow-on sales.

For these reasons, you must create a different strategy in serving nonkey accounts. In order to maximize profit, you should use a mix of two strategies. For the 20-percenters, sell as a consultant. For the 80-percenters, create standardized, ready-to-install, off-the-shelf systems; these can be cost-effectively sold or leased as commodities.

In order to consult with a customer operating manager on how he can improve his contribution to profits from an investment he makes with you—in something you may call your "solution"—you must counsel with him in his own terms. These are not the vendor's terms of product features and benefits or price and performance. They are, instead, the basic language of business management in its most elementary form: Business Management 101.

At the customer manager level, "business-ese" is the only language spoken. It is transaction talk, the language of money being transacted. It is charged with action verbs: funds being *invested*, investments being *returned*, cash *flowing*, payback *occurring*, profits *improving*, costs being *reduced*, revenues being *increased*, and market share being *gained*. But these are simply ways of expressing what is happening to the subjects of these verbs, the dollars themselves. Customer manager talk is money talk.

What do you have to know in order to "talk money" well enough to be conversant in "business-ese?" There are two requirements. One is to know how money is classified. The other is to know a customer's current money base of costs and revenues and how much you can affect them.

Classifications of Money

Money is classified into six major categories:

1. *Investment*—what a customer pays out.
2. *Return*—what he gets back on what he pays out. The rate of return is the ratio of return to the investment.
3. *Payback*—when he gets his investment back.
4. *Net profit*—what he makes on his investment, or his increment over and above payback.
5. *Cost*—an investment on which there is no return.
6. *Opportunity cost*—the profit he could have made on a different investment.

Customer Money Base

Consultants ask for incremental investments, money that is over and above the basic fixed-cost investments in the business as a whole. In return, they propose incremental profits. Incremental investments are discretionary. Customers choose among them on the basis of the best combination of muchness, soonness, and sureness that meets their needs.

Most consultative sellers propose incremental profit improvement. The rate of return is calculated only on the incremental investment in the proposal, which tends to make it exceedingly high. The customer's total investment in the business as a whole, or its total corporate return, is irrelevant. Consultative Selling takes place in the arena of a customer's microeconomics.

For that reason, the customer's balance sheet and income statement are neither causes nor effects of Consultative Selling. They will rarely, if ever, suggest leads. Equally rarely will they be impacted by a consultative seller's incremental improvement of any one business manager's contribution to profits. Yet, for the individual business manager whose profits are improved, the consultant's contribution can be a matter of life or death.

The consultant's micro impact makes a customer's annual report and 10-K interesting background reading but generally unproductive in targeting leads for Profit Improvement Proposals.

While it is true that all improved contributions to corporate profits flow to the corporate bottom line, they cannot be found there in annual or quarterly reports. In businesses of medium size on up, incremental profit improvements are subsumed in total profits. This makes annual or quarterly reports worthless as scorecards. For the same reason, they are also worth very little as lead targeters. Even when individual lines of business are broken out separately, the breakouts are almost always too large to be able to identify operation-specific cost problems or revenue opportunities for PIPping.

As background for operation-specific lead targeting, only the income statement offers anything of value. It shows whether profits are going up or down. The president's letter tells you the official reasons why. It may also indicate corporate priorities into which you can tie a PIP's business fit.

The income statement will also let you learn if total earnings are growing by giving you the information to calculate profit margins. If you divide annual net income by annual sales for the past three years, you can see if margins are shrinking even if sales volume has been rising. This will tell you that business is being bought rather than sold and that your profit improvement projects must be structured to help restore income.

If you divide the cost of goods sold by total sales, you may see additional evidence that profit improvement is needed if cost as a percent of sales has been rising over the past three years.

The ability to interpret an annual or quarterly report's data, more so than the data itself, is a key resource. When a customer announces an earnings gain of 15 percent, it is easy to see it as a growth company. But if you compare the rate of earnings growth to revenue growth, you may see that earnings are growing faster than revenues. If so, earnings are coming from cost management, especially cost-of-sales management, and not from sales. The challenge to grow the top line, which is the key performance indicator of a growth company, is going unmet.

If you want to predict how likely it is that top-line growth will increase in the short term, you can try to estimate the short-term growth potential of current sources of revenue. In the case of Hewlett-Packard, most of its growth revenues are from low-margin products like personal computers and printers that are subject to continuing price erosion. If H-P's market continues to shift to lower-priced models, both revenues and earnings growth will come under increasing pressure.

The data you need to qualify and quantify a customer's consultative needs cannot be found in reports. It is business-line–specific and business-function–specific and consists of two categories of data:

1. In a profit-centered line of business, what contributions to its revenues and earnings being made by its critical products and services can you affect? What is the gap between the current contribution of a product or service and the line manager's objective to increase it? Can you help him close the gap enough to make you a compelling partner?

2. In a cost-centered business function, what are the current contributions to the function's costs being made by its critical factors that you can affect? What is the gap between the current contribution of a factor and the function manager's objective to reduce it? Can you help him close the gap enough to make you a compelling partner?

When you know the answers to these questions, you will be ready for your first conversation in "business-ese" with a customer manager. Your objective will be to reposition both of you: your customer into a client and yourself into a consultant.

ZEROING IN ON CONSULTATIVE TARGETS

In order to be able to improve the profit contribution of a customer's business or business function, you must know three things:

1. The current values in the customer business or function that you can affect—the dollar values of a customer's current costs, current productivity levels, and current sales
2. The prospective dollar values that you can add
3. The net worth of your added dollar values when subtracted from the investment required to realize them

Knowing Current Customer Values

All customer operations are cost centers. Only one, the sales function, can also be a profit center if profits from sales exceed the cost of sales. Customers have a choice of three strategies for managing their operations. One is to avoid or reduce costs while maintaining productivity. Another is to increase productivity while maintaining, reducing, or even increasing costs. The third is to eliminate an operation altogether, either spinning it out as an independent profit center to remove it from the corporate books or outsourcing it.

- In order to consult with a *customer business manager,* you must be expert in the customer's markets. This means that you must have three kinds of smarts. You must be *process smart,* knowledgeable in the flow of the customer's products through their distribution processes and where their critical values are added. You must be *applications smart,* knowledgeable in how to apply your products and services to the customer's sales and distribution process so that revenues or margins can be increased. And you must be *validation smart,* knowledgeable in how to quantify your contribution.

"Knowing your customer's business" means having all three types of smarts. In the areas of your expertise, you must know how a customer's distribution process flows. You must be able to chart it from start to finish. You must know the 20 percent of its critical success factors that contribute up to 80 percent of its income and earnings. You must know the value of these revenues and profits. You must know your norms for the products and markets that account for the majority of profits and by how much the customer's earnings deviate from them. You must know how to bring the customer's profits closer to a norm if they are below it or keep them above it if the customer is doing better than the norm. You must know by how much you can do this and how soon. When you know all these things, then you can say that you know the customer's business as far as the products and markets you affect are concerned. Anything less is vendor selling.

- In order to consult with a *customer function manager,* you must be expert in his or her operation. This means that you must have three kinds of smarts. You must be *process smart,* knowledgeable in the flow of the customer's process and where the critical costs cluster. You must be *applications smart,* knowledgeable in how to apply your products and services to the customer's process so that costs can be reduced or productivity can be increased. And you must be *validation smart,* knowledgeable in how to quantify your contribution.

"Knowing your customer's business" means having all three types of smarts. In the areas of your expertise, you must know how a customer's process flows. You must be able to chart it from start to finish. You must know the 20 percent of its critical success factors that contribute up to 80 percent of its costs. You must know the value of these costs. You must know your norms for these operations and by how much the customer's costs deviate from them. You must know how to bring the customer's costs closer to a norm if they exceed it or keep them below it if the customer is doing better than the norm. You must know by how much you can do this and how soon. When you know all these things, then you can say that you know the customer's business as far as the operations you affect are concerned. Anything less is vendor selling.

Vendors like to say that they are value adders. Yet all they can usually quantify is the value of the cost they add when a customer buys from them. Rarely, if ever, do they know the value of the customer costs they reduce or the productivity they increase or the new revenues and profits they contribute to. Yet these are every supplier's most crucial values. Unless you know them, you are selling blind. You will only be as valuable as your most recent discount.

Even worse, you are selling costs, not improved profits, when you vend. If you do not know the value you add to a customer, you must sell what you know: your product's cost and its justification. As soon as you sell cost, you will come under the control of the customer's purchasing function, whose primary purpose is cost control. You will be imprisoned in vending.

In Consultative Selling terms, a *sale* is a transfer of values: A customer's resources—time, talent, and money—are transferred for the contribution to customer profits made by a supplier's products and services. In the same terms, a *sales call* must be an exchange of values as well. The customer must come away with new knowledge: He must be aware of the supplier's norms for profit contribution and how the current contributions of his operations compare with them. The supplier must come away with new knowledge as well, consisting of data on customer businesses or business functions whose profit contributions can be brought closer to the supplier's norms—in other words, he must come away with *leads.* Unless the supplier comes home with data on which to base a Profit Improvement Proposal, or with an approved proposal itself, he has not made a sales call. He has been socializing on company time.

All value is customer value. Adding value does not take place at the factory. It takes place in a customer's business. If you are going to add to a customer's value, you must first know what it is without your addition. This is the customer's "before." The new value will be the customer's "after." The difference between before and after is the *value added by your business.* In truth, it *is* your business. It is what you do and the reason why you are in business to do it.

For the purposes of Consultative Selling, the value you add must become the product you sell. You must become a value-added seller. This means that you must know your "product," the value that you represent.

In common with all products, value has its own specifications. These give it its performance capability, that is, what it is able to do inside a customer's business. Your performance capability is customer-dependent and will vary for each customer application. Each of your "products" will be unique to its customer. Except by chance, no two values will be the same. As a result, you will no longer be able to print a price list. As values differ customer by customer, moving up and down within the range that establishes your norms, the price you require in the form of a customer's investment to achieve each value will also differ.

Value has three specifications:

1. *It has "muchness":* You will be able to add a lot of value or only a little.
2. *It has "soonness":* You will be able to add value quickly or not for a while.
3. *It has "sureness":* You will be able to add value with a high degree of certainty or you will hedge.

A mix of "muchness," "soonness," and "sureness" forms the value benefits that you will be able to offer to each customer. You must be able to quantify each one. Otherwise, if all you can say is something like, "We are pretty sure that we can provide a lot of value to your operation very soon," you will be saying nothing. Once you have quantified your value, then you will be able to know your most important sales tool: what your added value is worth to your customers.

Knowing the Worth of Your Added Values

If you are able to offer your customer the added value of one dollar as the result of doing business with you, what are you really offering him? The dollar has three values. One is its money value. A dollar is a dollar. Another value is its time value. A dollar today is worth more than the same dollar will be worth tomorrow. Finally, the dollar has investment value. It can be invested at a rate of return that will multiply its original value several times.

Your value is worth what a customer can do with it—a function of how much he gets from you, when he gets it, and what he does with it. This is the ultimate worth of your dollar. Like value, dollars appreciate only inside a customer's business. In order to create new worth for a customer, you must therefore get into the customer's business—into his critical lines of business and critical business functions—and help him manage them. You cannot create worth without him. Nor can he achieve the added worth you offer without you. To magnify the worth of a business, you and your customers need each other. This congruence of need makes you partnerable.

As a consultant, the most important knowledge you can have about your business is *your value* to your customers; that is, how much you typically contribute to their profits and how long it typically requires to make your contribution.

When you know what your value is worth to a customer, you and your customer can tell what kind of consultant material you represent. If your value is the same as what the customer can obtain working alone without you, you are not consultant material. If your value is worth more than what the customer can obtain working alone or with any other supplier, you may be prime consultant material.

If you want to be a customer's consultant, you must offer him the prime value. Nobody must be able to offer him better value specifications—as much value or as soon or as sure. If you can achieve this position, your value will become the industry standard. Not only will you deliver the greatest value but it will be worth the most to your customers.

When that happens, you will have a new basis for your price. No longer will your price need to reflect cost or competitive market value. You will be able to relate your price to the worth of your value on a return-on-investment basis. The customer's added worth becomes his return. Your price becomes his investment. A premium return to the customer is all the justification you need to require a premium investment.

If you sell without knowing your value, everything else you know is rendered valueless for margin building. What price would you charge—or, in Consultative Selling terms, what investment would you require—for sixty two-way wireless radios installed on the manufacturing floor of an engine maker's plant? If you guess $150,000 because you do not know that the customer's first-year cost savings from reduced downtime is $1.5 million, what kind of a deal would you have made if you had given your product away while its value-to-price ratio was 10 to 1? You would have booked the sale, but you would have made yourself a philanthropist.

VALUE-BASING CUSTOMER INVESTMENT

Whatever a price is attached to is called the product. It is the thing sold; it is what the customer is asked to pay for. Vendors affix a price tag to hardware or software or a system that combines both of them. Consultative sellers eliminate the concept of price, replacing it with an investment to apply products, services, or systems at a profit to their customers. In this way, the investment is repaid by the value that comes out of it. The cost to the customer—the price—is zero.

Once price is eliminated, cost vanishes. So does fair market value set by competitive prices as a pricing standard. Value to the customer becomes the basis point for his investment, a way of doing business that Becton Dickinson has discovered about its hypodermic needles sold to hospitals. When purchasing agents were the customers, they complained that 10 cents was too much to pay for needles that they buy from competitors for 7 cents. Becton's vendor reflex was to wage a profitless price war. But a value analysis showed that accidental needlesticks cost a hospital an average $400 each in time and paperwork charges even if there were no complications or legal expenses.

What if Becton could reduce the costs contributed by needlesticks by more than the 3 cents difference in the price of needles offered by a competitor? What is Becton's value to the customer? What is a fair investment for a customer to make to acquire it—fair in proportion to the value of the return, not to the price of the hypodermic needles? Should Becton sell needles on price or on the value of needlestick prevention derived from advanced needle technology, training programs for hospital staff, and consultative expertise in safety program implementation?

Hewlett-Packard has made a similar discovery. In the same quarter that its earnings fell 46 percent because "pressure on gross margins prevented revenue growth from being translated into earnings"—in other words, price competition was eating up margins—an analysis of H-P's added value showed how much margin potential H-P was leaving on the table by vending its computer systems on price and performance:

- For one customer, each $100,000 paid to H-P contributed $1.2 million in reduced costs, for a value-to-price ratio of 12:1.
- For another customer, each $250,000 paid to H-P contributed $8.75 million in new revenues, for a value-to-price ratio of 35:1.

The alternative to knowing your value and selling it is discounting your price. Once you give away your margin to make a sale, you never get it back. Discounting is relentless in the way it destroys profits:

- If you start out with a 50 percent margin and you discount it by 10 percent, you must sell 25 percent more products in order to realize the same revenues.
- If you start out with a 35 percent margin, you must sell 40 percent more.
- If you start out with a 20 percent margin, you must sell 100 percent more.

Another way to look at it is if a product's costs remain steady at 91.9 percent of its $1.00 sales price, a 3 percent discount reduces profit from 8.1 percent to 5.1 percent—a 37 percent loss on the new price of 97 cents.

It is a myth that you can "make it up on volume." The cost of sales goes up with volume, nullifying increases in revenues. If a 3 percent discount produces an average 5 to 6 percent increase in volume, for example, it takes four cycles of 3 percent discounts to get a 20 percent increase in volume when unit costs first begin to fall. In other words, sales must increase by one-fifth just to get back to where you started.

The only way to avoid discounts is to sell your added value and not your product or service. In the same way that you cannot make it up on volume, you cannot get around it by other, less visible price offers such as sweetened payment terms, additional warranty coverage, or free training giveaways that are simply discounts in disguise.

NORMING YOUR VALUE

When you average your added values on an application-per-function–per-industry basis, you come out with your *norm* for your ability to add value to that function in that industry with that application: your *normal value.* A norm is the distillation of your consultative expertise in improving customer profits. Consultative sellers who sell from their norms are routinely able to say provocative things to their customers:

"According to our norms for the optimal layout for a print shop of your volume and type of production," 3M can say, "your current layout is depriving you of up to $1 million in profits every twelve months of operation."

"According to our norms for an optimal receivables collection system for food processors," AT&T can say, "you can improve the profit contribution of your current system by an average of $500,000 a year."

Norms are the consultative penetration tool. All consulting professionals work from norms, which represent their track record—their single most important possession and the foundation of their repute. When their norms are the industry standard, they can use them to issue a "norm challenge" against a customer's current norms as well as competitive norms. The challenge develops leads. Here is the standard of performance for this critical success factor in this business function or business line, it says. *How do you compare?* If my norms are better than yours, ask me *how* I can bring you closer.

IBM sales representatives walk along the manufacturing lines of pharmaceuticals makers and can say:

> Our model design for automating a process like yours can help you reduce up to $200,000 in labor. According to our norms, your manning is excessive by five work-

> ers. Your control process is also slower than our standard in spotting and alerting you to deviations from specification. This will be reflected in added costs for quality assurance, scrap, and downtime. You can avoid these costs by computerizing your product testing and quality assurance. The difference between our models in these areas and your operations can yield you up to three quarters of a million dollars in the first year.

Unless you know the norms that a customer manager uses to make decisions and address them head-on in your PIPs, you can never achieve a one-to-one acceptance ratio of PIPs proposed to PIPs closed. Airbus learned this lesson when it came to Bob Crandall, when he was CEO of American Airlines, to propose a purchase of its 600-passenger jet based on a lower cost per seat mile than the Boeing 747. Crandall never looked at the Airbus cost-benefit analysis. Because he rejected the criterion on which it was based, it was irrelevant whether or not its numbers added up. "Big planes pay off only when they fly full," he said. "People don't want to get into an airplane that has 600 people and go to a place where they have to stand in line for two hours to get through customs." As a result, he concluded that "the fact that it's cheaper to fly per seat doesn't make any difference. The real cost is how much it costs per passenger."

Airbus may turn out to be more accurate than Crandall in assessing the market for big planes. It makes no difference. Crandall may be wrong about cost per passenger being more important than cost per seat. It makes no difference. As long as Crandall's key performance norm is cost per passenger, that is where—and only where—he will look for a signal to buy.

Your norms announce what is special about you: You know how to improve the profits of certain types of business operations. You know the standard specifications of what their profit values can be for these business functions; indeed, you are probably the discoverer and maker of many of them. If a customer already exceeds your norms, you can help him maintain competitive superiority. If your norms are better than a customer's current performance, you can help bring the customer up to your standard values.

Your norms—not your products—must become your consultative stock in trade. You sell consultatively by superimposing them over the current norms of customer businesses. A customer's new product norm may be only a plan. It does not matter. The plan contains a pro forma financial projection of the business-to-be. This is its *as-if* norm: as if it were up and running. Your norm is an *if-then* model: *If* the customer adopts your solution, *then* the customer norm will more nearly approach your own. The customer will become improved.

At any given time, you can assess your competitive advantage as a consultative seller—in other words, the value of the net profits you normally contribute to your customers—by checking out your norms according to three criteria:

1. *Are they better than enough customers' current performance?* If so, you will have continued proposal opportunity.
2. *Are they better than your customers' industry average performance?* If so, you may have a competitive advantage over other consultative sellers to bring customers up past their industry average.
3. *Are they better than or as good as each customer industry's best practices?* If so, your norms are the industry standard of performance for all customers who want to achieve best practices.

Templating Proposable Leads

A consultative seller's database must be compartmentalized into three modules that he or she can scan left to right to target proposable leads:

Our Norm	**Industry Average Norm**	**Current Customer's Norm**

For the seller, Our Norm must be better than Industry Average Norm in order to be the norm leader. Our Norm must also be better than the Current Customer's Norm performance in order to have a proposal opportunity, either to improve a customer to the level of industry average or to bring him closer to "our norm."

Mack Hanan's Fast-Lead Targeter™ makes it easy to identify PIPpable opportunities by instantly comparing Our Norm against current customer performance for each operation to which a consultative seller has proven that he or she can add value.

The Fast-Lead Targeter enables a seller to discover at a glance the potential for a value proposition by asking just two questions:

- How does current customer product development cost compare to Our Norm? If our norm is lower, we have a lead.
- How does current customer same-day order fulfillment compare to Our Norm? If our norm is higher, we have a lead.

Fast leads give a consultative seller the vocabulary to speak in business-ese like this:

- Our Norm for average cost of recordkeeping of purchase orders, inventory reconciliation, and other related transactions in your product category is X dollars. Your cost is three times higher than our norm.
- Our Norm for average sales per square foot in your product category is X dollars. Your sales are five times lower than our norm.
- Our Norm for out-of-stock in your product category is X times per quarter. Your out-of-stock is six times greater than our norm.

Reverse-Valuing Past Profit Improvements

Figure 1-1 shows how to go back into the customer operations where you have installed your products, services, or systems and reverse-value the additions they have made to revenue generation or cost control. If you follow this process with a minimum of three customers, all where you have made the same application to the same operation in the same industry, you can average the re-

Figure 1-1. Reverse valuing. (From Mack Hanan's Fast-Value Calculator™.)

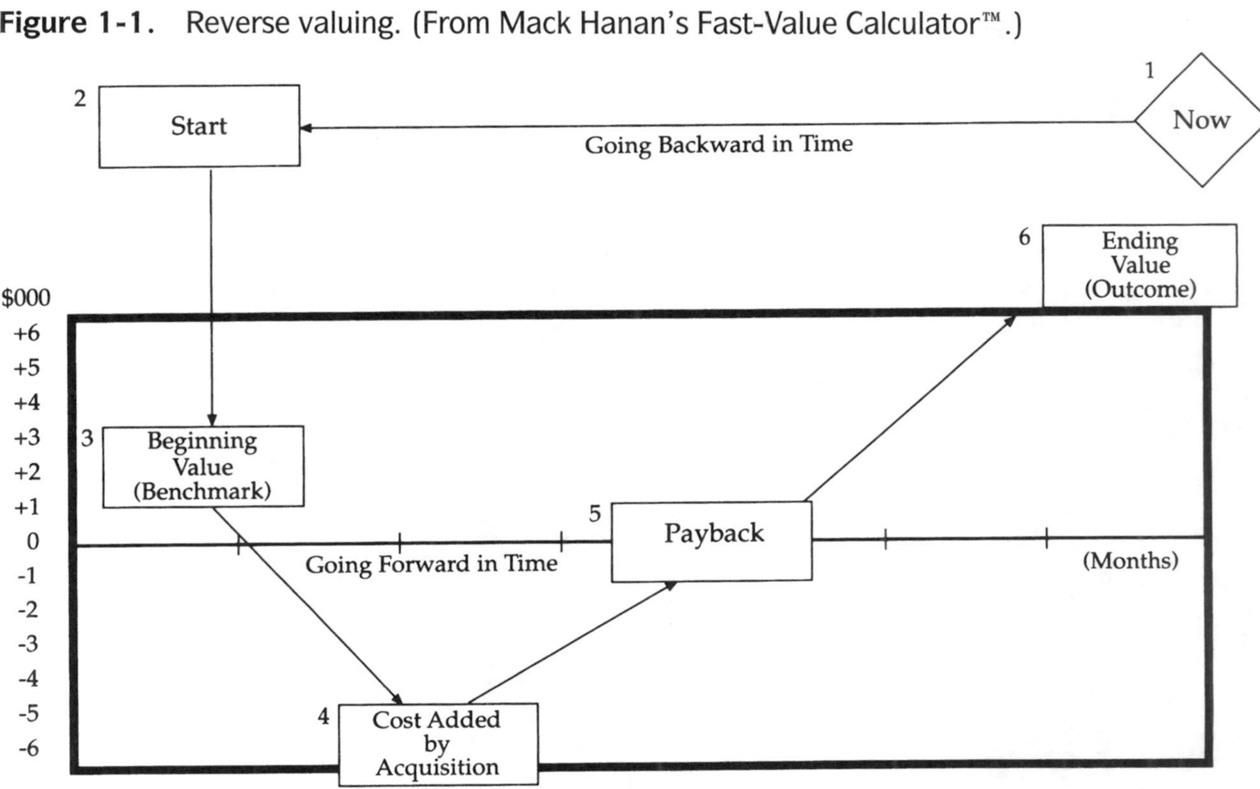

sults into a range of prenorms. Using them as templates, you can follow this four-step procedure to "get to proposal":

1. Assess your added value.
2. Target leads by applying your added-value norms to similar operations in the same industry.
3. Propose to add your normal value to managers of operations that need to remain competitive or to regain competitive advantage.
4. Close proposals based on the improved profits from your added value.

PIPping applies your norms to a customer manager's actual performance, highlighting their comparative values. Whenever a deviation between a manager's "actual" and your norm is favorable to your norm, a lead opportunity is automatically triggered.

Figures 1-2 and 1-3 show how the past values assessed by reverse-valuing are recorded in terms of increased revenue contributions or contributions to decreased costs.

Using norms, a consultative seller can get a handle on a customer's perception of the values that can be added by conducting challenging dialogs like these:

- "It takes you 3.0 hours to complete a design cycle. Our norm is 1.7. What is the value to you in costs saved and faster revenues for every 30 minutes we can bring you closer to our norm?"
- "It takes you 72 minutes to make a die changeover. Our norm is 46. What is the value to you in costs saved and faster revenues for every 10 minutes we can bring you closer to our norm?"
- "It takes you 3.6 years to introduce a new model. Our norm is 2.9. What is the value to you in costs saved and faster revenues for every 30 days we can bring you closer to our norm?"

Your norms are your value metrics. They say that there is a better way than the one the customer is currently practicing. The

Figure 1-2. Past value-added form for increased revenue contribution. (From Mack Hanan's Fast-Value Calculator™.)

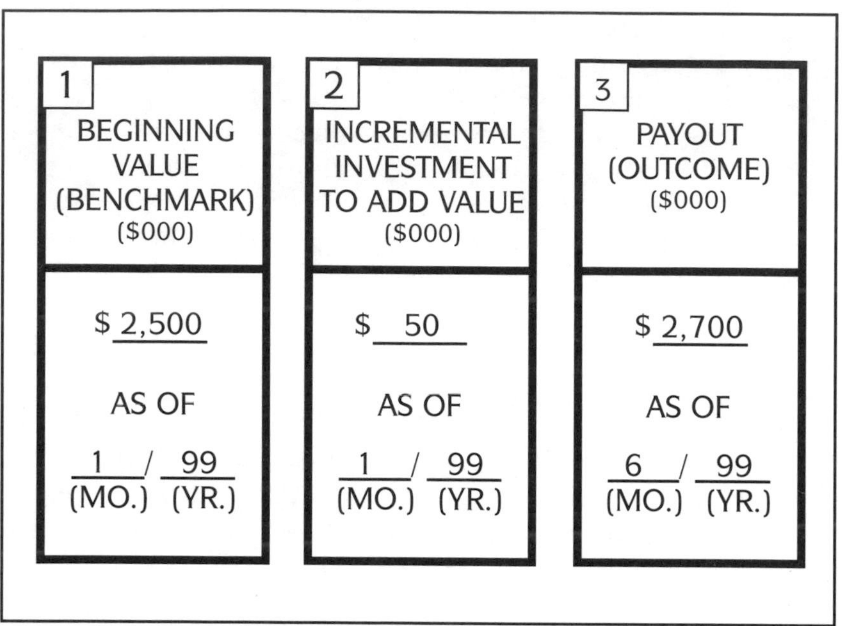

profit difference between the customer's way and your norm represents your added value. If you can enable a customer's new product, for example, to enter its market one month earlier than its plan, the dollar value of that month's earnings and the advance of one month in achieving payback of the product's funding represent your added value.

The first thing that you should propose to a customer is your norm for the customer's business or business function. "If your operation can more closely approach my norm," you can say, "some or all of the added value representing the difference between them can be yours."

What you do not ask is as important as what you do ask. You do not ask, "Do you want my product, service, or system?" Nor do you ask, "Do you want my solution?" or "Do you want to buy from me?" You need only ask whether the customer wants his operation to more closely approximate your norms. When you ask that question, you are proposing to sell in a consultative manner.

Figure 1-3. Past value-added form for decreased cost contribution. (From Mack Hanan's Fast-Value Calculator™.)

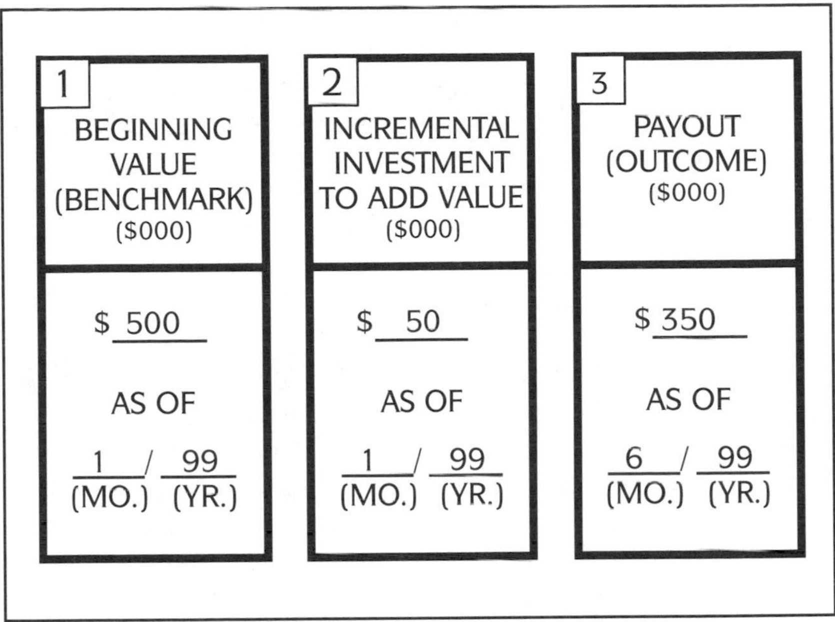

When the customer asks *how* he can make his operation come closer to your norm, he has begun to "buy" from you.

As soon as you know your normal benefit on an application-per-function or application-per-operation or per-process basis—they are all ways of saying the same thing—you can use it in two ways:

1. To target leads fast in customer operations whose current revenue performance is below the level of your norms or whose current cost performance is above them.
2. To get to proposal fast by presenting a preliminary benefit that can bring the customer's current performance closer to your norms.

You want to be able to say something like this to command a customer manager's attention:

> We are experienced in improving the contribution to profits made by your operation. Our norms show that managers who implement our solution can increase their revenue contribution or decrease their cost contribution by approximately *$x* within *y* period of time. How do these norms compare with your current performance? If performing closer to our norms can make you more competitive, what if we can work together the way we are proposing to achieve a $000 minimum improvement within the next 00 months?

Making Norms Industry-Specific

The norms you work with come into play as soon as you choose a category of performance you want to improve in a customer operation whose contribution to profits you believe you can bring closer to your normal performance. At that point, you compare the customer's current performance against your norms. If your norms are superior, you have a lead to prepare a Profit Improvement Proposal. Figure 1-4 shows a "subway map" of the lead targeting stations along the route to a PIP for reducing monthly scrap production in a telecommunications customer's manufacturing process.

A matrix for warehousing your norms on an industry-specific basis is shown in Figure 1-5. For each line of business or business function that you sell to, enter the major operations within it that you affect across the horizontal axis and your major applications that can improve their performance down the vertical axis. Where each application intersects each operation, the matrix will show your normal range of added value. Your norms that rank as a customer industry's best practices identify the categories in which you can be the "category killer"—the owner of the standard value of its outcome. Killer norms are your brands, your "product line" of high-margin earners in return for their high added value.

Norms that are not best practices identify your commodity applications. They earn you less and cost you more to sell because you must compete against someone else's category killers.

When a customer operating manager calls out, "Who owns

Figure 1-4. PIP process "subway map."

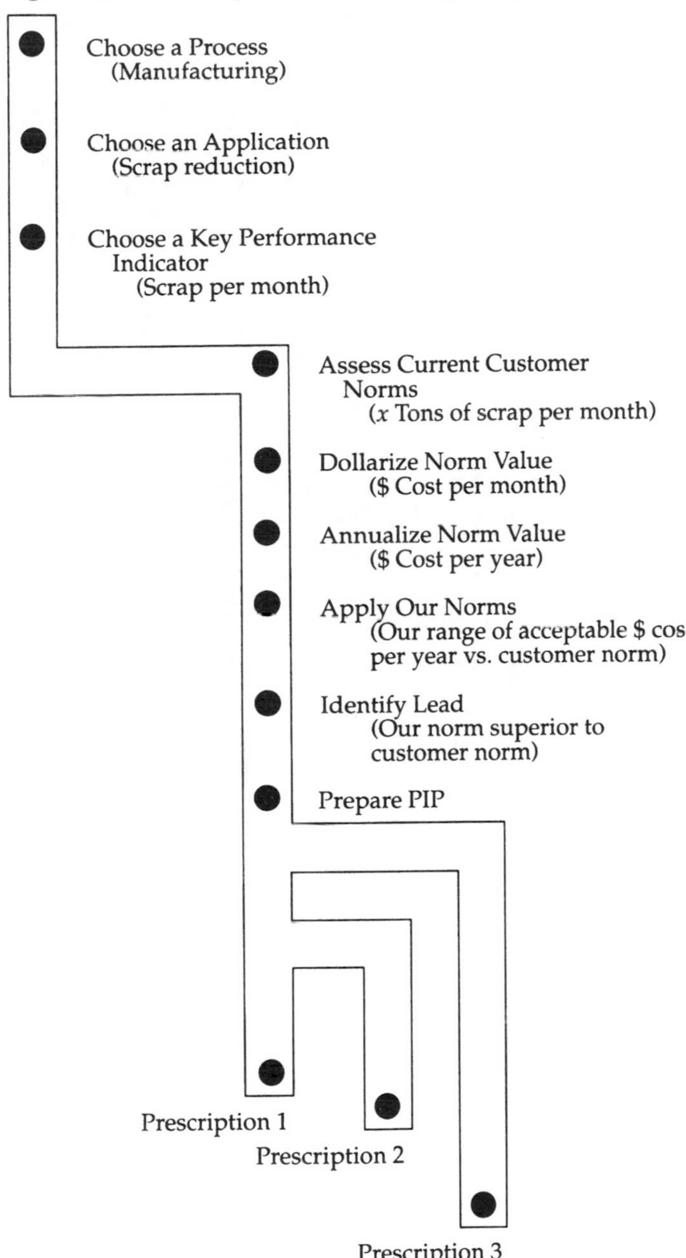
Choose a Process
(Manufacturing)
Choose an Application
(Scrap reduction)
Choose a Key Performance Indicator
(Scrap per month)
Assess Current Customer Norms
(x Tons of scrap per month)
Dollarize Norm Value
($ Cost per month)
Annualize Norm Value
($ Cost per year)
Apply Our Norms
(Our range of acceptable $ cost per year vs. customer norm)
Identify Lead
(Our norm superior to customer norm)
Prepare PIP
Prescription 1
Prescription 2
Prescription 3

Figure 1-5. Norm matrix.

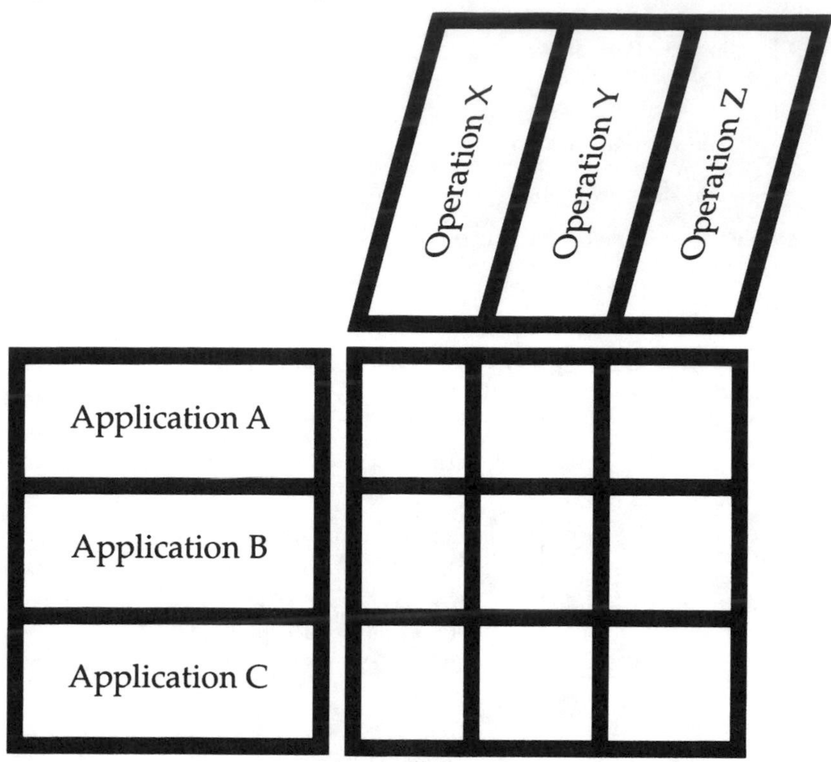

the norms for my performance in this category?" your voice must be the only one to answer if the question addresses one of your category-killer applications. If someone else answers, you may be redundant. If everyone else answers—which means that no one owns the norm—you are a vendor even if you call yourself a consultant.

Norms are meaningless unless they are industry-specific. Industry designations do not get specific until they are defined by a three-digit Standard Industrial Classification (SIC) code, such as the seven classes of Primary Metal Industries:

SIC Code	*Industry Subcategory*
331	Blast Furnaces and Basic Steel Products
332	Iron and Steel Foundries
333	Primary Nonferrous Metals
334	Secondary Nonferrous Metals
335	Nonferrous Rolling and Drawing
336	Nonferrous Foundries

Within each 3-digit code are 4-digit subclasses. The code 3321 contains gray and ductile iron foundries, while 3322 contains malleable iron foundries. As a general rule, 3-digit norms suffice. But if you do a lot of business in a 4-digit subclass, it will pay you to correlate your norms to its improved outcomes. Otherwise, a niche specialist can beat you.

Your norms must average the aggregate values you contribute to a specific operation in a line of business or business function in the industry as the result of each application.

Applications must be equally specific. The exact specifications, configurations, or installation requirements of an application may vary even within the same industry. Your norms should account for them by being prefaced with predictive modifiers, such as:

- Above/below average engineering changes
- Above/below average specification deviations
- Above/below average labor content
- Above/below average use of multiple materials
- Above/below average production of multiple parts
- Above/below average generation of multiple product variations that cause multiple customized setups
- Above/below average length of production runs

If you sell to manufacturing customers, you should create a correlate to the SIC classification system with an SPC Index for Standard Process Classifications and an SCC Index for Standard Cycle Classifications. You can model them like this:

Standard Process Classifications

001 Information Systems Workflow
002 R&D Workflow
003 Engineering/Product Development Workflow
004 Manufacturing Workflow
005 Inventory Workflow
006 Sales & Service Workflow

Standard Cycle Classifications

101 Product Design & Development Cycle
102 Production Cycle
103 Inventory Cycle
104 Order Entry/Shipment Cycle
105 Billing & Collection Cycle
106 Sales Cycle

A norm's worth is derived from its specific application-to-operation nature. This is the only way that your norms can act as shorthand representations of your ability to solve customer business problems: your norms for costs saved by reducing labor content or reducing scrap in a manufacturing operation, or your norms for revenues gained by speeding up product design and development cycle times in R&D.

Selling based on customer industry norms is commodity selling. Industry norms are commodities. They are available to you and to your competitors alike. They give you no meaningful differentiation. Nor do they give your customers the competitive advantage to take leadership even if you succeed in improving their current norms to the industry level. Industry norms are competitive floors, not ceilings. To perform at or near the industry norm is merely a customer's entry pass into competition, not a badge of superiority. Competitive parity is signaled by the industry norm. Competitive advantage takes place above it.

As a norm leader, you can offer customers a demonstrable advantage over their competitors by bringing them closer to your norms, which should be significantly superior to the industry average. This ability—to help your customers compete more cost-effectively—is your own competitive advantage as a consultant. It transcends your product price and performance, your deals and discounts, features and benefits, or any other aspect of your business and its sales propositions. It is the added value that your customers buy when they buy from you.

The superior level of your norm value—superior to both the industry average and your customer's current performance in an operation's dollar contribution to profits—should brand you as the partner of choice. By contrast, your competitors who sell from industry norms will be selling commodities. Even though they can propose customer improvement, they cannot propose *leadership*.

Maintaining a superior norm margin is crucial to your branding. Every time you perform below it, you lower it; every time you lower it, you come back to the pack of competitive commodity suppliers. This is your main incentive to work at your best. It also warns you to work only with customers who want as badly as you do the growth that your norms promise, who have the managers and support staffs who can partner additively with you, and who will be impressive references for your track record as norm leader.

A model set of norms, in this case "norms on a card," is shown in Figure 1-6. The information on this three-by-five–inch card represents the normal savings that an automated process controls supplier can make in the major cost contributors to a pulp mill's operations.

Figure 1-6. Norms on a card.

Critical Success Factors	*Norms for Cost Contrib/YR* ($000)*
Labor	4,000
Chemicals	4,600
Wood	2,300
Energy	2,100

*250,000 Ton/YR Mill

POSITIONING AS THE MIXMASTER

Each customer business function is a mix of costs and opportunities. Can you optimize the customer's mix—that is, can you help it more nearly deliver its optimal contribution to profits? If you can learn how to master the mix of customer costs in an industry's manufacturing process, for example, you can ensure your role as the industry's standard-bearer.

Every customer allocates certain resources to each of his businesses and their functions. This is his asset base—actually, his cost base. Some of these resources are supplied internally. They consist of his own people and the capital they use. The rest of his resources come from outside—the products, services, and systems that are acquired from a variety of suppliers. Taken together, these internal and external resources form the customer's current operating "mix." In order to partner, you will have to help create a mix that can contribute higher profits.

All customer businesses operate with a mix. Some mixes are simply conglomerations of products. Others add services such as training or maintenance. Still others are composed of systems that, in turn, are composed of subsystems or, when amalgamated, contribute to networks. You must determine where you fit in every mix, what value you can add to it, and what the worth of that value can be to you and a customer.

The mix becomes your market. It is where you fit, where you operate, where you belong. It will become the arena of your expertise. You must know how to make it produce profits in the most cost-effective manner, and you must know this better than anyone else. You must master the mix so well that you can position yourself with customers as their industry's "mixmaster."

Customer mixes usually lag behind the optimal mix. They frequently represent a sizable investment. They are also hidebound to a customer's learning curve. People have learned how to operate the current mix and have become familiar with its capabilities and its quirks. Training programs have been built around it. Cost and production schedules are established for it. Psychologically, it has become "the way we do things around here," a part of the gruel of corporate culture. It must be approached remedially but respectfully. You must not want to run your customers' businesses. You must want to partner with them so that *they can run them better.*

There are three main strategies for optimizing a customer's operating mix:

1. You can supplant one or more elements in the current mix. If the mix is labor-intensive, for example, you may be able to reduce labor content by substituting an automated process or eliminating an operation altogether. Or you may be able to combine multiple processes such as forecasting and inventory control, thereby eliminating overlapping and duplicated costs.

2. You can substitute your product or process for a competitive product or process that is part of the customer's current mix. The basis for your recommendation must be that improved financial benefits will accrue to the customer if the mix is altered—not simply that more advantageous performance benefits will be realized.

3. You can manage the mix as its systems integrator or facilities manager, working under a profit-improvement contract with a customer.

The specific strategies for partnering by means of optimizing a customer's mix will depend on the industry you serve. If you sell personal care products to supermarket and drug chains, you can penetrate by optimizing the mix of the number of facings that stores allocate to your products compared to competitors', the locations of your facings, and the type of displays. The proof of your optimization will have to be quantified in financial benefits, such as profit improvement per square foot, overall improvement from personal care department contribution per store, or improved profit contribution from related item sales. Or you may propose to optimize a customer's mix by taking on the role of manager of the personal care product category.

If you sell financial services such as stocks and bonds, insurance, real estate investments, or money market funds to affluent individuals, you can optimize the mix of their portfolios in terms of growth potential, risk, and current payout. The proof of your optimization will have to be quantified in dollar benefits, such as higher earnings, lowered taxes, or increased net worth.

Customers are preoccupied with growth. In business, you grow or die. Without growth, costs overtake you, new technologies outmode you, and competitors outmarket or outflank you. Customer managers take partners precisely to hedge against these risks.

All consultants discover that it is easier to reduce a customer's costs than to expand sales, and it is a good deal easier to quantify the resulting improvement to profits from cost reductions. But consultants quickly learn that no customer business exists to control costs. Customers are in business to make money, and the only way to make money is through sales. A consultant who is positioned as a cost reducer can be important to a customer. But a consultant who is positioned as a sales developer is vital.

New profits from increasing a customer's volume at the same margin or increasing margins at the same volume are the stuff of which growth is made. As a result, a customer can control more of a market and become the profit leader if not the leader in market share. There is nothing wrong with being the low-cost producer. But if a consultant is expert in cost reduction, he should learn how to translate his impact into its effect on revenues so that he can be positioned as a growth contributor.

All cost reductions can be translated into their sales equivalent. A reduction in the cost contributed by unnecessary inventory expense can be interpreted as the equivalent of a corresponding increase in sales revenues. This is equally true for a decrease in the cost contributed by scrap from off-specification production, from rejects or rework, from failures to make same-day delivery, from late billing, and from late collection of accounts receivable. If these costs are reduced, their earnings equivalent is the dollars saved or avoided: How much profit on how many dollars' worth of how many units sold over how much time stated as "the equivalent of profits from the sale of 500,000 cartons each week—or 1,000 carloads every seventy-two hours—or ten additional aircraft operating each day at an 80 percent load factor."

2

How to Penetrate High Levels

Top-tier customer management rarely deals with vendors, and then only under duress. They speak different languages. Vendors speak price and performance; management speaks value and profit. Vendors speak of their competitors; management is concerned about its own competition. Vendors wonder when management will ever buy; management wonders when vendors will ever leave.

Vendors who stand before their customer's top tier will not do so for long, or soon again. For consultative sellers to make a stand, and make it again and again, they must be prepared to speak the language of management, address customer concerns instead of their own, and put to work their knowledge of the customer's business so that a demonstrable improvement—not just a shipment of goods—takes place.

Key account sales representatives who want to penetrate the top customer tier must position themselves to discuss, document, and deliver their answers to the question, "How much profit will you add?"

In order to be accepted as profit improvers, sales representatives must pledge allegiance to the Consultant's Credo, reproduced in Figure 2-1. Only by understanding the consultant mindset—which is the mirror image of the customer manager mindset—will you be able to partner at the Box Two level shown in Figure 2-2. The customer business line managers and business function man-

Figure 2-1. Consultant's Credo.

Consultants sell money, not products. They transact returns from investments, not sales. Their price is an investment, not a cost. Their performance is measured by the amount and rate of the customer's return, not by product performance benefits. They work inside their customer businesses as partners, not from the outside as vendors. They relate directly to customer line-of-business managers and business function managers, not purchasing agents. They work at these middle management levels on a long-term, continuing basis, not from bid to bid. Their focus is not on competitive suppliers but on competitive profitmaking for their customer partners and for themselves.

agers are concentrated at this level, reporting directly to Box One, where the funds are.

By partnering at Box Two, you can capture customer managers to act as your "economic sellers"—there is no such thing as "economic buyers," since Box Two managers do not buy—who will help you do your job so that you can help them do their jobs more successfully.

If you are a Box Two manager, what constitutes success? It means always improving your contribution to profits. For a business line manager, it means expanding revenues or increasing margins. For a business function manager, it means reducing costs. And where does the money come from to do these things? It comes from Box One. What is your role in this process? You must help your customer partners get more funds, and get them more quickly and more surely so that they can increase more revenues or margins and decrease more costs.

As Figure 2-2 shows, Box One is the keeper of the keys to the corporate treasury. Box One is Box Two's funder, open to suggestion twenty-four hours a day, seven days a week, from his Box Two managers on how corporate funds can be invested more cost-effectively—in other words, how to get "the biggest bang for the

Figure 2-2. Customer-manager hierarchy.

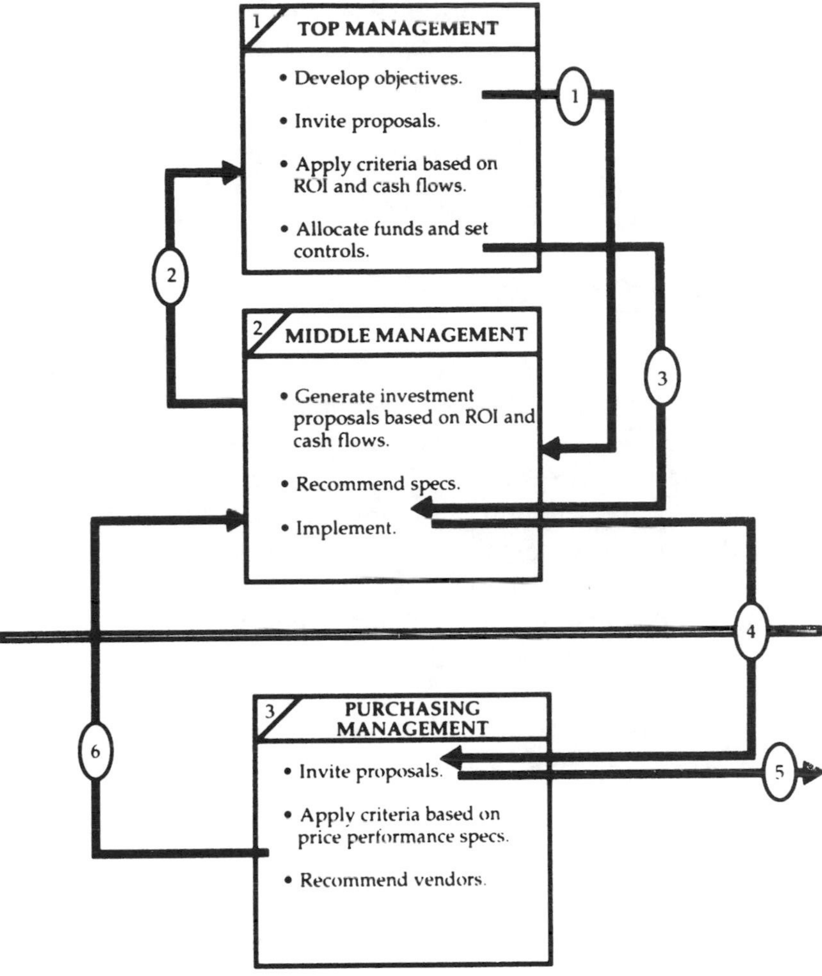

buck." Box Two managers are always in a proposal mode with their Box One funders, claiming a stake in the funding process for their own businesses or functions. Box One favors them on the basis of the strategic fit of their proposals with corporate growth policy and their adherence to financial objectives for each dollar invested with them. What rate of return will be achieved? When will the investment be paid back? How abundantly will the cash flow? What is the degree of risk?

With every release of funds to a Box Two manager, a control procedure goes along with it to make sure that the invested funds are, first of all, paid back on time, and then maximized for the greatest return. The Box Two managers who get the most funds the most often are the best internal sellers. If you can help them get even more, or more often, they will "go partners" with you to do it again and again.

ALLYING BOX TWO

Consultative sellers succeed or fail on their ability to ally themselves with their Box Two counterparts. They cannot sell without them because Box Two *sells for them* in ways that they cannot. Their alliances are founded on creating an ongoing stream of Profit Improvement Proposals for the customer managers to sell internally, thereby obtaining the funds to support the consultative seller's strategies. In order to act consultatively, the seller must conform to the requirements outlined in Figure 2-1.

Box One thinks, feels, and acts in ways that are standard operating performance for all Box One managers, emulated by all Box Two managers who interface with them, and virtually unknown to everybody else. Box One's position self-description is that of a money manager.

As a money manager, Box One is preoccupied with financial stewardship, the management of other people's money. This involves making prudent, duly diligent investments, the control and fractionalizing of risk into small, survivable bites, and a conservative management style that emphasizes certainty over the chance for a windfall, incremental gains over breakthroughs, and consistency over flashes in the pan.

Your alliances at the Box Two level depend on the same standards of performance as your Box Two counterpart's internal alliance with his own Box One: the contributions that you make to competitive profit making. When you work in partnership with a Box Two function manager, the added contribution you make to him becomes incremental to the contribution he has committed to make to Box One. That is why he will partner with you. The incremental value of your contribution becomes his test of how much you are worth as a partner.

The definition of *business partner* is therefore the customer manager's definition: someone who can add incremental value to the manager's contribution to profits. If you are going to qualify as a consultant partner, you must make yourself incrementally valuable to a business manager. This means you must deliver one or more of three types of added value:

1. You must enable your partner to *add more profits* than he would be able to contribute without you.
2. You must enable your partner to *add profits sooner* than he would be able to contribute without you.
3. You must enable your partner to *add profits with greater certainty* than he would be able to contribute without you.

These "deliverables" set the standards of performance for consultative sellers. You will be judged for your partnerability by the manager's answers to three questions: *How much* value do you propose to add? *How soon* do you propose to add it? *How sure* can I be that you will add as much value as you propose as soon as you propose to add it?

These are very different questions from the traditional ones raised at the Box Three purchasing interface. When vendors make their sales calls there, they are asked how much performance they can propose and how little price they can charge for it. But Box Two does not buy products; he invests in value. Box Two does not buy at all; he sells proposals to obtain funds for his own operations. The Box One managers he sells to are your customer's ultimate buyers. They buy investment opportunities that can put their money to work at the highest rates for the surest return within the shortest periods of time.

They judge their Box Two operating managers by how good they are as money managers. "If I give you one dollar," they ask in effect, "How much more will you give me back? How long before I get it? How sure can I be?" A manager who partners with you as his consultative seller is betting that you can help him enhance his performance by enabling him to return more money than he could alone, or return it faster, and return it more surely.

When you reduce one of a Box Two manager's critical cost factors, you can help him improve the contribution he returns from his operation. When you increase one of his critical revenue factors, you do the same. These are the mutual objectives of your cooperative partnerships because they are the achievements that improve your mutual profits.

A customer manager who meets the standards of performance for cooperative partnerability is called the *Alpha Manager,* the consultative seller's co-manager on the customer side. The Alpha Manager is the owner of the contribution from a customer operation. The Alpha's name is signed in blood on the operation's business plan. He runs, supports, or supplies a line of business and is not to be confused with vendor selling's usual list of barnyard suspects like the political fox, the coaching goose, or the gatekeeper gander.

There is only one Alpha Manager per consultative seller per customer operation. This makes it crucial to partner him; once lost to a competitor, the consultative seller is effectively denied penetration.

EMPOWERING BOX TWO WITH VALUE

Box Two managers have a simple set of needs:

1. They want money.
2. They want it now—yesterday would be even better.
3. They want money so they can make more money with it.

In order to position yourself for Consultative Selling, you must be able to prove to a customer manager that you can help him get his hands on money, that you can help him to get it soon, and that you can supply him with a steady stream of investment opportunities that will enable him to make more money. These are the empowering features and benefits that will make you compellingly partnerable.

As your products and services become more closely replicated by competition, their features and benefits can no longer be differentiated enough to command a premium price. This places the burden of differentiation on you. Can you help a customer manager make or save more money than your competitors can? Can you help him make or save it faster? Can you make him more certain by working with you? *Yes* answers are your sole competitive advantage because they provide the sole competitive advantage of your customer managers.

Vendors sell by asking purchasing managers at the Box Three level to let the seller do his job: "Buy from me." Consultants sell by helping their Box Two partners do their own jobs better: "Win with me." If you put your money to work with me, the consultant's position says, you will have more money back sooner and surer. At the same time, you will have a greater market share of a current market or you will have gained entry into a new market or you will have a reduced cost burden in an important operation or greater productivity. You will be competitively advantaged as either a market share leader or as the industry standard of value as the low-cost producer.

The Box Two connection is vital. It is the essential linkup that makes Consultative Selling work. Without it, vendors remain vendors at the Box Three level, as these comments—typical of trying to sell consultatively to an untrained and unpartnered purchasing function—show:

> "The customers have not responded. We try and try but at the end of our product demos, the same questions are still raised: what is the price and how much of a discount does it represent?"
>
> "We must be qualifying opportunities far too late in our customers' decision process. We have no time to PIP; just enough to propose a quote."

The true value of the competitive advantages you bring to a customer is not in new profits themselves but in their investment value when he puts them to work. How much more can he make on what he has just made with you? Funds always seek work. Idleness incurs opportunity cost. For this reason, you must have your next investment proposal in your hip pocket—actually, in your Account Penetration Plan—ready to present as soon as your current project has reached payback. This maintains your position squarely in the flow of funds while simultaneously repositioning your customer for the next round of being competitively advantaged by his partnership with you.

As your customer partner positions you, you are an optional investment opportunity. This is how you must come across to him. It tells you how you must define the nature of your business with him:

- If you are in the telecommunications business, you must not simply be in telecom. You must not sell switches, networks, or rates.
- You must not be simply one more "problem solver." You must not just sell "solutions."
- You must not simply be a "consultant."

You must be a *profit improver*, a partner whose expertise and experience in the customer's business can help the customer increase the amount, speed, and certainty of the profits he contributes to his top-tier managers in Box One. You must understand the world that your partner lives in. If he is "in manufacturing" and considering robotics, he lives in a world of cost contributors, such as Figure 2-3 shows. Which of them can you help him control? Your contributions are your tickets of entry into his world. How much you can contribute, how soon, and how reliably will determine whether you will be invited to live in your customer's world as his partner or will just be passing through.

COMPETING AGAINST A CUSTOMER'S COMPETITION

Vendors compete against each other. Their customers pay their Box Three managers to manage this competition, playing one vendor off against another to get the best—that is, the lowest—

Figure 2-3. Robotics cost checklist.

Acquisition Costs

- The robot and its tooling
- Facilities, equipment revisions, and rearrangements
- Application engineering
- Process and product changes
- Training and transfers
- Installation
- Direct labor costs

Life Cycle Costs
(Costs of Ownership)

- Cost of capital
- Taxes and insurance
- Maintenance labor, supplies, and spare parts
- Energy
- Training
- Scrap and rework
- Safety and potential cost of disability

price. Competition, whether among vendors or others, is based on comparison. When vendors compete for Box Three, they compare themselves against their competition product by product, feature and benefit by feature and benefit. When all the distinctions without a difference cancel out, vendors compare their performance to their price. In this way, they force debate on the relative merits—or, to say the same thing in other words, they force competition on themselves. The winner makes the sale but, in the process, trades away his margins.

It is not uncommon for the margin loss to exceed 50 percent. In one typical case, a sales representative "sold" a $3 million order for computers to a retailer at a 54.75 percent discount that, the customer was told, would "elevate your awareness of the benefit of doing business with us by increasing your overall profitability." The discount was composed of a 46 percent price break plus free cooperative advertising funds, prepaid freight, the services of a team of marketing and sales representatives together with a product trainer, and a rebate program. As the representative said who made the sale, "The customer practically sold himself."

The transcendent objective of Consultative Selling is to maintain premium margins. To do this, consultants must create a new concept of competition; that is, they must sponsor a different set of comparisons, none of which is with "other vendors." In addressing Box Two, consultants can position two types of comparison for their customers to evaluate:

1. For profit center managers who run customer business lines, consultants can create a comparison between a manager's current sales and share of market and the consultant's norms. When the consultant's norms are superior, he can propose to add value to the customer by helping to increase volume or margins.
2. For cost center managers who run customer business functions, consultants can create a comparison between a manager's current operating performance and the consultant's norms. When the consultant's norms are superior, he can propose to add value to the customer by helping to reduce or avoid costs.

In both cases, the consultative seller is challenging the customer to compare his current competitive advantage with a proposed superior advantage. Is a competitor taking greater advantage of a market opportunity than you are? If so, I can help you come closer to equality or leadership. Are unnecessarily costly operations taking needless advantage of your profits and preventing you from being a lower cost producer? If so, I can help you come closer to equality or leadership.

When a customer focuses on comparing what it is costing him now, in both direct costs and opportunity costs, to be competitive with what it could cost him if he were partnered with the consultant, his concentration is on his own competitive position and not the consultant's. Other vendors are driven from his field of vision. They are out of sight and out of mind because the questions the customer asks himself have nothing to do with "the best price." He is, instead, preoccupied with questioning the deal at hand. Is it credible—can I believe the numbers? Is it sufficient—will it make enough of a difference? Is it doable—can the proposed people and systems and strategies do the job? Is it realistic—can I reasonably expect to get the predicted rate of return on my investment within the promised time frame?

What if he asks, "Are there other suppliers who could do the same thing or do it more cheaply or better or faster?" He already knows the answer: "Perhaps." He also knows that because time is money, he will risk opportunity cost if he wants to find out. He will be far more concerned with evaluating today's opportunity today—the bird in the hand—and not speculating about tomorrow. All he can ever be sure about is today. Today's opportunity taken tomorrow is already operating at a competitive disadvantage.

PARTNERING WITH BOX THREE

Consultative Selling permits you to move up from a vendor relationship with a customer's Box Three purchasing manager to a partner relationship with a Box Two business manager. In the process, you must be careful to avoid alienating the Box Three manager. The best way to ensure his participation and support—or at least his passive permission—is to offer to take him with you.

You must make your offer in Box Three terms: What is in it for him? These are four potential advantages:

1. Increased visibility at the Box Two and Box One levels
2. Increased access to knowledge about the business issues that drive purchase requirements
3. Increased mobility on the corporate career path as a result of increased visibility and knowledge
4. Decreased demand on his budget when Box Two managers make investments from their own budgets to fund consultative projects

It is a business paradox that it may be easier for a Box Three manager to move up with you rather than alone in his own company's hierarchy. This is true because the Consultative Selling process provides him, just as it offers you, the opportunity to add value at the Box Two level. Instead of relating primarily outward with vendors, Box Three can relate upward with his own managers, who have been his users and customers but who can hereafter be his partners.

By offering to include Box Three in your Box Two consultancies, you risk nothing. Box Three may say *yes,* which is the best case, or he may say *yes, but;* he will remain a passive participant who wants to be kept informed as a member of the loop but prefers to take no active role. This is the next-best case. A certain number of Box Three managers will say *no.* This gives you the option of trying to convert them or working with a company whose Box Three will say *yes* or *yes, but* and trying to convert them later.

Because of its continuing nature, your relationship with Box Three managers is important to you. What do you say to them when you create a two-tier sales strategy by which you sell at both Box Two and Box Three? You have nothing to lose and much to gain by proposing to partner with them in the following way:

> It is our intent to continue to sell to you as we have in the past, responding to your requests for proposal with quality products at fair prices. It is also our intent to seek out additional opportunities to serve you. We anticipate finding these opportunities in your lines of business and cost centers where they may be unknown even to their managers or where the cost-effectiveness of doing something about them may not be realized. We would like to share our discovery of these opportunities with you and invite you to partner with us and your business managers in diagnosing the opportunities and proposing profit-improvement solutions for them. What do you say?

What if only one Box Three manager wants to go upstairs to Box Two with you or take you there? What if only one Box Three manager does not want to go himself but is willing to let you go? You will have enough agreement to get started.

The Box Three types who are easy to partner have a broad-banded business orientation and a desire to expand their role as business managers. By contrast, Box Three types who are more difficult to partner have a technical orientation, often quite provincial and parochial, are cost-conscious more than value-driven or profit-sensitive, and are defensively protective about sharing customer knowledge. They may also have an acute vendor orientation, keeping all suppliers at arm's length as "outsiders" and being afraid of criticism if it appears that a supplier is doing Box Three's job. New young purchasers can be unusually aware of their prerogatives and jealous of a supplier's superior knowledge or expertise. This can make them just as stubbornly resistant as older managers, close to retirement, who are reluctant to change because they perceive no benefits to the remainder of their career lifetimes.

Box Three will partner you if his own purposes are served. Is there value to him in gaining visibility upstairs, or in learning more about the business objectives of the products and materials he purchases, or in playing a role as a profit improver instead of merely another cost center? If so, you can sell these values consultatively to him in terms of both personal profit improvement and the opportunity to make an enhanced contribution to business profits.

Under your mentorship, he can learn how to convert his appropriations requests for funds into value propositions that will position him—like you—as a profit improver instead of a cost center. You can then go upstairs together rather than trying to go over or around him.

3

How to Merit High Margins

For both consultative sellers and their customers, profit is the name of the game. While the game is the same, the role you play in it is very different from that of your customer.

Setting profit objectives is the customer's business. It cannot be abdicated, nor can the customer delegate it to anyone outside the company. No one who is external to a company can ever know enough about total corporate assets and liabilities—financial, operational, or human—to set business objectives based on them. Besides, your concern with a customer's business is rarely an overall one. It is concentrated on the application or use of the product and service systems with which you yourself are involved. As a result, your role is concerned with the additive effects that the value of your product and service systems can have on the customer's profitability. You are each customer's *incremental profit improver,* not total profit maker.

A customer's primary management function is to develop strategic and tactical plans that can achieve profit maximization. Your role is limited to profit betterment. This means that you will propose your contribution from the point at which customers have finished developing their own profit plans. The end point of the customer's profit objectives becomes your point of departure.

Every value that a PIP adds to a customer is incremental to the customer's current values. This means that the overhead of fixed costs already being funded by the customer can be made to contribute additional values without adding to it. PIPs require no additional plants to be built, no new R&D facilities to be developed, and no new customer sales managers or representatives to be hired. PIPs make the customer's current overhead more productive and less costly, leveraging small investments into significantly higher returns.

This is why consultative sellers propose in terms of "contribution." It is not their own ability to contribute profits they are proposing. Instead, they are being consultative in helping their customers produce a greater contribution from current assets.

GENERATING PROFIT IMPROVEMENT PROPOSALS

A consultative seller's day-to-day work is the generation of Profit Improvement Proposals. Each PIP adds value to your customer's profit objectives through the application of your product and service systems to the customer's business operations. Through such added value, you are able to merit added margins in return.

The process of generating profit proposals must be a continuing one. Once it begins, it can go on without end because the profit-improvement opportunities in a customer company are limitless.

You will find the task of selecting your profit-improvement portfolio easier if you apply five criteria. They will steer you toward PIPs that have the greatest chance of succeeding.

1. *New profits should be achievable within 365 days.* Longer time frames incur unpredictable risks; they not only defy ready calculation but invite disenchantment or cancellation of PIP projects already under way.
2. *New profits should be significant for both you and your customer.* Shared profit improvement should not be confused with equal profit. The first objective—profitability for both—is a vital aspect of the concept of partnership. The second—equal profit—is both impossible and unnecessary.
3. *New profits must draw on a major product or service ca-*

pability to be profitable for your company. Similarly, in order for your customer to profit, your proposals must affect a major product, service, or operation.

4. *New profits must be measurable* in terms of a net increment or a decremental investment in operating assets. If it cannot be measured, or if no provision is made to quantify it, agreement on whether improvement even took place may be impossible to obtain.
5. *New profits should not be an isolated entity* but a module that leads naturally to the next infusion of profits and then to the next one after that.

Box Two business managers are managers of cost centers or profit centers. Whatever operation their particular business function may perform or whatever markets their line of business may sell to, they are essentially in the business of asset management. They are funded by their Box One managers with assets in the form of cash or credit. They are expected to invest these assets in their operations to turn a profit on the original investment, which they will allocate to fixed and operating assets "under management." How good they are at this determines how much they will get the next time.

A consultative seller can take on the role of contributing to his Box Two partner's success as an asset manager in three ways:

1. He can help his customer manager improve his ratio of selling successful proposals to Box One by adding high-quality investment opportunities to the manager's portfolio and helping him to obtain more funds.
2. He can help his customer manager improve his turnover rate of accepted proposals to Box One by adding more investment opportunities to the manager's portfolio and helping him turn them over faster.
3. He can help his customer manager improve his success ratio of implementing projects by adding expertise that will help earn more profits or earn them sooner and with greater certainty.

Consultative Selling is based on a universal management principle: Never add an asset to a customer operation without an asset management program to reduce its cost of ownership or to earn back more than its price.

In business, money has one purpose: to make more money. To be a consultative seller, you must position yourself as adding the values of "more money faster and surer" to your customers. This is the supreme product. All customers need it all the time. There is always demand—no matter what you sell—because no matter how much money is on hand, there is always a short supply. There is never enough soon enough; "more money yesterday" is the only answer a Box Two manager ever gives to the question, "How much do you want and when do you want it?"

Every dollar that a Box Two manager has is on loan to him. The loan, in the form of allocated funds from Box One, is callable on the date that the manager's proposal has pledged to achieve payback on Box One's investment. But that is only the beginning. Box One does not invest to achieve payback. His objective is to maximize the return on his investment and to do so as quickly as possible. In this sense, the funds he lends to the Box Two managers who report to him are trust funds: Box One trusts his Box Two managers to return them at a profit.

Proposing Profit Improvement

Proposing is a three-step process: definition of a customer problem to be solved or a customer opportunity to be capitalized; prescription of the profit-improvement benefit from solving the problem or capitalizing on the opportunity; and description of the operational and financial workings of the system that can yield the improved profit.

Step 1: Problem/Opportunity Definition

Your initial task is to establish consultant credibility. Initial credibility comes only from displaying knowledge of a customer's business. Until a customer can say, "That supplier knows my business," the customer will rarely be inclined to say, "That supplier can improve my profit."

In fact, you must be knowledgeable about two areas of a customer's business. First, you must know the location of significant cost centers that are susceptible to reduction. Second, you must know how a customer's customers can be induced to buy more from the customer. In the first instance, you must prescribe a system that will reduce customer costs. This is a problem-solving system. In the second instance, you must prescribe a system that will increase customer sales. This is an opportunity-seizing system.

Defining a customer problem or opportunity has two parts: what you know, and how you know it. The second part documents the first by citing the sources of your knowledge. It also reinforces your credibility. There are three likely sources of knowledge about a customer cost problem or sales opportunity. One is that the customer revealed it. This is the "horse's mouth" source. A second source of knowledge is past experience with the customer, with other companies in the same industry, or your track record symbolized by its norms. Or knowledge can come from homework. This is the "midnight oil" source.

Step 2: Profit-Improvement Prescription

The objective of the first step in a consultative presentation is to say to a customer, in effect: "You have a situation that is detrimental to your profit. Either you are incurring unnecessary costs or you are failing to capture available sales revenues." The objective of the second step is to say, "Working together, we can reduce some of those costs or gain some of those sales as a cost-beneficial investment."

In this way, you further reinforce the perception of being knowledgeable about the customer's business by framing the system's benefit in businesslike terms of return on investment. By quantifying an added value the system can make to the customer's operations, you are creating a business-manager-to-business-manager context for customer decision making in contrast to a vendor-to-purchaser context.

The prescription for customer profit improvement must specify the positive return that can predictably result from installation of your system. The return should be specified as both a percentage rate of improvement and its equivalent in dollars. These quantifications, the end-benefit specifications in money terms, rather than specifics about the system's performance or components, are the ultimate specifications of the consultant's system. These are what a customer will or will not buy. They are therefore what you must prescribe for delivery.

IBM consultants approach top-tier management of key retail customers on behalf of IBM's computer-assisted checkout station. The consultants prescribe profit improvement benefits of reduced costs and increased sales like this: "For a store with gross weekly sales of $140,000, savings are projected at $7,650 a month by faster customer checkout and faster balancing of cash registers." The time required to check out an average order is said to be reduced by almost 30 percent. In addition, IBM sales representatives claim that the elimination of time and cost expenses of correcting checker errors can contribute annual savings of more than $91,000 per store.

If a store is growing, its total savings every year can approach one week's gross sales at the $140,000 level. The net value of these savings falls directly to the store's bottom line. The essential contribution made by IBM is providing added growth funds that supplement revenues from sales and can be invested for still further growth. In the course of making its contribution, IBM consultatively sells computers.

Step 3: System Specification

The third presentation step is to specify the system that will deliver the promised profit-improvement mix and to justify its premium price by interpreting price in terms of investment in the new mix. Customers must not be asked to buy systems; you must invite them to improve profit. They are not quoted a system's price; you must promise them a positive return on the investment in their system.

The purpose of defining the system is not to sell it, but rather to present proof that the promised benefit is derived from known capabilities that have been prescribed precisely because they will contribute in the most cost-beneficial way to the customer's profit improvement. The system substantiates your promise. Its capabilities, plus your personal expertise in applying them, are the means of conferring new profitability on the customer.

Defining a customer problem or opportunity should condition a customer to relate to you as a business manager. The next presentation step, prescribing a quantified benefit, should condition a customer to regard the system as a profit-making investment, not as a cost or a collection of components. Defining the system and justifying its price should condition a customer to credit the prescription as believable and achievable.

The final step in a system's presentation is to set down the standards by which you will progressively monitor the system's ability to deliver the promised benefit in partnership with the customer. At least three control standards should be set so that a working partnership can be confirmed between consultant and customer:

1. Time frames for the accomplishment of each installation and operational stage
2. Checkpoints for measuring the impacts of phasing the system into customer business functions
3. Periodic progress review and report sessions to head off problems and anticipate new applications and opportunities for system extension, upgrading, modernization, and replacement

COMPARING COSTS AND BENEFITS

The comparative analysis of a customer's costs to improve his profits by doing business with you and the benefits he can expect to receive are the heart of Consultative Selling. Cost-benefit analysis, which should really be called "investment-return analysis," tells the customer how much he must lay out for how much he can get back. The basic format for costing the benefits of a profit improvement project with a five-year commercial life is shown in

Figure 3-1. Compare it with Figure 6-1, which shows a similar analysis of an investment's costs and benefits in the software format of Mack Hanan's PIPWARE™.

Figure 3-2 is a glossary of guidelines to analyze the relationship between costs and the benefits that flow from them.

MANAGING PROFIT PROJECTS

A PIP is a profit project. Its site is a customer's premises, either one of his business lines or a business function. A PIP is a money-making project. It says to the customer, Here is where you are incurring unnecessary costs or missing out on realizable revenues. Here is what it is costing you. Here is how much you can save or earn. Here is what it will take to obtain the improvement and how long it will be before you can see it on your bottom line.

PIPs are designed to affect a customer's economy. To do this, they require adding the value of a supplier's products or services along with information in the form of advisory services and training. Sometimes financing is involved as time payments or a lease. But the essential ingredient in every project is its manager.

The art of managing a profit-improvement project is a consultative seller's prime skill. To manage it means to make it pay off as proposed, in full and on time. This requires the seller to be a good diagnostician, making sure he or she has sized up the project correctly from the outset. The seller must then be a good prescriber in order to propose the most cost-effective solution for the problem or opportunity he has diagnosed. Then he must be a good installer, implementer, and applier to fit the solution seamlessly into a customer's operations so that it becomes a part of their natural flow. He must be a good planner, exactly meeting each milestone along the way from startup through payback to realization of the proposal's objective. And at every step of the way, he must be a good partner with his customer's people, without whose cooperation he can accomplish nothing.

Customers who are being PIPped must perceive that they are being invited to invest in the improvement of the contributions their operations make to their profits—not that they are being

(text continues on page 80)

Figure 3-1. Cost-benefit work flow.

Investment	Y0	Y1	Y2	Y3	Y4	Y5
Cash One						

Contribution From Increased Sales	Y1	Y2	Y3	Y4	Y5
Cash In					

Contribution From Reduced Costs	Y1	Y2	Y3	Y4	Y5
Cash In					

Net Cash Flows	Y0	Y1	Y2	Y3	Y4	Y5
Cumulative Cash Flow						
Total Profit Improvement						

Net Present Value (NPV$)	
Payback (MOS)	
Return on Investment (%)	

Figure 3-2. Glossary of cost-benefit guidelines.

Investment	Represents a customer's total incremental expenditure to obtain our solution, including but over and above his costs to do business with us: capital equipment and materials, software, services other than annual maintenance, training, and other variable costs that will have to be expensed. It is assumed that the total investment is a one-time cost that will be paid out in full in Year 0. Total investment is the "cost" in the cost-benefit analysis. Multiply the total investment in capital equipment by the current depreciation rate permitted by the accelerated cost recovery schedule (ACRS). Subtract the resulting cash flows generated by cumulative annual depreciation from the total investment.
Cash Flow	Represents the incremental cash benefits generated by the savings and revenues from our solution. They are calculated on a recurrent annual basis that can be accumulated at the end of the useful life of the total investment. Cash flow is the "benefits" in the cost-benefit analysis.
Payback	The cumulative cash flows to date have exactly returned the customer's total investment so that he is released from risk and made whole again. After payback, cash flows become positive so that profits can occur.
Net Present Value (NPV)	Represents today's current value of the sum of all the future cash flows after they have been discounted for annual

(continues)

Figure 3-2. (Continued)

	opportunity loss based on what the same total investment might have saved or earned if invested elsewhere. Annual opportunity loss is calculated over the useful life of the total investment. (The Year One net present value of $50,000 by the time it will be received in Year Two is $41,667, which represents $50,000 discounted by the factor of 0.83333.)
Return on Investment (ROI)	Represents the ratio of a customer's total profit improvement to the total investment required to generate it. In order for a deal to be done, ROI must equal or exceed a customer's minimum hurdle rate for incremental investments. The hurdle rate is generally set at 2/3 to 3/3 of the customer's cost of capital.

asked to buy the consultative seller's products, services, or systems. They have no vested interest in the seller's products. Their only interest is in the assets that they already own and how to improve their contributions.

A project in profit improvement begins when a customer closes the seller's proposal. The project ends not with the one-time delivery of products and services but with the on-time delivery of improved customer profits. In between, the seller must manage the flow of work. Even more important, he must manage the flow of new profits.

As project manager of a profit proposal, the consultative seller must have the answers to questions like these on the tip of his tongue on a day-in, day-out basis:

- *"How's it going?"* This means: Are we on plan so that we will make our objective when we said we would?

• *"Is everything under control?"* This means: Are our control procedures proving that we are proceeding according to plan or are they picking up variances?

• *"Any problems?"* This means: Has our diagnosis been changed by the discovery of facts we did not know beforehand or by new events that have arisen since we began?

There are three parameters to good project management. They all concern money. Even the parameter that refers to time concerns money because that is what time is.

1. The manager must bring the project home *within budget.* He must not overrun the customer's investment.
2. The manager must bring the project home at *full realization.* He must not deprive the customer of his expected return.
3. The manager must bring the project home *on time.* He must not prolong the length of the customer's investment cycle or delay the onset of awaited funds.

It takes a tightly controlled manager to achieve these three hallmarks of good management with consistency. He must control his project's resources in order not to overinvest them and hike up the project's costs so that its payback is postponed. He must control his project's cash flow on a milestone-by-milestone schedule in order not to come up short. And he must control the clock in order not to run out of time. Managing tightly is essential from a project's start to finish. Managing tightly only at the end after a careless or profligate beginning is a recipe for failure.

The ability to diagnose heretofore unsolved customer problems in such a way that they can now be solved is an enviable asset for a project manager. So is the ability to conceive a simplistic solution that, for the first time, enables a customer problem or opportunity to be dealt with cost-effectively. But the greatest ability is *dependability.* Can the project manager be depended on to control the project, to keep it from getting out of hand, to pick up deviations quickly and remedy them at once, to avoid cost overruns, and to be free of surprises? If the answers are either no or, even worse, sometimes, no amount of creativity or simplistic problem solving will atone for the absence of reliability.

No two consultative sellers have the same intellectual capital or employ their capital in the same way. Given identical customer operations, customer objectives, and commodity products and services, one consultative seller will always propose what a customer regards as the single best solution—the most cost-effective way of solving a problem or realizing an opportunity. How can you become the proposer of the winning PIP and, consequently, the manager of the winning project?

The secret of Consultative Selling success is your personal ability to come up with an optimal mix of muchness, soonness, and sureness of benefits for each PIP. In other words, how much better than the next consultative seller is your intellectual capital when you apply it to bring together your technology smarts with your process smarts about a customer's operations?

The value basis for Consultative Selling can be summed up in a single sentence: *Consultative sellers are in the business of selling a dollar's worth of value for 50 or 60 cents on the dollar.*

This is more than any vendor can get for selling a dollar's worth of cost.

Selling dollars is crucial because no one can make margin on products anymore. Yotaro Suzuki of the Japan Institute of Office Automation asks, "How do you assign prices in a world where quality is perfect?" Hiroshi Yamauchi of Nintendo concludes that "there is no way to charge a premium on hardware." In the United States, the most common assessment of suppliers by their customers is, "They make a great machine. So what?"

Part II

Consultative Proposing Strategies

4

How to Qualify Customer Problems

The high margins that accrue from Consultative Selling are your reward for knowing more about the customer operations you affect—and being able to improve them—than your competitors do. Margins are merited by mastery of how a customer runs the business lines and functions that are your sales targets. The more you know about them, and the better you are able to implement what you know into proposals for performing them more cost-effectively, the greater your value will be; accordingly, the higher the price you will deserve.

Consultative Selling is industry-specific. Within each industry, it is operation-specific. Business operations in customer companies are your end users, your true markets. According to the way they operate, they create the costs that you can reduce or do away with entirely. They can add new sales revenues or productivity if you can show them how. Your customer's business operations are the sources of the problems you will have to solve and the showcases where the value of your solutions will give testimony to your capabilities. Scoping their ways of operating should therefore be your constant preoccupation.

If you are going to sell in a consultative manner, customer business operations will be the subject matter of your consultation. The only alternative is to talk about your own processes and the products or services they produce. In that case, you will be talking to the purchasing tier and selling on a basis of competitive performance and price. Your opportunity for high margins will have vanished.

DEVELOPING BUSINESS OPERATIONS PROFILES

All business operations have a flow—they have a beginning, a middle, and an end. Manufacturing begins with raw materials and ends with finished goods in inventory. Data processing begins with raw information and ends with reports. There are costs at both ends; in between, there is nothing but costs.

Consultative sales representatives should be able to chart the flow of the critical customer business operations they affect. They should be able to assign appropriate costs to the most critical success factors in each process—the 20 percent that contribute the 80 percent—and be able to prescribe the optimal remedy to reduce their contribution to costs or expand their contribution to revenues.

Some of these remedies will be therapeutic; that is, they will lower an existing cost. Other remedies will be curative; they will alter a process, combine it with another, or eliminate it from the flow. In still other cases, the remedy will be to change the architecture of a process so that a completely new set of cost or revenue centers will result.

In most customer operations, work flow is cost-ineffective. It incurs unnecessary cost or it processes work ineffectively. If you can optimize it, you can improve its contribution to profits. Every dollar of cost you take out can drop to the customer's bottom line. Every improvement you make in productivity can also lower operating cost and raise the output from each dollar invested in labor, energy, and materials.

There are two ways to scope a customer business line or business function. One is to scope its funding to determine where it ranks in its company's flow of investment funds. A second way is to scope its process flow to determine its critical success factors.

1. *Scoping funding.* Nothing happens in business until funds flow. Once funds are allocated, they can be drawn down at the

Box Two level and put to work; that is, invested. If a consultative seller wants work, he or she must go where the funds are flowing, which will always be to a customer's cost center and profit center managers whose success is critical to corporate strategy.

"Go where funds flow" prevents your coming up dry by being told, "We have no money," and having proposals turned back that are effectively stamped "insufficient funds."

2. *Scoping process.* When funds flow to a profit-centered line of business or cost center, work can flow through it. You must know how this takes place. You must be able to identify the critical success factors in all customer functions that you affect, you must know their current contributions to function costs or revenues, and you must know if you can add value to them and at what rate of return for a customer's investment.

Figure 4-1 shows the critical functions that determine the success of a supermarket chain's business. Where are costs higher than necessary: Is inventory stocking or order assembly inefficient? Where are revenue opportunities remaining undercapitalized: Can backhaul trucking be made to contribute, or contribute more, to profits?

The work flow for an aerospace manufacturer is shown in Figure 4-2. This process begins with the marketing function. How can it turn over more projects faster? Are design analysis and testing roadblocks to turning over the process as a whole? Is time wasted, and therefore money, in moving along the projects that marketing brings in? What if model testing could be accomplished one month faster? One week faster? What value would that add to delivery, the time when an aerospace manufacturer is paid in full? In other words, what would the added value be of reducing the cycle time of receivables collection by one month for each project?

All PIPs prescribe a solution for work flow problems or cycle time problems, sometimes both. A PIP can propose to reduce the number of work stations in a process or re-engineer the way they operate or how they are organized. Other PIPs can propose to reduce the time required for a workstation to complete its operat-

(text continues on page 90)

Figure 4-1. Supermarket chain work flow.

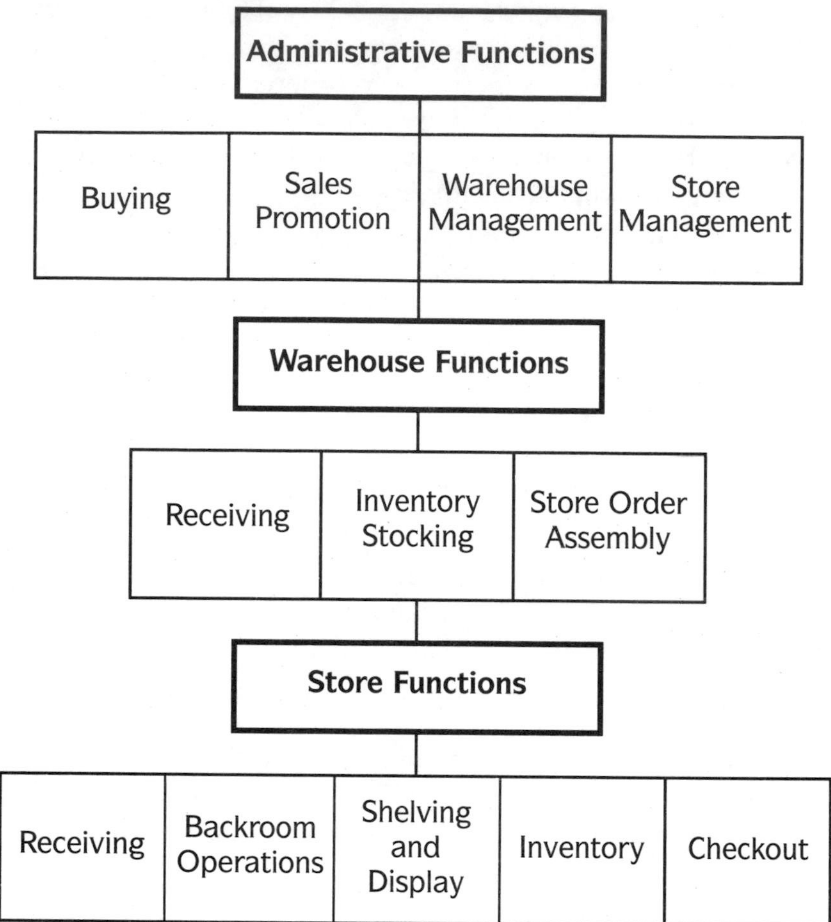

Figure 4-2. Aerospace manufacturing work flow.

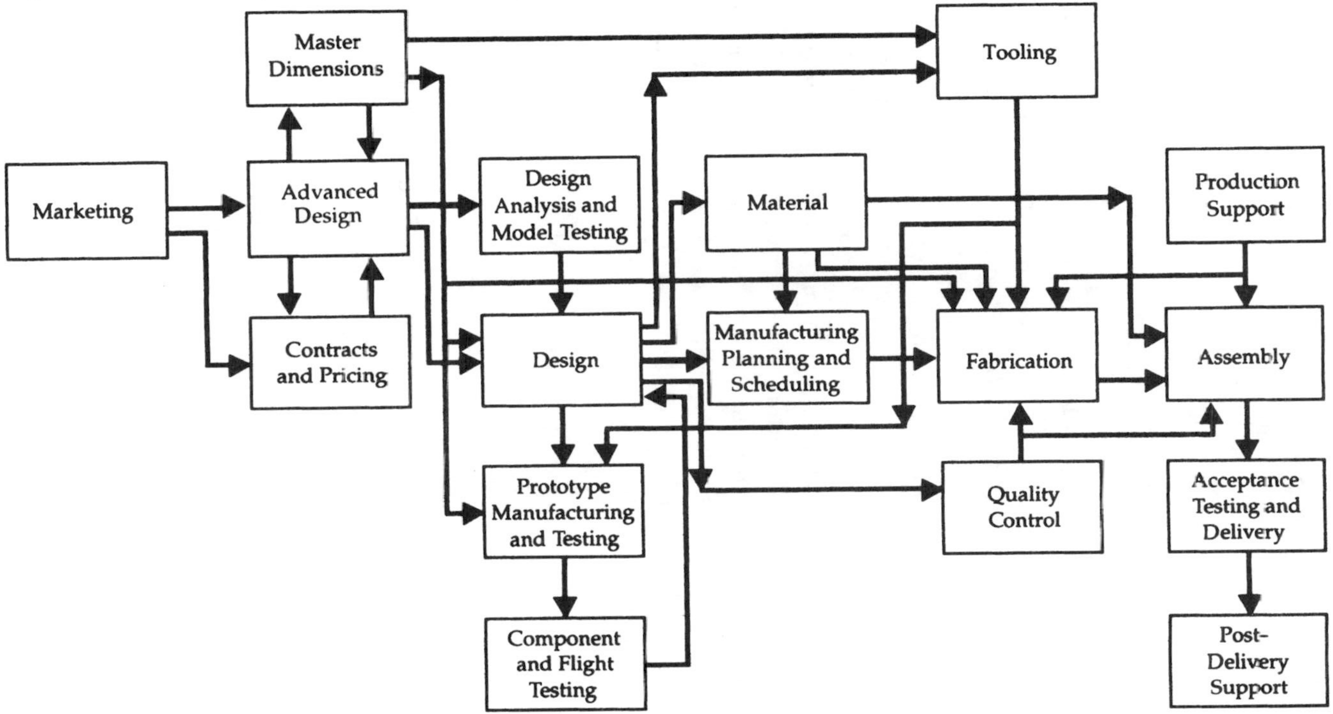

Marketing

Master Dimensions

Advanced Design

Contracts and Pricing

Design Analysis and Model Testing

Design

Prototype Manufacturing and Testing

Component and Flight Testing

Material

Manufacturing Planning and Scheduling

Tooling

Fabrication

Quality Control

Production Support

Assembly

Acceptance Testing and Delivery

Post-Delivery Support

ing cycle, speeding up work flow but leaving essentially unchanged the way the process is engineered.

DATABASING FROM CUSTOMER SOURCES

To vend, you need to know your own costs. To sell in a consultative manner, you need to know customer costs. To vend, you need to know your own sales opportunities. To sell as a consultant, you need to know customer sales opportunities. Realizing that you must come up with a cost-reducing or revenue-adding option, how can you learn a customer's current costs in the business functions that are important to you? How can you get a fix on the customer's unachieved sales potential? In profiling customer operations, how can you quantify with reasonable accuracy the problems and opportunities that will form the base of your penetration plans?

You will need to develop three databases, storehouses of information that will become the basic resources for value-based selling to key accounts:

1. An *industry database* on each of the industries in which you serve key customers
2. A *customer database* on each key account customer you serve in an industry
3. A *customer's customer database* on your key accounts' key accounts

From your industry database, you will learn average costs, average profits on sales, average inventories and receivables, and other industry norms. The information in each of your key customer databases will allow you to compare customer performance against industry averages. In categories where a customer falls below the norms, you may find sales opportunities.

Your individual customer databases will teach you the concentration and distribution of customer costs. Where do they bunch up? Are these the same places for the industry as a whole? How heavy are they? What are their trends? Are they rising or are they coming under control? What variable factors affect them most significantly?

The best answers to all of these questions always come from customers themselves. Supplementary and complementary data can be found in public information sources listed in Figure 4-3.

Your customer databases will also provide you with knowledge of where potential new sales opportunities for a customer may be found. These may include existing products, new products, combined products, new or enhanced services, superproducts, or systems. How can your customers sell more? How can they sell at higher prices? How can they extend sales into closely adjacent markets? How can they invade new markets that offer superior profit opportunity? How can they anticipate or turn back a competitive thrust?

Figure 4-3. Public information sources.

Customer Information

- Quarterly, annual, and 10-K reports
- Investment analyst research reports
- *Standard & Poor's Corporate Records*
- *Standard & Poor's Register of Corporations*
- *Thomas Register of American Manufacturers*
- *Ward's Business Directory*
- *Dun & Bradstreet Reports*
- *Value Line Investment Surveys*
- Compustat database on public companies
- Internet *Alta Vista Document Search*
- AOL/America Online *Hoover's Business Sources*
- *Lexis/Nexis* Online

Financial Ratios

- *Almanac of Business and Industrial Ratios*
- *Dun & Bradstreet Industry Norms and Key Financial Ratios*
- *Standard & Poor's Analyst's Handbook*
- *Robert Morris Associates Annual Statement Study of Financial and Operating Ratios*

In order for you to know your customers' businesses, you must know more than the performance and cost characteristics of the internal business functions that you can affect. You must also know the markets your customers sell to. They are your customers' opportunity. Their needs cause many customer business functions to operate the way they do: to manufacture the kinds of products they make, to advertise and sell the way they do, to communicate inside and outside their businesses with the telecommunications and data processing technologies they use. Only when you know your customers' customers can you understand the full range of sales opportunities that can be enlarged as well as costs that can be reduced.

The essential elements of information you will need to know about your customers' customers are exactly the same as the data you must develop on your customers themselves. You will have to learn the major cost areas your customers affect in their own key account businesses and the main sales opportunities they help them achieve.

In order to induce a customer manager to share his or her numbers with you, there is one immutable rule to follow: *To get customer numbers, you must offer your own numbers first.* The numbers you offer must be the best projection of your norms onto your best estimate of a customer's current performance.

Being sure of your solution means more than just being sure that it will work. Does it yield the best financial reward—in other words, do the dollar values work best? If you are wrong, millions of dollars may be sacrificed, as one customer discovered:

> We make hundreds of components that can be configured in thousands of ways to make an unlimited number of customized products. One vendor wanted to set up a just-in-time inventory of all our components. Another one gave us a system to determine the optimal configuration for each product based on customer requirements. The JIT inventory would have saved us between $3 and $5 million. But the second vendor saved us roughly $18 to $20 million per year in manufacturing costs by reducing the number of false orders for unneeded components.

PROPOSING THE POWER OF ONE

The number one, which is the smallest whole number, can have enormous power. One more product sold every day, one more percentage point added to current revenues or profits every week, or one more day gained every month in the collection of accounts receivable can yield astonishing amounts of improved profits for a customer. Applying the power of one also appeals to customer comfort. Most managers can deal with increments of that magnitude without incurring a disruption of the business whose costs and inefficiencies can nullify the gains. Furthermore, the number one has the power of credibility. Most customers will readily concede that they can improve performance, productivity, or profits by 1 percent.

The power of one is the basis of PIP power. It is your power base for a customer's profit improvement. If the power of one is powerful enough, it may also be your end point. If you propose to increase an inventory manager's turnover cycle, you need to know the power of improving the number of turns by one a year. If your customer were IBM, with a $10 billion inventory that was turning over 2.8 times a year, each additional turn can save $2 billion in cash that no longer needs to be tied up financing unsold computers. If you propose to decrease an airline manager's operating costs, you need to know the power of reducing costs by each cent. If your customer were Delta, each 1 cent reduction in the cost of flying one seat one mile can earn the equivalent of $600 million a year in new revenues.

Multiple-Sourcing the Power of One

The power of one's value can come from multiple sources. By reducing inventory overstocking by 1 percent, the value can come from a combination of reduced interest cost on the capital invested in inventory, reducing carrying charges for slow-moving and stationary items that together can add up to 25 percent or more of total inventory contribution to distribution costs, and reduced write-off for obsolete products.

What if the customer's inventory problem is being out of

stock, and you can reduce it by 1 percent? The value can come from several sources:

- Higher turnover of the highest profit-contributing products that yield more than 80 percent of annual revenues
- Accelerated billing and collection cycle from increased same-day order fulfillment
- Reduced lost orders, reduced lost customers, and increased customer satisfaction
- Reduced take-down and set-up manufacturing costs for small make-up runs

The power of one can show up in the added purchasing power of one new customer for your own customer. If you find yourself proposing that your own customer should invest $1 million with you in new equipment, stop before you go any further and ask what you should be consultatively persuading him to buy. It must not be the equipment. What the customer is buying is an extra $1 million in annual sales at a contribution margin of $250,000 that is enabled by the enlarged capacity the equipment can provide. Before you can propose, you must know two things:

1. $1 million worth of incremental annual demand exists.
2. The return on the customer's investment compensates him for the incremental cost at or above his hurdle rate. This means that you must know that the customer's 25 percent marginal return exceeds his minimum acceptable return of 20 percent on investments of $1 million.

If the demand exists and the investment's return is minimally acceptable, then all it may take to close a PIP is the annual income from one additional customer. This one customer's business is what you are actually proposing.

If General Valve Company sells its Twin Seals at $100,000 and a competitor comes in at $70,000, General must try to justify the extra $30,000. If it is not selling consultatively, it will vend the features and benefits of Twin Seals and end up discounting their value. But with Consultative Selling, General can earn more than its originally proposed $100,000.

When General sells to a petrochemicals refiner, its account manager goes looking for leaking valves. When he finds a valve that is leaking contaminants into a premium fuel facility, he has a closeable proposal opportunity. The refiner's potential loss on premium fuel that has been downgraded into regular fuel is $.03 per gallon. This can add up to an annual loss of $75,000 in each of the refiner's ten 2.52 million–gallon tanks for a total loss of $750,000 a year, year after year. Capturing this money converts a performance-to-price ratio to investment-to-return, making $100,000 irrelevant against the added value of $750,000 to infinity. If payback of the customer's investment can occur within 12 months, the investment becomes the equivalent of a short-term loan at the ROI's rate of interest.

General's account managers do not have to wait to discover leaks in a refiner's processes. They can anticipate their negative contributions to maintenance cost and revenues according to their norms. Ball valves and gate valves are always cheaper than General's Twin Seals. On initial purchase price alone they would win. But their costs of ownership can be prohibitive. If one of them leaks only 0.01 percent of a pipeline's total throughput, 28.8 barrels of marketable product will be lost. This amounts to 10.5 thousand barrels lost per valve per year. At an average product price of $10 a barrel, the annual cost of a ball valve or gate valve is actually over $100,000. When the price of oil rises, the valve's cost of ownership goes up with it. Refiners who deprive themselves of the benefits of Twin Seals can be shown to end up constructively "buying" them over and over again without ever enjoying their contributions to improved profits.

Codifying the Power of One

Some consultative sellers have codified the power of one in their businesses. For every 1 percent of cost reduction we can help a customer achieve, such a business can say, we can propose a 5 percent improvement in customer profits. For every 1 percent of added sales revenues we can bring to a customer, we can propose a 4 percent improvement in customer profits. For every 1 percent of added margin we can help a customer command, we can propose a 9 percent improvement in customer profits.

If you can help a manufacturing customer eliminate one part from a major product, you can free the business from ten contributions to cost. The customer will not have to:

1. Design it.
2. Assign a part number to it.
3. Inventory it.
4. Shelve it.
5. Inspect it.
6. Assemble it.
7. Repair it.
8. Package it.
9. Handle it.
10. Deliver it.

If you partner with customers to help them expand sales, can you enlarge their market opportunity by a factor of one? If you can start new mothers using a customer's baby foods one month sooner, when their babies are five months old instead of six, you can open your customer to millions of dollars worth of incremental annual sales.

Figures 4-4 and 4-5 are laundry lists of general opportunities to apply the power of one to revenue expansion and cost reduction. Somewhere in these lists may be your own best opportunities, the things you do exceptionally well that help customers improve their profits and that therefore become the definition of "what you do" as a business. These elements of "your game" target the critical success factors in customer businesses and business functions that identify the arenas where you can make the partnership contributions that must become your industry's standards for adding value.

The power of one applies equally across the board of customer operations, as in the following examples for information systems:

Figure 4-4. Revenue expansion opportunities.

1. Add operational flexibility.
2. Add manufacturing or processing quality.
3. Add volume.
4. Improve effectiveness of sales department.
5. Introduce new sizes, shapes, or materials or new and improved products.
6. Reduce customer returns.
7. Apply creative sales promotion strategies.
8. Speed up production and distribution.
9. Reduce or eliminate unprofitable products, customers, warehouses, or territories.
10. Improve market position.
11. Add brand name value.
12. Add customer benefits.
13. Extend product life.
14. Expand into new markets.
15. Increase distribution.

Figure 4-5. Cost reduction opportunities.

1. Reduce number of operations.
2. Reduce cost of one or more operations.
3. Combine two or more operations.
4. Automate operations.
5. Reduce labor.
6. Improve production scheduling.
7. Reduce operating time to speed up production.
8. Reduce insurance costs.
9. Reduce materials consumption.
10. Recycle materials.
11. Substitute less expensive materials or otherwise reformulate product.
12. Reduce raw materials inventory.
13. Reduce parts inventory.
14. Improve controls.
15. Simplify product and package design.

- If an airline's reservation system goes down for one hour, it can cost an average of $100,000 in lost sales.
- If a manufacturer's mission-critical network goes down for one hour, it can cost an average of $80,000 in delayed transactions.
- If a Wall Street brokerage's distribution system goes down for one hour, it can cost more than $6 million in stock and bond purchases.

For each of these examples, the Consultative Selling opening questions are the same: "What if we start to reduce downtime one hour at a time? What is the smallest number of hours that can make a significant difference in revenues? What is their dollar volume? If one hour is significant, as in the Wall Street brokerage example, what if we start with that?"

The world of costs is changing. Whereas labor has traditionally contributed the major share of a manufacturer's costs, now it rarely exceeds 10 to 20 percent. While the hard-core costs of capital equipment have traditionally been a principal area of customer investment, or at least have been perceived as such, this is no longer the case in businesses in which information-intensive services are natural accompaniments of equipment. In buying computers, for example, a common rule of thumb is to allow $100 for training expenses for every $1 of hardware cost. In networking computers and telecommunications equipment, the support costs of making everything work together as a single coherent system normally outruns the equipment cost by five times. These customer costs for integration and application are more important to reduce, in many cases, than are the costs of the hard goods they add to.

GETTING TO PIP

Nothing happens in Consultative Selling until you get to PIP. At the PIP point, you make your preliminary PIP to a customer manager and begin your partnership. This begins the process of putting you in business with him. It positions you as potentially partnerable, permitting the belief that you may provide him with a compelling reason to work with you. At the same time that a preliminary PIP starts the selling phase of the sales cycle, it also forecloses to your competition the customer problem or opportunity you have projected for improvement.

The sooner you can get to PIP, the better. Until you do, you are vulnerable to opportunity cost from not being able to sell. You are also open to preemption by a competitor who can get to PIP faster or by the closing of the opportunity window if customer priorities change, managers change jobs or their positions become consolidated, or funds run out or become reallocated. Simultaneously, your customer is also suffering lost opportunity and may be preempted in industry advantage by his own competitors.

When you sell improved profits, time becomes your enemy. Time downgrades the value of money, which has a time value as well as a dollar value. The rule of thumb about money is that a dollar today is always worth more than the value of the same dollar tomorrow because today's dollar can be invested today to make more dollars. Tomorrow's dollar must wait for tomorrow. This is as true for your business as it is for your customer. The longer it takes you to get to PIP, the less money you make and the more money you spend in cost of sales to make it.

Customer managers are in business to do deals. A deal is an investment that yields positive return. Profit Improvement Proposals are invitations to deal by making an investment in an application of your products, services, or systems to improve customer profits.

From a customer's perspective, there are six major hurdles that your PIPs must clear in order to be considered a good deal:

1. The *expected return,* expressed by the customer's question, "How much do I get out?" There are two ways of proposing your answer. One is the cash flow from year-one expanded revenues or reduced costs. The other is the net present value of all future cash flows beyond the first year discounted back to the present and calculated over the productive life of the investment.
2. The *proposed investment,* expressed by the customer's question, "How much do I have to put in?"

3. The *internal rate of return,* expressed by the customer's question, "What is the ratio between how much I get out and how much I have to put in?" The answer is the annual percentage return per dollar invested.
4. The *payback,* expressed by the customer's question, "How soon do I recover my investment?"
5. The *opportunity cost,* expressed by the customer's question, "How much do I lose by saying no?" The answer is the total net positive cash flow payout over the productive life of the investment.
6. The *earliest point at which risk can be controlled,* expressed by the customer's question, "If I don't like it once I'm into it, how soon can I get out?" The answer is the first checkpoint at which results are measured.

A PIP becomes closable because it is more advantageous for a customer to live with your solution than to go on living with his current problem or inability to take advantage of an opportunity.

Closable PIPs are delivery vehicles for "killer apps": or applications of a supplier's technology to a customer's operation that maximize improved profits. A killer app kills off a problem or kills off competitive proposals to realize the same opportunity. It kills off procrastination because, operationally and financially, its results are compelling. When a killer app is first proposed, it stops debate dead in its tracks. Its top-line and bottom-line contributions make customers want to get their hands on them. The new profits seem realizable. The operating improvements that enable them seem achievable. Delay seems unjustifiable.

At first sight, many killer apps appear to be no-brainers. Quite the opposite. They come out of a consultative seller's grey matter: the ability to reach into his or her database on customer operations along with their needs and objectives, and especially their current contributions to revenues and costs, coupled with the knowledge of how supplier technology can best be applied to affect them. This ability to mix and match reveals the "matrix mind" of the consultative seller. In a continuous filtering manner, the seller is screening customer operating norms through the templates of supplier improvement norms. Killer apps come into being when the two intersect.

Your PIPs must reek of credibility in the advantages they propose. They start out with one strike against them. Every customer manager knows about—or even worse, has lived through—the $250,000 investment that grew to $500,000 in order to save a $1 million return that was promised to be twice as much but shrank to less than half of that by the time it was realized.

Every manager's common experience also includes the six-month payback that stretched out to sixteen. There are three ways to make your PIPs credible. One is to make all your preliminary calculations on the conservative side, leaving yourself "wiggle room" when you work with your customer's numbers:

- Overestimate all costs by 20 percent.
- Underestimate all revenues by 20 percent.

The second way is to promise a small number of benefits. It is easier to achieve the correction of a customer's parts shortage all by itself than to combine it with improving productivity, enhancing customer service, and speeding up inventory turns all in the same PIP. The third way is to work with your customer's numbers. If you propose to reduce a customer's inventory, start with his current cost of goods sold—for example, $3 million. Then put his numbers to work like this:

- The customer values his current inventory at $800,000.
- The current turn rate is therefore 3.75, the result of dividing the cost of goods sold by the inventory value.
- If you propose to reduce inventory by 10 percent, or $80,000, leaving an inventory value of $720,000, the improved inventory turn rate is 4.16.
- If the customer agrees that his cost of carrying $80,000 worth of inventory is 25 percent [to account for handling, insurance, shrinkage, damage, space, obsolescence, taxes, and the opportunity cost of tied-up cash], the total savings come to $20,000.

The customer will buy this number because his own numbers have gone into it.

PIPPING IN THE "RED ZONE"

If you are going to have a norm of 1:1 for PIPs closed to PIPs proposed, you must get into a customer manager's "red zone," where he is compelled to take action on each PIP you present. It is not enough to say that your proposal "certainly made him sit up and take notice" or that the outcome of your presentation was that you made him think. A thinking manager is not a closing manager. Your outcome must be to get a close. What will get you into the red zone where you can score?

A customer manager's red zone is where his key performance indicators (KPIs) are located. Each PIP must fit one of them in order to link it to the manager's contribution to business strategy. This is called a PIP's business fit. A statement of business fit sounds like this:

This proposal contributes to realizing your business objectives to:

1. Increase your sales volume by $4.5 million (42.4 percent) over the next three years.
2. Increase your market share by 4.1 points (10 percent).
3. Increase your net operating profits before tax (NOPBT) by $2.3 million (9 percent).

In the course of your partnering, you will learn each customer's business objectives. Your PIPs must tie their contributions to these objectives by quantifying how much of each objective you can help realize: for example, contributing $864,000 (4 percent) toward the customer's sales volume objective of $4.5 million and increasing NOPBT by $69,000 per year to contribute 30 percent of the operating profit objective.

KPIs compose a customer manager's "plan." The manager's current performance is called "actual." If plan exceeds actual, the manager is "off plan" and at risk of becoming competitively disadvantaged. Disadvantages can become your leads if your norms represent an improvement over a customer's actual performance when it is below a KPI.

The performance indicators that you choose to improve for

your customers provide them with their definition of your business. The KPIs you decide to "own" position you with customer managers in terms of exactly *where* in their operations you can partner with them and *why,* because of your norms, they are compelled to partner with you. The "where" is your entry point.

If you want to make yourself compelling to IT managers, for example, nothing will do it faster or on a more businesslike basis than to issue norm challenges like these:

- Do your operating costs exceed our norm of 1 percent of the dollar value of all the purchases you make? If so, what if we can work together to bring you closer to our norm?
- Does your staff exceed our norm of 2.2 per each $100 million to $150 million worth of purchases?
- Does your number of instances of delayed shipments exceed our norm of four to six total yearly deliveries from each supplier?

If you want to compel a hospital manager to do business with you, challenge him with your norms for his KPIs for capacity utilization expressed in terms of patient occupancy rate and average length of stay for patients in each disease category. You can also challenge other KPIs for the percent of outpatient revenues to total revenues, gross revenues per discharged patient, cash flow per bed, and the percent of salary and benefits expenses of hospital employees to the hospital's total expenses. Comparing labor costs to total costs shows how well a hospital is controlling its workforce content. Cash flow per bed shows how aggressively the hospital is recruiting patients, and their average length of stay shows how well the hospital is managing its turnover. If your norm for labor costs is 51 percent of total costs while a hospital manager can do no better than 56.6 percent, you have a lead for a PIP to improve his performance.

If you sell IV systems for intravenous drug delivery to health care organizations as IVAC does, you may need to know the key performance indicators of more than one class of customer manager. In IVAC's case, critical care and neonatal unit heads are major users, as are general service IV team leaders. Pharmacy managers are involved as well, in addition to hospital administrators and their chief financial officers. In IVAC's initial incarnation as a vendor, it was assumed that the critical success factors influencing sales were competitive price and performance, salesperson skills, timing, and supplier reputation. After reincarnation as a consultative seller, the chief factor critical to IVAC's sales success has become the contribution that IVAC can make to key users' KPIs.

At the Box One HMO and hospital administrator level and at the Box Two midlevels, there are several performance indicators to choose for improvement:

- Capacity utilization, such as the number of beds in service, occupancy rate, and average length of stay, all of which IVAC can affect
- Revenues and expenses, such as cash flow per bed, total profit margin, and return on assets
- Productivity and efficiency, such as the ratio of personnel per patient and total assets turnover, as well as outcomes in terms of patient discharges in compliance with disease-category standards for length of stay

LEAD TARGETING WITH KPI NORMS

Key performance indicators come in two types:

1. Dollar values, expressed as minimum revenue or maximum cost objectives
2. Ratios, expressed as percentages

Some KPI classifications are standard across all industries. They are part of a manager's position title. Other KPIs are industry-specific.

KPIs for Profit Center Managers

Position title predicts the key indicators for every profit center manager's performance. He or she is evaluated by financial and working capital indicators of line-of-business performance such as:

- Total revenues, which are total receipts from sales
- Total operating income, which is gross profits minus total operating expenses
- Total operating expenses, which are costs of sales plus G&A plus R&D
- Cost of goods sold, which is sales compensation plus sales support and sales training
- Inventory turnover, which is the ratio of annual net sales compared to end-of-year inventory
- Accounts receivable turnover, which is the ratio of annual net sales compared to average receivables outstanding

Profit center managers are also evaluated by how well they handle key indicators of their operating performance:

- Gross profit, which is total revenues minus cost of goods sold
- Net profit, which is after-tax net income minus net sales
- Productivity, which is sales revenue minus cost of labor
- Selling efficiency, which is expressed in several ratios that compare sales revenues against selling expense, finished goods inventory, order backlog, same-day order fulfillment, and accounts receivable

If your customer manages a soft drink bottler, any significant deviations between the key indicators of his performance and your norms for them can become a proposable lead:

- How much of his capacity is he utilizing?
- How many cases per employee is he shipping?
- How much of his run time is interrupted by downtime?
- How much gross margin is he earning per case?
- How much of his sales revenue is held up in accounts receivable?
- How much of his customer base is he satisfying?

KPIs for Cost Center Managers

A cost center manager has function-specific KPIs:

- If he manages R&D, he is evaluated—among other indicators—by a ratio comparing the number of products developed to the number of products commercialized.
- If he manages manufacturing, he is evaluated by a ratio comparing the number of hours downtime to the number of hours uptime.
- If he manages inventory, he is evaluated by a ratio comparing the number of orders shipped the same day to the number of orders received.

Once you know what your customer managers are held to perform, you can propose to help them by targeting any indications that their actual performance lags your norm for their performance in categories like these:

Lead Targeting From Key Financial Performance Indicators. A customer's current financial performance can indicate opportunities for three kinds of profit improvement projects:

1. *Total Revenue Raisers.* You can propose to raise total revenues by speeding up time to market, increasing the turnover rate of the new product development cycle, improving forecasts or reducing inventory, adding distribution, or accelerating the billing and collection cycle.
2. *Total Operating Income Raisers.* You can propose to raise total operating income by increasing sales or decreasing operating expenses for cost of sales, G&A, and R&D.
3. *Cost of Goods Sold Reducers.* You can propose to reduce cost of goods sold by improving sales force productivity, reducing the sales cycle, adding distribution, opening up new sources of demand, or re-engineering sales strategy.

Lead Targeting From Key Operating Performance Indicators. A customer's current operating performance can indicate opportunities for four kinds of profit improvement projects:

1. *Gross Profit Raisers.* You can propose to raise gross profit by increasing sales volume and expanding market share, speeding up the sales cycle, adding distribution, increasing the turnover rate of the new product development cycle, or reducing manufacturing costs.
2. *Net Profit Raisers.* You can propose to raise net profit by increasing margins or reducing the cost of sales.
3. *Productivity Raisers.* You can propose to raise productivity by reducing labor content, increasing automation, or improving workforce training.
4. *Selling Efficiency Raisers.* You can propose to raise selling efficiency by reducing cost of sales, finished goods inventory or order backlog, or by increasing same-day order fulfillment and accounts receivable collections.

Lead Targeting From Key Working Capital Performance Indicators. A customer's current working capital performance can indicate opportunities for two kinds of profit improvement projects:

1. *Inventory Turnover Raisers.* You can propose to raise inventory turnover by reducing inventory or helping to turn it faster.
2. *Accounts Receivable Turnover Raisers.* You can propose to raise accounts receivable turnover by helping to collect receivables faster.

5

How to Quantify Your Solution

Customer profit improvement begins with knowledge of how customers make the profits that you are going to improve: how they make their money right now. This is the starting point for Consultative Selling. Unless Consultative Selling strategies can improve the profits a customer can make, the customer will not be a prospect for high-margin sales.

A customer makes money based on five principles:

1. Circulating capital
2. Turnover
3. Contribution margin
4. Return on investment (ROI)
5. Payback

Applying the Circulating Capital Principle

Profit is made by the circulation of business capital. Every business is founded on capital, or funds that start in the form of cash. The objective of business is to make the initial cash grow into more cash. This is accomplished by circulating the capital, the initial cash, through three transfer points. Each transfer adds value:

1. The initial cash circulates first into *inventories*.
2. Then the inventories circulate into *receivables*.

3. The receivables finally circulate back into *cash,* completing one cycle.

This three-step process demonstrates the principle of circulating capital. Every business depends on it for its income.

Circulating capital is the current assets of a business. They go to work in profitmaking as soon as cash is invested in accumulating inventories. Every time raw materials are purchased or processed, inventories come into existence. Another name for production scheduling could really be inventory conversion. Manufacturing adds further to the value of inventories, and so do all the other processing functions of a business that transfer value from cash to product costs on a dollar-for-dollar basis.

Figure 5-1 shows the profitmaking process that occurs as capital funds circulate through a customer's business. At *A* the funds are in the form of cash. As the business operates, the funds change form. The initial cash is transferred into inventories as raw materials are purchased, labor is paid, and finished goods are manufactured and transported from plant to warehouse.

When sales occur at *B,* funds flow from inventories—the manufactured goods—into receivables. As they flow, the magnitude of the funds increases because inventories are valued at cost and receivables are valued at selling price. This increase represents the gross profit on sales. The greater the gross profit rate, the greater the increase in funds during each rotation of the capital circulation cycle.

At *C,* the funds earned by the collection of receivables flow back once again into cash. Before they do, they are reduced by the sales and administrative expenses that have been disbursed throughout the operating cycle.

At this point, one full cycle of capital circulation has been completed. It has resulted in an increase in the number of dollars in the circulating capital fund. This increase is the difference between gross profits and selling/administrative expenses. In other words, a profit is made when the circulating capital of the business turns over one cycle. The more cycles through which you can help turn your customer's circulating capital during an operating year, the greater the profit the customer can earn. This is the principle of *turnover.*

Figure 5-1. Profitmaking capital circulation.

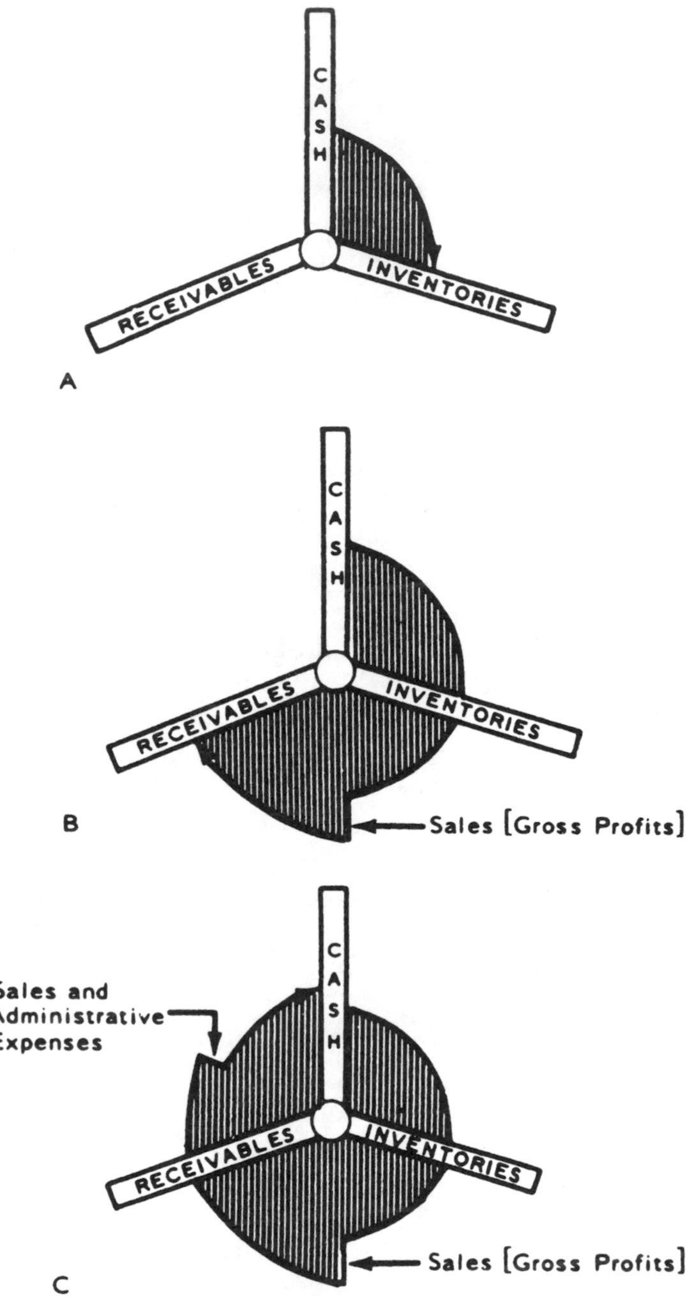

APPLYING THE TURNOVER PRINCIPLE

The circulation of capital funds in a customer's business takes on meaning only when it relates to time. Since capital funds turn over in a complete cycle from cash to inventories, then to receivables, and finally back into cash again, their rate of flow can be measured as the rate of turnover. The faster the turnover, the greater the profit.

Stepping up a customer's turnover rate through profit improvement is the consultative sales representative's most important function. Unless your profit projects are by and large directed to improving the turnover of the capital employed in your customer's business—especially the capital that is in the form of inventories—you cannot accomplish your mission.

Turnover will generally offer more opportunities than will any other strategy for profit improvement. The most common way to improve turnover rate is through increased sales volume and lowered operating fund requirements. In some situations, turnover may be improved by decreasing sales or even increasing the investment in operating assets.

You are in excellent position to help improve a customer's turn of circulating capital since, as Figure 5-2 shows, the drive wheel that rotates capital is sales. You must continually search for the optimal relationship between your customer's sales volume and the investment in operating funds required to achieve it. At the point where the optimal relationship exists, the turnover rate will yield the best profit.

In Figure 5-2, the circumference of the sales wheel represents $200,000 worth of sales during a twelve-month operating period. The sales wheel drives a smaller wheel representing circulating capital. The circumference of the circulating wheel equals the amount of dollars invested in working funds, in this case $100,000. Enclosing the circulating capital wheel is a larger wheel, also driven by sales, that represents the total capital employed. It includes the circulating capital of $100,000 plus another $100,000 invested in plant and facilities. Thus the circumference of the wheel representing total capital employed is $200,000, equal to the sales drive wheel.

Figure 5-2. Profitmaking turnover.

Basic Relationship

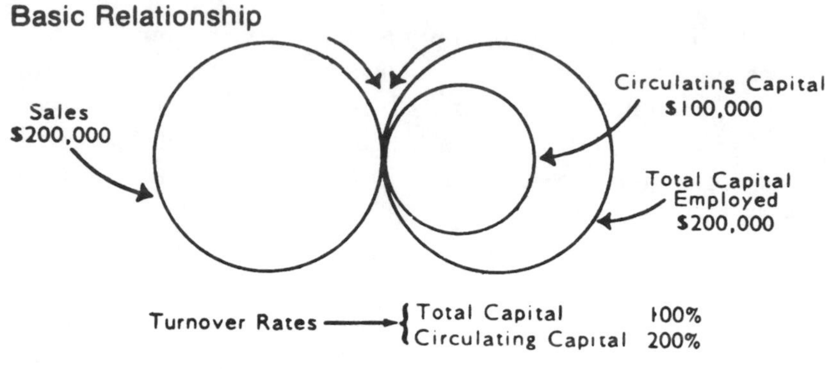

Option A: Increase Sales

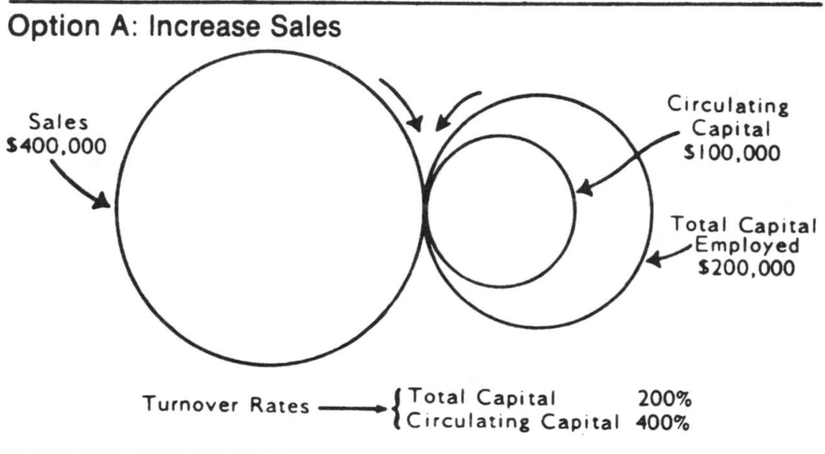

Option B: Decrease Capital

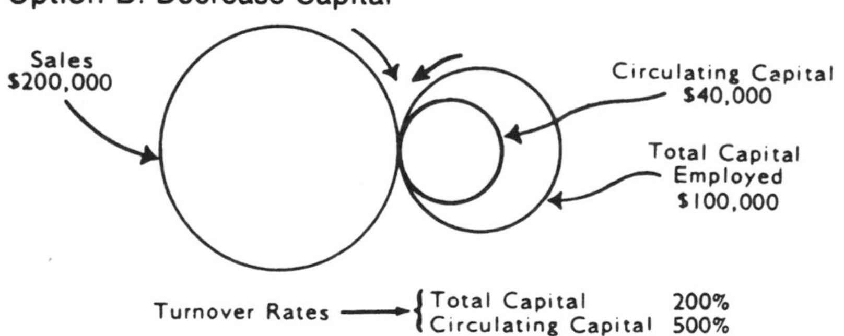

When annual sales are $200,000 and total capital employed in the operation is $200,000, the annual turnover rate of total funds invested is 100 percent, or one turn per year. The portion of the total that is circulating capital, amounting to $100,000, will turn over at the rate of 200 percent, or twice a year.

Each of the three elements of circulating capital—cash, receivables, and inventories—will have its own individual turnover rate. Inventory turnover is calculated according to the number of months' supply on hand. A six months' supply would represent two turns per year, or a 200 percent annual turnover rate. Turnover of receivables is expressed as the number of days' business outstanding. If ninety days of business are outstanding, the receivables turnover is four turns per year, or 400 percent.

Since circulating capital increases every time it completes one turn, your job is to find ways to increase customer turnover through the use of your product and service systems. You can exercise two options for improving turnover. One way, option *A*, is by increasing sales. The other way is by decreasing the amount of money invested in circulating capital, option *B*. Figure 5-2 shows an opportunity to double customer sales to $400,000 per year without increasing the $200,000 of total funds employed in the business. This is option *A*. The turnover rate will be increased from 100 to 200 percent. At the same time, the turnover rate of circulating capital increases from 200 to 400 percent.

If the consultant cannot increase the customer's sales, option *B* offers an alternative opportunity to improve turnover. Even though sales remain at the same annual rate of $200,000, turnover can be increased if total capital employed is reduced from $200,000 to $100,000. This includes a parallel reduction in circulating capital from $100,000 to $40,000. These reductions help the consultant improve the turnover rate of total capital employed from 100 to 200 percent and that of circulating capital from 200 to 500 percent. This strategy for improving turnover means that the operating funds of the customer's business are being worked harder.

The profit improvement created by options *A* and *B* can be readily appreciated by multiplying the increase in funds generated at each turn of the operating cycle by an increasing number of turns. If the operating profit from one turn in the basic relationship shown in Figure 5-2 is $50,000, the profit realized by option *A* would be doubled to $100,000. In option *B,* profit would remain at $50,000 but $100,000 of funds would be released from operations that could be used to generate additional business or reduce indebtedness.

Opportunities abound for improving a customer's turnover. The reason is simple. The sum total of funds employed in a customer's business represents the many individual funds that make up circulating and fixed capital. An improvement in the turnover of any one of these funds will correspondingly improve the turnover of the total funds employed. Therefore, you can zero in on any component of a customer's "turnover mix" without having to consider any of the others or their sum total. For example, improvement in the turnover of any single item in a customer's inventory—including your own product—will improve total turnover and consequently contribute to profit improvement.

APPLYING THE CONTRIBUTION MARGIN PRINCIPLE

The key to profits is contribution margin—how much margin each product line or business unit contributes to a customer's total profits. Affecting a customer's contribution margins is a key objective of Consultative Selling. There are two ways to do this. You can help increase sales volume at the current contribution margin. Or you can help increase contribution margin at the current volume of sales.

Figure 5-3 shows how contribution margin works. It is calculated by subtracting variable costs from sales revenues. In the example, a customer's total contribution margin is $.095. That means that each single dollar of sales is currently contributing a margin of 9.5 cents to cover the customer's fixed operating overhead of $221,000. It takes a lot of $1 sales to contribute enough 9.5 cents' worth of margins to cover $221,000 of overhead. Even when sales do that, the customer merely breaks even. That is where you come in. If you can increase sales or decrease the vari-

Figure 5-3. Analysis of profit contribution by product line ($000).

	Total	Product Lines A	B	C
1. Sales	$2,600.0 100.0%	$1,742.0 67.0%	$650.0 25.0%	$208.0 8.0%
2. Cost of sales	$2,106.0 81.0%	$1,440.0 82.7%	$520.0 80.0%	$146.0 70.0%
3. Gross profit (1–2)	$494.0 19.0%	$302.0 17.3%	$130.0 20.0%	$62.0 30.0%
4. Wages	$221.0 8.5%	$134.0 7.7%	$65.0 10.0%	$22.0 10.5%
5. Other	$26.0 1.0%	$10.0 0.6%	$13.0 1.9%	$3.0 1.5%
6. Total (4 + 5)	$247.0 9.5%	$144.0 8.3%	$78.0 11.9%	$25.0 12.0%
7. Contribution margin (3–6)	$247.0 9.5%	$158.0 9.0%	$52.0 8.1%	$37.0 18.0%

able costs that subtract from sales revenues, you can improve customer profits.

The consultant's choices are shown in Figure 5-3. If you want to work on product line *A*, you can improve profits best by improving sales. While it has only a 17.3 percent gross profit, it also has a 9.0 percent contribution. Any increase in sales volume will produce new profits. On the other hand, if you work on product line *B*, you will have to reduce its variable costs. Its 20 percent gross profit exceeds that of *A*. But it is making only an 8.1 percent contribution after variable expenses. If you can reduce its expenses, you can improve its contribution even without increasing sales volume.

APPLYING ROI AND PAYBACK PRINCIPLES

When you present a PIP to a Box Two manager, what questions can you anticipate?

- *What is the net present value of this deal?* To get the answer, the manager will discount your proposal's future cash flow projections at the rate of his company's cost of capital. The manager will then calculate the cumulative value of these cash flows in terms of today's dollars in order to arrive at their present value. Finally, he will subtract the investment you are asking from the present value to learn the net value.
- *What is the return on investment from this proposal?* To get the answer, the manager will multiply margin by expected turnover. If margins have been declining and you propose to improve them, you can leave the rate of turnover alone. If you cannot increase margins, the manager will look to see if you are proposing to increase turnover.
- *What is the payback period on the investment that is being proposed in the PIP?* Payback calculates the return *of* the investment, not the return *on* it. The manager will want payback as soon as possible in order to limit risk. He will usually calculate it by dividing the initial investment by the projected cash flows. Alternatively, each period's cash flows may be added together until the investment has been covered.

Customer managers use a business shorthand to appraise your PIPs quickly in order to qualify them for serious consideration. They use two criteria in rapid-fire order to make a quick study of the key things they have to know up front:

1. How much money can they most likely earn if they invest in your proposals?
2. How soon will they be able to realize it?

These two quick screens will tell them if they are interested in going further with you, which means finding out how sure they can be about the "muchness" and "soonness" you are proposing.

Criteria of "How Much"

Customer managers use three criteria of muchness to determine how much they will get out of an investment in one of your PIPs:

1. *Net present value (NPV)* indicates the net value of all the future cash flows you will help them earn over the commercial life of your proposals, discounted back to their present value today so they have a common denominator of value. Bringing future values back to their present value, which discounts them, is made necessary by the time value of money. A dollar in the manager's hands today is always worth more than the value of the same dollar in his hands tomorrow. Every manager has a minimum NPV standard for accepting proposals. You must PIP him above the standard to merit consideration.

Net present value is the prime index of value. Consultative Selling is NPV selling. The improved profits that a consultative seller sells are improved NPV. Nothing else tells the seller or a customer the true value of what is going to be returned on the customer's investment.

Net income by itself, representing cash flow, ignores the cost of the assets required to generate added revenues. Revenues by themselves ignore their costs. Return on investment by itself can inflate the perception of the return when the investment is comparatively small.

2. *Return on investment (ROI)* indicates the ratio of a customer's total profit improvement to the total investment required to generate it. In order to do a deal, ROI must equal or exceed a customer's minimum hurdle rate for incremental investments—generally two-thirds or more of the customer's cost of capital.

ROI is a ratio of the dollar income generated by a PIP compared to the dollars invested. Two other formulas for evaluating return differ enough from ROI to deserve their own definitions. IRR (Internal Rate of Return) is the average annual percent return from each dollar invested over the commercial life of a PIP, adjusted for the impact of time. ROCE (Return on Capital Employed) is profit before taxes divided by the dollar value of all the capital employed in inventory, accounts receivables, and net investment.

3. *Aftertax cash flows* indicate a proposal's profit after subtracting for taxes and adding back depreciation and other noncash outlays. Cash flow is net income, commonly referred to as the bot-

tom line. Cash flow is vital to every business. It can be even more important than profits because it pays for the continuity of ongoing operations. Depreciation is the reduction in asset value from use or obsolescence. It is based on periodically writing down a portion of an asset's original value so that it can contribute to the reduction of taxes, thereby influencing aftertax cash flow.

Criterion of "How Soon"

Customer managers use *payback* as their criterion of soonness to determine how soon they will be able to recover their investment in your proposals. The payback period is computed by dividing the total amount of an investment by the expected aftertax cash flows. Payback is an important determinant of the relative merits of competitive proposals. Once payback has occurred, the customer manager is "clean," removed from risk. From that point on, his interest will focus on the net present value, accounting rate of return, and aftertax cash flows of your proposals.

Criteria of "How Sure"

The soonness of payback is a key indicator of how sure a customer manager can be of receiving the muchness and soonness of a PIP's proposal. The sooner the payback, the surer the deal. The major contributors to sureness beyond payback are your norms, which validate your track record, and your PIPs' Cost-Benefit Analyses, which prove your Prescriptions.

ROI is an analytic tool that has three qualities in its favor for your purposes: (1) It is a fair measurement of profit contribution; (2) it is helpful in directing attention to the most immediate profit opportunities, allowing them to be ranked on a priority basis; and (3) it is likely to be readily understood and accepted by financial managers as well as sales and marketing managers of your customer companies.

Figure 5-4 represents the two formulas for calculating ROI. The formulas relate the major operating and financial factors required in profitmaking to the rate used to measure the profit that is made: the rate of profit per unit sales in dollars; the rate of

Figure 5-4. Return-on-investment formulas.

A. Options for Improving ROI by Improving Turnover

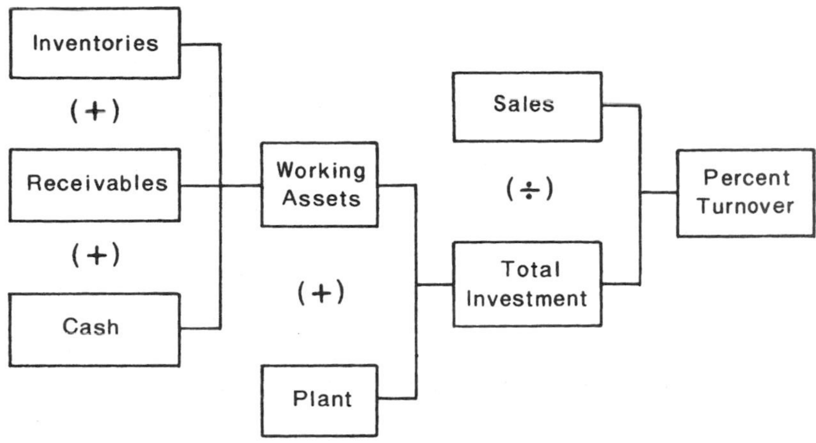

B. Options for Improving ROI by Improving Operating Profit

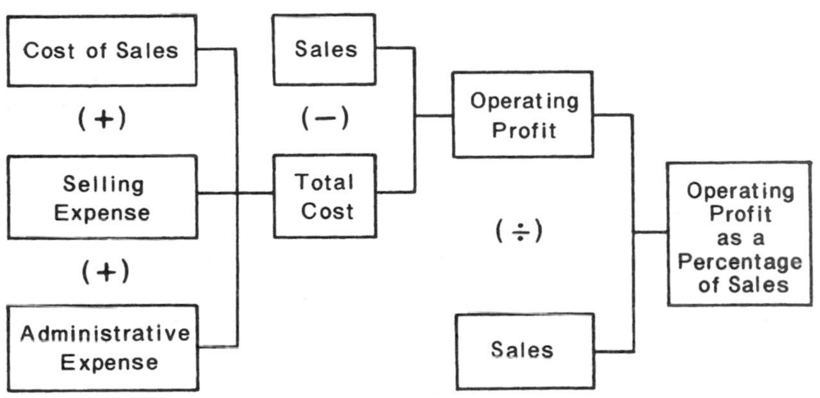

turnover of operating funds, the funds required to finance business operations; and the total investment of capital employed, including working assets, plants, and facilities.

The customer's sole economic justification for investing in your profit-improvement projects is to earn a superior rate of return on the funds invested. This truism must be interpreted in two ways. One is in terms of income gained. The other is in terms of costs avoided in obtaining investment funds, costs of retaining such funds, and costs suffered by denying their use for alternative, potentially more profitable, projects.

Diagnosis is the heart of consulting. Diagnostic techniques based on ROI are the heart of diagnosis. As Figure 5-4 shows, ROI is the product of the rate of operating profit expressed as a percentage of sales and the rate of turnover. Any time you want to improve a customer's ROI, you must first diagnose a problem in the customer's operating profit rate or an opportunity to increase the customer's turnover.

Part *A* of Figure 5-4 shows the ingredients of ROI expressed as turnover. If you examine each of those ingredients, you will find profit opportunities that can improve turnover. You can, for example, recommend a project to reduce your customer's receivables. This will reduce the amount of funds invested in working assets, thus reducing the customer's total investment base. As a result, you can improve your customer's profit without increasing sales volume.

Part *B* shows options for diagnosing profit improvement if your objective is to increase operating profit. You can recommend a project to lower the customer's cost of sales. This will reduce total costs and enable the customer to show an increase in operating profit.

CO-MANAGING A CUSTOMER'S ASSETS

When a customer invests his money to acquire your products or services, he obtains an asset. His goal is to turn it over as quickly as possible so that it will revert to cash. Then he can reinvest in another asset with you and start the process over again. If he makes good investments with you, he will end each investment cycle with more money than he started with. Asset turnover is the secret to making money. The more assets that are turned, and the faster they turn over, the more money will be made.

Accounts receivable and inventory are a customer's two major current assets. Current assets, by being turned over, are more quickly convertible to cash than are fixed assets. Anything you can do to speed up a customer's asset turnover in these two areas will make money for both of you. If you and a customer allow these assets to build up—if a customer's sales decline and inventories grow or if your customer's customers delay paying their bills—both of you will be in trouble.

Ideally, customers would like to have zero investments in accounts receivable and inventory. Every day that you can help them condense their collection period is money in the bank. Every additional turn of inventory also improves profits. An item that turns over 1.7 times a year sits in inventory approximately seven months before being sold. If you can help move it in six months, using the power of one, you can accelerate its contribution to earnings by one-seventh.

Asset turnover is especially important in selling to a customer's profit center managers. One of their key performance indicators is ROI, which is calculated by dividing their earnings by the investment in their asset base. The higher their ROI, the greater the investment that top management will continue to make in their profit centers, and the higher the reward each center's manager will receive.

The ROI of your customers is a good index of how good a co-managing partner you are. If you have the ability to affect inventory, but you let them stock out on their highest margin products, you are a poor co-manager of your customers' assets. If you have the ability to affect collections, but you let their money languish in accounts receivable, you are more of a mismanager than a co-manager. Increasing inventory turns and decreasing collection cycles will make you better.

Whenever you make a proposal to a customer, you are challenging him to assess a risk. If you ask him to invest with you to expand his capacity to produce his existing products, you are offering him a median risk. All other types of investment will have a higher or lower risk. Investments for replacement or repair are the safest. Past experience can accurately help foretell their probable cash flows. Cost reduction investments are somewhat riskier. No one can calculate the exact magnitude of their potential savings. The riskiest type of investment concerns new products or new market development, where neither the costs nor the revenues can be predicted with certainty.

As soon as a customer invests with you, he incurs an opportunity cost equal to the return he could have earned from an alternative investment of the same funds. The opportunity cost is in addition to the direct cost he pays you and the indirect costs he incurs in implementation. The further away you take him from his median risk, where he knows the return he can expect, the more risk-averse he will be and the more proof he will demand and the closer partnership with you he will expect.

Whenever risk increases, a customer will balance it against its return. In high-risk situations, he will be more interested in whether the return is sufficient to justify the risk than the rate of return itself, however high it may be.

The risk-return trade-off is the basis of management. The only fully known sum of money in any transaction is its investment. Future benefits are always uncertain. As risk increases, the anticipated return must increase with it. If a manager is confronted with two equal investments that promise a similar return, he will probably choose the investment with the lower risk—that is, the one with the higher net present value per dollar invested.

Where risk is equal or minimal, it is not a factor. Under these conditions, it will be better to make an investment rather than let money sit idle—and thereby incur opportunity cost—as long as a positive net present value can be returned. This means that it must equal or exceed the customer's cost of capital. As long as it does either one or the other, the investment will be acceptable. This is simply another way of calculating the worth of an investment based on its net present value. According to NPV, investing $50 million today for a stream of future cash flows with a value today of $59.755 million is an acceptable investment. In effect, the customer is paying $50 million for an asset worth $59.755 million, gaining $9.755 million of new value. Since the NPV is well over zero, this is a good investment. If it were only zero, the customer's wealth would be unchanged and his time would be wasted, consumed by opportunity cost.

Invoking Opportunity Cost to Accelerate Closing

Risk, no matter how minimal, increases over time. That is one reason why a dollar today is always worth more than a dollar in the future. Two other reasons why money has a time value are inflation and the opportunity cost that is incurred when money is not productively invested.

Because money has a time value, every dollar returned by an investment is worth less as time goes on. In the way that customer managers think about investments, they say that if I have 91 cents on hand today, I can invest it at 10 percent interest and it will grow into one dollar within one year. Is this the best deal available to me at this time? Can I get a better rate of interest anywhere else? Can I get a quicker payback? Can I get a larger return?

The fear of opportunity loss can be a powerful motivator to commit. Consultative sellers always calculate the value of a lost opportunity to invest with them, reminding their customers of how much it is costing them for each day, week, month, and quarter of deliberation and delay in co-managing a PIP. This puts a penalty on "missing out on a good thing" and, conversely, awards brownie points for biting the bullet.

In traditional vendor selling, time is always on the customer's side. The longer that a purchasing cycle is allowed to run on, the lower the eventual price. For this reason, delay is a more profitable strategy for a customer than closing quickly. While prolonging price negotiation is in the customer's self-interest, the opposite is true for his suppliers.

Whenever a vendor negotiates price, he loses twice. Loss of time is loss of money. As time is lost, the vendor loses even more by discounting his price. Until he reaches the price point where the customer calculates it will no longer be worthwhile to trade more time for an even greater discount, no close will take place.

Vendor prices are always initially unacceptable to customers because time will bring them down. Quick discounts rarely move a customer to close. He knows they will become successively deeper. In reality, vendors never make a close. Their customers control closure, allowing it to take place when they perceive that each additional unit of waiting time will earn them a diminishing return of discounted price.

When the value of time has such a different meaning for a customer and a supplier, there is no way that their relationship can be anything but adversarial. Talk of partnership by vendors is gibberish.

Consultative selling makes partnership possible by endowing time with a mutual value. With a PIP proposal process, immediate closing benefits customers and suppliers alike. If the customer stalls in closing a PIP, he incurs a calculable opportunity cost from postponing today's profits until tomorrow. The dollars themselves can usually be made up; year 5 cash flow may have to wait to be recoverable until year 6. But because money has a time value in addition to a dollar value, the worth of each dollar tomorrow will always be less than the worth of the same dollar today.

For the supplier, delay is also expensive. Any value proposed today will begin to depreciate as soon as it is PIPped. PIPs are enabled by the application of technology, which is perishable. From commercialization forward, all technology is obsolescent. As its value depreciates, its once-exclusive ability to make a contribution to customer profits may become equalized or superseded by a competitive technology. As a result, a PIP's value proposition must be revised downward at the same time that its customer's opportunity cost is rising: It is lose-lose.

The unwillingness on both sides to absorb opportunity cost drives quick PIP closure. Each party is motivated by self-interest in wanting its money now. The customer wants to maximize the net present value of time. The supplier wants to maximize the net present value of technology. A waiting game would be a losing game for both of them.

Guaranteeing Results and Gainsharing Rewards

Once a PIP has been accepted, even before its value has been realized, the consultative seller's customer is already counting on the new earnings he has just contracted for. He will find sources of investment for the project's earned funds just as soon as they are available, not wanting to waste a minute in putting them to work. He will depend on their being available on time and in the amount promised. If they are not available, the customer will suffer a shortfall. He will also suffer a lost opportunity.

Since funds still "on the come" are already invested as if they were real as soon as they are proposed, it is easy to see why failing to realize them can be a catastrophe. The funds are planned for. If they are not going to be delivered, the customer will be surprised. It is not necessary to say "unpleasantly surprised." Managers learn early in their careers there is no such thing as a pleasant surprise; all business surprises are unpleasant.

It is easy to see why there is no substitute for guaranteed results. When you guarantee your solution, you are acting as a co-guarantor, a co-signer of your proposal. Your Box Two partner is the actual guarantor. He or she is the true receiver of corporate funds, choosing to invest them with you. This makes each Box Two manager the ultimate responsible party whose career success or failure is at stake and whose reputation as a "good manager" will be enhanced or downgraded by your proposal's effectiveness. Simply by the act of endorsing your proposal and going public as its sponsor—your internal "economic seller"—a customer manager is implicitly guaranteeing that he will return his company's funds plus a profit. When you partner with him, you inherit the same obligation.

Guaranteeing your results is the ultimate answer to the customer's question: How sure? By establishing a floor for your payoffs, it allows you to eliminate the ceiling on your reward. Once you achieve your guarantee, you can ask to share in any gains over and above it.

Gainsharing is an alternative to price. It is based on an understanding between a supplier and customer that their business together should be a mutual value exchange. The supplier should grow the customer by adding value in the form of increases in his revenue capabilities and cost savings. In turn, the customer should grow the supplier by adding value in the form of enhanced margins at high volumes.

A supplier and customer who cannot make money *with* each other—not *on* or *off* one another—cannot grow each other. If they cannot grow each other, they cannot partner because mutual growth is what partners do day in and day out.

Gainsharing is the partnering strategy for growing value and for mutually participating in its gains. It rewards the partners' mutuality of objectives, their mutual strategies to realize them, and their mutual acceptance of risk. It positions suppliers as growth consultants whose essential capability is to add value. As an opportunity-seizing and problem-solving approach to doing business, gainsharing dedicates suppliers to wealth creation, not just to the creation of products or services. It puts them in the business of manufacturing and marketing wealth.

The emergence of a basis for gainsharing at Boeing illustrates the incremental but nonetheless progressive nature of the change. Originally, Boeing would go into the market to "find the supplier with the lowest bid and monitor him so he doesn't screw up." Then Boeing began to "find the supplier who makes the best product and make him part of the process." Boeing's emergence will be complete when it sets out to "find the supplier who can create the most new wealth with us and partner with him by sharing the gains."

Gainsharing is neither a supplier strategy nor a customer strategy. Both benefit; neither incurs a downside. The mutual nature of the reward should drive both of them to gainshare whenever a unique value can be added to a customer operation that contributes to a superior gain.

Other factors along the lines of avoiding or diminishing negative outcomes also favor gainsharing and, in some cases, tend to make it inevitable:

- No supplier will be able to recover enough margin on product sales to refertilize his R&D with sufficient funds to ensure continuous short-term innovation cycles. Product acquisition has become a cost-control function, pushing suppliers' price points inexorably downward toward zero cost.

- No customer is going to be able to achieve and maintain best practices as his industry's low-cost manufacturer or high-share market leader by relying only on standard solutions produced by his suppliers. Standard solutions yield standard practices. Yet no supplier can afford to provide custom solutions at cost-controlled price points and still achieve low-cost supplier status for his own business. The only way to obtain funds for custom solutions is through gainsharing.*

• Person-to-person negotiation between customers and suppliers on price has become cost-ineffective, adding both direct and opportunity costs to the customer's cost-controlled process of acquisition and adding to a supplier's cost of sale. It is only a matter of time before it will be unaffordable to both parties to allow sales representatives and purchasers to negotiate commodity transactions based on price. When human beings are involved in negotiations about exchanging value, gainsharing will be the only affordable subject to debate.

APPLYING YOUR INTELLECTUAL CAPITAL

Gains for sharing come about as the result of applications of one or more of three forms of capital:

1. Intellectual capital in the form of the expertise required to initiate and manage a profit-improvement project
2. Financial capital in the form of investment
3. Operating capital in the form of products, services, and systems

Applying intellectual capital to create profit-improvement projects, not simply stocking them with operating capital, is becoming increasingly recognized by suppliers as what their business is all about. But ideas in themselves are worth little, being nothing more than raw materials that rank at the bottom of the value curve. By adding values from application and implementation, information and education, and consultation and evaluation of results, intellectual capital can realize whatever opportunity it may have for capitalization.

The *gain* in *gain*sharing is net present value [NPV]. It is calcu-

*The complete guide to sharing in the contributions made to customer profits is available in *Gainsharing™: Alternative to Pricing* by Mack Hanan and Jon Feinstein, (New York: The Greymatter Group Inc., 1999).

lated as the present value of a wealth creation project plus the worth of all future values when they are discounted back to the present. This takes into account the reduced value of money over time. In addition to NPV as the key indicator of gain, payback is a measure of the exposure to risk in realizing the NPV. The longer the payback, the greater the risk. A third indicator is the relationship of reward to risk that is calculated by the rate of return on investment [ROI].

Penetrating Your Customers' Value Chains

In order to share in the gains you contribute on a PIP-by-PIP basis, you must find a customer problem or opportunity that will let you realize three results:

1. The maximum gains from a product, service, or system application can be contributed.
2. They can be accumulated in the least time.
3. They can be accumulated at the highest level of cost-effectiveness.

As a consultative seller, you must seek out customers who can gain the most from your PIPs so that there is maximum gain for both of you to share. Customers who can gain the most are called "gain-sensitive." A customer can be gain-sensitive no matter where the business may be on an industry's value-creation curve:

- A customer who is ahead of the industry curve can be gain-sensitive because he wants to stay ahead.
- A customer who is behind the curve must be gain-sensitive because he wants to move up before he drops off.
- Customers who are in between are gain-sensitive because they must move up to become one of the top three competitors or face up to two business-altering options: consolidate by acquiring or being acquired, or vacate their market.

Fitting In as a Value-Adding Partner

If you want to gainshare instead of price—in Consultative Selling language, "propose an investment"—you must be able to answer the customer's question, "Where do you fit as a partner in the gains of my business?" In order to answer, you must know where you can add value. Since you are not offering yourself as a partner in the entirety of a customer manager's operation, your positioning is crucial in helping him determine if he has a partnerable vacancy that you can fill.

- A supplier who positions himself as a *moneymaker* is fitting himself primarily into a customer's sales, marketing, and distribution operations. He may also fit into the parts of a customer's product development, market research, manufacturing, or inventory control operations that affect sales. Moneymakers can range up and down value chains, intervening in operations where they are capability-specific for improving contributions of revenue.
- A supplier who positions himself as a *moneysaver* is fitting himself differently into customer support and supply operations. Instead of acting as a sales builder or market builder, he adds value by reducing an operation's contribution of costs.

Of the two platforms for gainsharing—one to expand revenues and the other to reduce costs—the proposed gains from cost reduction are easier to calculate and propose than revenue improvements. Customers accept potential cost savings more readily than a prospect of newly generated revenues. Costs, being internal, can be better controlled. Markets, the sources of revenues, are more ephemeral since they are outside customer control and defy prediction. Besides, customers are almost always better at control than at expansion. Yet revenue improvements are almost always significantly greater contributions to gain for sharing.

SPECIFYING INSTEAD OF BEING SPECIFIED

As a consultant, you should be proposing improved profits as a result of solving a customer's business problems by the application of your technology to his operations.

You are not selling your technology. Nor are you selling solutions to a customer's business problems such as "improving materials flow" or "decreasing production backlogs." You are selling improved profits; they are your product, and your proposals must set them forth in their major specifications of how sure your customer can be that he will receive the "muchness" and "soonness" in your proposal. A customer will not have the comfort level to partner with you if only you are sure. Your sureness is unimportant. You must make the customer feel sure. Unless you do, he will tell you that he is not comfortable. If he stays that way, you will not partner him to sell for you.

There are many short-term comfortable partners. There are fewer long-term comfortable partners. But there are no long-term uncomfortable partners.

You make a customer manager comfortable when you give him the evidence to prove where the return on his investment will come from and how it will flow. You may think, quite naturally, that the investment causes the return. Actually, it is the other way around. It is the promise of the return that causes the investment to be forthcoming, making the investment the result. If you do not make customers comfortable with the cause of their new profits first, they will be unable to envision a result.

When a customer signs off on a transfer of funds to you, he is committing to incur an asset. He owns something new. Its cost becomes a part of his balance sheet, increasing his indebtedness. The only valid trade-off for his debt is the added values he can receive from the improved operation, process, or function in his business that you will help him achieve.

To make this trade-off measurable, a consultative proposal is modeled after proposals commonly prepared by Box Two for presentation to Box One. When you present it to your Box Two partner, you will be playing his role. He will be playing the role of Box One. The more closely you replicate your Box Two partner, the more closely he will relate to you as partnerable and the more readily you will be accepted into his internal hierarchy.

You, like Box Two, will become a specifier of profit-improvement solutions. Box One, who allocates assets to maximize their profitable return, will sit in judgment of both of you. Together, you will follow the official business proposal approach: First, diagnose a problem or opportunity in business terms; second, prescribe a solution in business terms; third, prove how the solution will work in business terms; and fourth, commit to controlling the solution to make sure it works in business terms—that is, make sure it improves the proposed amount of profits on time.

A consultant can find many relatively simple ways to specify profit improvement. If you sell to supermarkets, you can show each chain's central headquarters or even individual store managers how an improved planogram, substituting your brands for others or increasing the number and location of their shelf facings, may improve profit per case or per $100 of sales.

Profit improvement for a manufacturing customer may depend on improving the profit of dealers' and third-party value-added resellers (VARs). By helping a customer's distributor organization increase its contribution—something the customer cannot directly control yet must nonetheless influence—you can help your customer raise the profit on sales made through channels.

A distributor's largest single investment is likely to be in inventory. The key to distributor inventory control is finding the minimum investment required to maintain adequate sales and service. One way of measuring the utilization of inventory investment is to compare a distributor's inventory turnover with his industry's average. Inventory turnover can be computed by using this formula:

$$\frac{\text{Cost of sales for one year}}{\text{Average inventory}} = \text{inventory turnover}$$

If a customer's distributors are in a business whose inventory turns an average of 4.5 times a year, or once every eighty to ninety days, you can help a distributor whose turnover is lower than average see his problem this way:

$$\frac{\text{Projected cost of sales}}{\text{Projected average inventory level}} = \frac{\$370{,}000}{\$100{,}000} = 3.7 \text{ inventory turnover}$$

To help this distributor increase turnover to approach the 4.5 industry average, you will have to help him reduce inventory investment. To do this, you must first find out what level of inventory investment can yield a 4.5 turnover. Divide the distributor's projected cost of sales by the desired 4.5 turnover, which results in an $82,000 inventory. It now becomes clear that you can help the distributor achieve profit improvement by reducing inventory investment by $18,000. Then you can turn your attention to optimizing the inventory mix.

The consultant's best approach to inventory reduction is usually through product line smoothing. Distributors almost always carry too many items in their lines. An inventory burdened by too many items can cause a dissipation of the distributor's sales concentration, extra handling costs, waste through obsolescence or spoilage, and, of course, higher inventory carrying costs, higher insurance costs, and overextended investment.

To analyze a distributor's inventory, you can simply rank the products in the line according to their cost of sales and then compute their inventory turnover. Such an analysis could look like this:

- Products A, B, C, and D account for 57 percent of the cost of sales but only 34 percent of inventory. These products turn over inventory by an average of 6.2 times a year.
- Products E, F, G, H, J, and K account for 43 percent of the cost of sales but 66 percent of inventory. These products turn over inventory by an average of only 2.4 times a year.

The inventory turnover analysis in Figure 5-5 shows what it costs the distributor to carry inventory. By comparing the carrying costs of inventory to forecast sales volume, you can begin to learn more precisely what inventory the distributor should maintain. The first four products are apparently well controlled. They have an average turnover rate of 6.2 percent and 1 percent average carrying cost as a percentage of sales. You now know that you must concentrate on reducing inventory whose average turnover rate is only 2.4 percent and average carrying cost is 2.6 as a percentage of sales. This will help bring the distributor's inventory down to the $82,000 level that should contribute to the projected 4.5 inventory turnover.

Figure 5-5. Inventory turnover analysis.

Product	Percentage of Sales	Average $	Percentage of Average	Turnover	Carrying Cost as Percentage of Sales
A	15%	$ 7,000	7%	8.2%	0.8%
B	17	9,000	9	7.0	0.9
C	14	11,000	11	4.7	1.3
D	11	7,000	7	5.8	1.1
Subtotal	57%	$ 34,000	34%	6.2	1.0
All other products	43	66,000	66	2.4	2.6
TOTAL	100%	$100,000	100%	3.7%	1.7%

MIGRATING INITIAL SALES

Key account penetration through Consultative Selling is a reciprocal process. Preliminary partnering makes possible initial entry at top-tier levels. Once entry has been accomplished, partnering should proceed apace so that migration opportunities open up beyond the initial sale. The purpose of preliminary partnering is to gain entry. The purpose of entry is to migrate, to penetrate a customer business in ever-expanding breadth and depth from your breakthrough point. The purpose of migration is to grow the customer's business and your business again and again.

In addition to the obvious benefit of providing ongoing high-margin sales opportunities, migration offers several other advantages. It helps amortize the investment in data collection. It helps develop new information sources about a customer business. It spreads awareness of your consultative positioning. And it helps deny opportunistic chances for competition to move in on a problem that you can, and should, solve. It helps prevent departnering.

Some migrations occur naturally—the solution of one problem leads progressively to the discovery of another, or a solution in one division stimulates customer interest about its transfer to a similar problem in another division. Other migrations will take place only as a result of effort. You will have to search out opportunities in the nooks and crannies of your customer businesses, relying on your customer process smarts to point up the most productive areas to explore.

The objective of penetrating a customer business in depth is to serve all major needs with your major products, services, or systems. This concept can be called maximizing "share of customer" as long as it is understood that it is not simply a volume criterion—it is a standard of the importance of your involvement. If you are significantly involved, you can become the preferred supplier of your customers' improved profits. Penetration in depth is inextricably tied to penetration in important areas of a business. Migration must be a selective policy whose aim is to consolidate your position as profit improver of the most vital functions you can affect.

The ideal migration timetable makes improving profit in one operation the jumping-off place for improving profit in the next operation. In this way, you can extract maximum learning value from each experience. You can also avoid stretching your resources too thinly across more assignments than you can handle. It pays to remember that migration works both ways. One significant success encourages permission to try another. One significant failure discourages permission to try anything more at all.

Installing an initial system should therefore be regarded as planting the seed for follow-on sales opportunities, not the end of the sale. Once a sale has been made, the consultant has acquired a major asset: a more profitable customer. You can benefit the customer even further by additional profit improvement through one or more of three types of migration. You can offer to *supplement* the initial system with added value. Perhaps some value may have been sacrificed for financial reasons at the time the original system was approved. Or perhaps a greater need has become apparent only after installation. As a second type of follow-up, you can offer to *upgrade* the original system, up to and including the ultimate upgrading, which is total replacement of the system. Third, you can offer to *integrate* an entirely new complementary system with the initial system.

These profit-improvement opportunities are not mutually exclusive. You can use all three approaches in sequence with the same customer. First, you can supplement the entry system. Then, at a later date, you can upgrade some of the original system. Finally, a complementary new system can be integrated with the original one. Then you can recycle the sales approach by offering to supplement the new system, then upgrade it, and eventually integrate a third system with the first two.

This recycling strategy is illustrated by the following scenario. It begins *after* an initial system is in place and producing prescribed profit-improvement benefits.

Cycle 1

1. Supplement initial system.
2. Upgrade initial system.
3. Integrate a complementary new system with the initial system.

Cycle 2

1. Supplement new system.
2. Upgrade new system.
3. Integrate a second complementary system with one of the existing systems.

Cycle 3: Repeat Cycle 2 and turn it faster.

The incremental value of a consultant's relationship with a key account customer is simple to calculate. At any given time, it is the sum total of earnings from all of a consultant's Profit Improvement Proposals. A few proposals will probably be spectacularly successful. But for the most part, steady, modest success is all that is required.

Each proposal should be successful in its own right. Beyond that, it should also lead naturally into the next successful project. As your profit-improvement contributions accumulate in a value-adding chain, you will be building equity. This equity will consist of the value of the portfolio of PIPs you have installed in each account. The reward for good work will be more work. By inviting you to remain in the game and try to improve profit one more time after each success, your customer is acknowledging a consultative partnership. As with all partnerships, "congratulations" is always followed by "you're vulnerable."

You, the consultant, are only as good as your last proposal. This should cause you to be financially conservative. Paradoxically, however, you will also have to be strategically daring in conceiving profit-improvement opportunities and planning to capture them. The net result of combining these two characteristics becomes the essence of your personal consultative style.

In planning to construct a profit-improvement portfolio, you should start small. At the outset, you must be content to make a single profit improvement in one business function or one product line in one account. Since the first proposal will probably be evaluated more critically than any of its successors, you must follow one injunction above all others: *The first time out, be successful.*

6

How to Sell the Customer's Return

The penetration plan is your annual blueprint for getting into and staying in the business of a principal customer. The way you get in is by improving the customer's profit. The way you stay in is by continuing to improve the customer's profit, extending it to the solution of new problems, and never letting go.

The process for penetration planning requires answers to three critical questions that can determine up to 80 percent of your profitability on sales:

1. Who is my customer?
2. What can I do to improve my customer's profit?
3. What will my customer do for me in return?

The answer to the first question is crucial. Your customer is never a company as a whole, nor is it even a division. It is a specific business manager within a division whose costs you can reduce or whose contribution to sales you can increase. If you are IBM, your customer is not PepsiCo. Nor is it PepsiCo's Frito-Lay division. It is the manager of Frito-Lay's inventory control function, for example, whose contribution to Frito-Lay profits you will be improving by improving his or her performance in a key indicator, such as same-day shipments.

Planning to penetrate divisions or departments of customer companies is a far cry from vending commodity merchandise to purchasing managers on a price-performance basis. It is a totally different process: data-dependent rather than persuasion-dependent. Its database must therefore be structured to support the differences in sales strategy that a consultative approach demands.

Opportunity databasing hinges on one central concept: maximizing contribution. Two kinds of contributions are involved. One is your profit contribution to a customer. You must maximize it. The other is a customer's profit contribution to you. You must maximize that also.

The role of a profit maximizer differs from the role of a needs analyst or a benefit provider or a problem solver. All these are intermediate steps. Through needs analysis, the provision of benefits, and the solving of problems, profits become improved. This is the ultimate step. If it does not take place, all the intermediate objectives can still be accomplished, but they will be in vain.

High-penetration objectives—superior profit objectives for your customer and for you as well—are financial objectives. Nothing supersedes them. They must come first in your penetration plan because they are the purpose of the plan. The only reason to plan is to be able to set and achieve high financial objectives.

The objectives of your plan should be databased in the manner of Mack Hanan's Fast-Penetration Planner™:

1. The most likely profit contribution that will be made *by you* to each customer
2. The most likely profit contribution that will be made *to you* by each customer

"Most likely" profits are a conservative estimate. They are somewhat more bullish than bearish, but only somewhat. They represent the contributions that can be expected if your strategies work according to plan and if there are no important hitches that have not been planned for. In practice, they should come out just about right.

If you help customers improve their profits from incremental sales, you may have to adjust the gross profits by the customers' effective tax rate before you commit to an objective. If you improve customer profits by cost savings that can flow directly to the bottom line, you can calculate the profits as net incremental gain. Only the net counts. Neither you nor your customers can take anything else to the bank.

The total annual contribution you expect to make to your customers will be the sum of all the Profit Improvement Proposals you plan to install in their business functions during a year. The contribution your customers will make to you will be the sum of your profits from the sale of each proposal that is collectible during the same year. Two ratios are helpful to monitor how effectively your resources are being allocated to obtain each customer's contribution. One compares profits to the expenditures required to achieve them; this is return on investment (ROI). The second is the more traditional ratio of revenues to expenses.

DEVELOPING YOUR "WHAT-IFABILITY"

The ability to propose a steady stream of investment opportunities or, more correctly, return opportunities to your customer partners is the engine that drives Consultative Selling. Proposals mean business. They make money for you and your customers, keep your learning curve strong by giving you access to new sources of information about customer businesses, and keep your partnerships active, alert, and alive. You should always have a minimum of three proposals in progressive stages of development. The one that you are working on should be on the table, the next one should be heating up in the oven, and the third should be in the freezer awaiting defrosting.

The proposals that are in the oven and the freezer represent your inventory. Until you sell them, they run up opportunity costs for you and your customers. You should turn them over quickly.

A consultative seller is continually diagnosing problems and opportunities and what-ifing solutions. Asking the customer "what if?" invites him to play strategic Ping-Pong with you. Each what-if should provoke either a "how?" or an enhanced what-if from your partner, building on your proposal or coming at it from a different cut. By presenting your proposals as questions, you circumvent most of the defensiveness that causes adversarial rejections and refusals to buy in. Instead, you open your proposal to the customer, asking him in, so he can add his values to it and make it partly his own. Unless it becomes "his" in this way, he will not sell it with you. As long as your proposals remain "yours," you will be a vendor.

For example, a consultative seller might ask a supermarket chain: "*What if* you can acquire the equivalent of a $500,000 order each week without incurring a single dollar for cost of sales? You can, if you can eliminate out-of-stock opportunity cost in a single best-selling brand in your dry cereals sections."

Or he might ask the same supermarket customer:

> *What if* you can offer your customers more advertised specials each week than your competitors can? In addition, *what if* you can also offer deeper price cuts on each of these specials? How much in new sales and profits can that earn for you each year, considering that every single dollar of new earnings will be net, because all costs of each special will be fully funded by us?
>
> The funds required to support our contribution will come from savings of more than $90,000 per store annually.
>
> On a per-store basis, the operating costs break down like this: For a store with gross weekly sales of $140,000, savings are projected as approximately $7,650 per month.

When your customer asks you how he can add the value you are proposing to his operation, he is opening your consultative sale. This answers the question "How do you open?" You do not. In Consultative Selling, the customer opens.

"How?" is the magic opener. It means "How can I be empowered?" "How?" comes in several forms. Some are nonverbal: facial expressions such as raised eyebrows, furrowed forehead, pursed lips, or quizzical looks and sometimes nods. Fingers pulling at noses or earlobes, hands going to chins or backs of necks, and body leaning forward are additional nonverbal ways of asking "How?"

Verbally, a "how?" can be asked directly or indirectly as an expression of envy for your other customers whose profits you have improved, a revelation of wishes and wants that would constitute an ideal solution and how your proposed solution compares to it, or a request for added comfort expressed as a "Yes, but" reaction.

A qualified "how?" is often expressed in the form of pseudo-problems that are designed to test and probe your solution, your experience, or your commitment. Customers also may want to know what their competitors are doing—"I wonder how they do this?"—or why their own people have not applied a similar solution long ago.

PIPPING A PIP A MINUTE

Automating the proposal process makes it easy to produce a continuous series of PIPs, improving your productivity as a profit improver a hundredfold while reducing your PIP cycle times close to zero. Mack Hanan's PIPWARE software program permits you to create "a PIP a minute." A new iteration of what-ifs can be prepared every sixty seconds in a professional business case format that can be closed right off the computer screen.

Figure 6-1 shows how PIPWARE software automates the calculations of costs and benefits whose work flow is shown in Figure 3-1. Figure 6-2 shows the ease of entering multiple *what-ifs?* into PIPWARE to calculate alternative outcomes.

The PIPWARE proposal is a ready-to-close request for an allocation of funds. It presents each proposal's business fit and its contribution to an objective that accelerates its realization in terms of net profits improved and annual cash flows. PIPWARE also documents each source of the customer's improved profits, the individual amounts contributed by revenue increases and cost savings, the rate of return on the customer's investment, and its payback period.

(text continues on page 144)

Figure 6-1. PIPWARE™ cost-benefit analysis.

Cost-Benefit Analysis

(000)	Year 0	Year 1	Year 2	Year 3	Year 4	Year 5	Total
Total Expenses (Net Cash Out)	($6)	($296)	($473)	($364)	($299)	($299)	($1,737)
Total Benefits (Net Cash In)		**$2,131**	**$2,131**	**$2,131**	**$2,131**	**$2,131**	**$10,655**
Gross Profit Improvement:	**($6)**	**$1,835**	**$1,658**	**$1,767**	**$1,832**	**$1,832**	**$8,918**
Less Taxes	$2	($642)	($580)	($618)	($641)	($641)	($3,121)
Net Profit Improvement:	**($4)**	**$1,193**	**$1,078**	**$1,148**	**$1,191**	**$1,191**	**$5,797**
Cash Flow	($1,354)	$1,463	$1,450	$1,412	$1,389	$1,389	$5,748
Cumulative Cash Flow	($1,354)	$109	$1,559	$2,970	$4,359	$5,748	
Net Present Value	**($1,354)**	**$1,330**	**$1,198**	**$1,061**	**$949**	**$862**	**$4,045**
Internal Rate of Return:	**103.8%**						
Payback (Months):	**12**						

Tax Rate: 35.0%
Hurdle: 10.0%

Depreciation Method: MACRS
Amortization Method: Straight Line

Page: Cost-Benefit Analysis | Edit | Preview | Present | Exit

Figure 6-2. PIPWARE™ what-if? options.

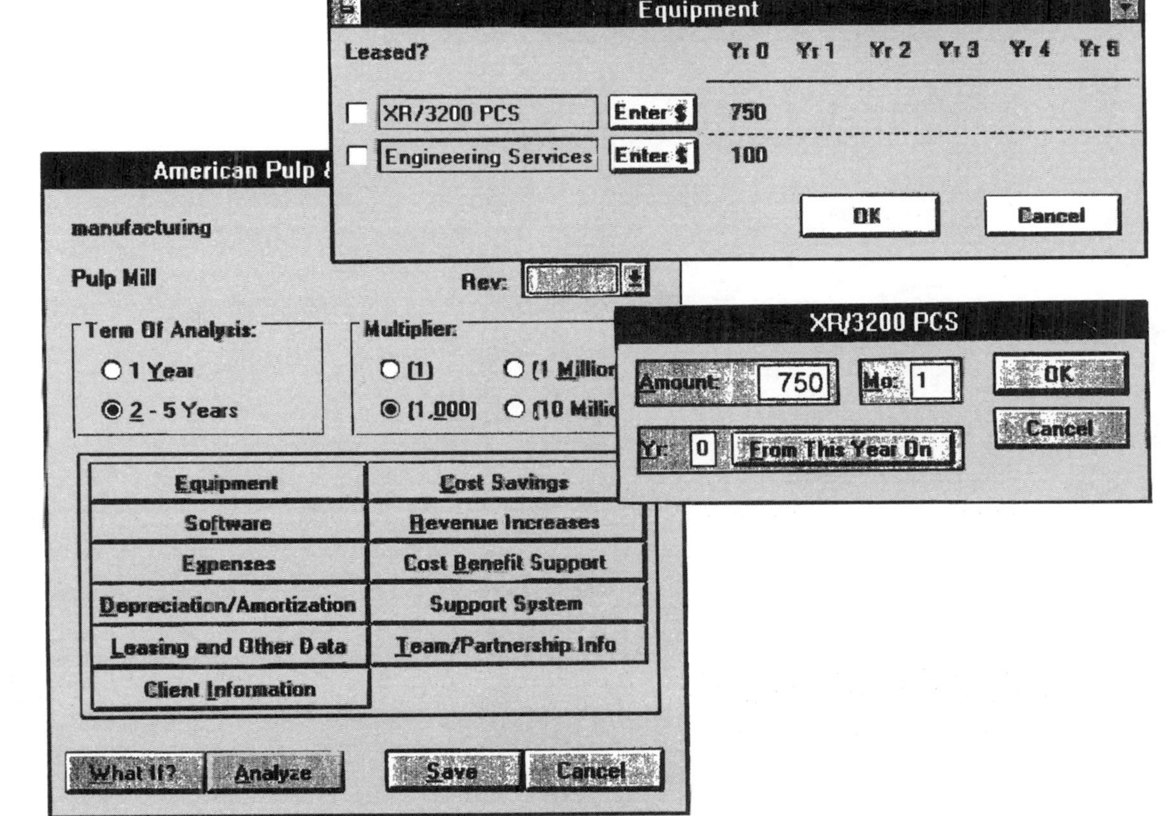

PIPWARE's cost-benefit analysis follows the same 1-2-3 rank order of internal customer requests for funds:

1. *The investment,* which is the "cost" in the cost-benefit analysis that includes the acquisition costs of the products, services, or systems you are proposing. If gainsharing is the method of customer investment, its amount can be bundled in the single line item on the Cost-Benefit Analysis called Total Expenses, or it can be highlighted as a Co-Management Share deducted from net after-tax profits.
2. *The benefits,* which include all future cash flows from incremental sales revenues and savings that the investment can achieve from reduced variable costs such as labor, materials, maintenance, scrap, or downtime.
3. *The rate of return,* which compares the benefits to the investment.

A cost-benefit analysis is not a cost justification, which is what vendors use to sugarcoat their costs. In Consultative Selling, there are no costs to justify. Because consultative sellers realize a return that exceeds their costs, all costs become investments of current funds that are made to bring in future flows of cash that pay them back and keep accumulating to show a profit. A positive return means that cost is zero. Once you can show that an investment will cause a positive return, the anticipation of the return compels the customer to make the investment.

Through PIPWARE, you and your customer can preview in real time every likely consequence you can think of for each proposal option over the course of a profit project's commercial life in ways like these:

- *What if* we cycle the investment over two or more years instead of front-end loading it in Year 1—does that make our project more fundable?
- *What if* we cut back on the investment in Year 1 to get to payback faster—does that make our proposal more closable?

- *What if* we cycle a series of short-term investments and plow back their returns so that we can self-fund 50 percent or more of each successive project—does that move us closer to the front of the line for approval?

Information technology applied to the PIP process has been revolutionizing Consultative Selling. PIPs are cycled faster. Meantime between PIPs is reduced. Arithmetic errors are impossible to make. *What-if* iterations can be made one after another in order to get to the optimal solution. PIPs can be presented electronically or telephonically, sent by E-mail or posted on a Web site. They can be stored in a corporate retrieval system for sharing. Sales managers can access them for coaching and counseling on-line. Suppliers and their third-party business partners and strategic allies can co-PIP no matter where they are in the world. Multiple customer locations can be PIPped simultaneously.

IT has become the enabler of PIP immediacy, continuity, and universality. In these ways, it acts as the multiplier of consultative sales force productivity. The number of "feet on the street" is meaningless. PIPs proposed and closed are what count.

PIPWARE mimics the consultative seller's thought process from the first moment of targeting a lead to agreeing with the customer on the single best solution to the problem or opportunity it presents. PIPWARE's built-in thinking goes like this: "Which of my customer's strategic business objectives can I fit into? What operation in a line of business or business function that I can affect must I improve in order to make a contribution to the objective? What is the revenue or cost target that my customer manager's performance is being measured on? What is the minimal improvement that will give him or her a significant competitive advantage? What is the most cost-effective solution to deliver the improvement?"

By tying each PIP to an objective of your customer's strategy, you enter into his business. In effect, you say something like this:

> Your business strategy commits you to internally finance the development of several new product line extensions. Here is a cost-effective way to bring in $25 million of

incremental cash flow over the next five years. This will pay for your total R&D costs plus a third of your test marketing for three line extensions.

PENETRATING HIGH LEVELS

Objectives are a plan's purpose. Strategies are the methods of achieving objectives. In Consultative Selling, strategies are packaged in PIPs. Each proposal represents a strategy to improve customer profit by solving a cost or sales problem. If the customer is a not-for-profit organization or a government agency, proposal strategies will focus on reducing costs and improving the dollar value of productivity. Either way, the mix of strategies must make a measurable impact on customer profit or operational performance, or both.

PIPs are the sales vehicles for penetration strategies. They are designed to penetrate the customer's business at high-level points of entry. Each proposal contains a strategy for solving a specific customer problem or realizing a specific opportunity. The sum total of profits contributed by each year's proposals constitutes the value added by Consultative Selling.

Many vendors remain in denial. At Motorola, Jim Caile of the Cellular Subscriber Group is still trying "to figure out how to put value back in the hardware." Motorola's Two-Way Radio people are doing the same, even though value has long ago been commoditized out of the hardware and relocated into customer operations. At a plant of Cummins Engineering, Motorola discounted a sale of its factory floor radios down to $100,000. Within the first 12 months, Cummins had saved $1.20 million in downtime costs by speeding up maintenance and reallocating raw materials and labor. In return for selling the performance value of its radios instead of the financial value of their application, Motorola came away with only a fraction of the 12 to 1 value-to-investment ratio of the radio system's contribution to improved profits.

Consultative Selling makes vendor selling schemes obsolete. Even when vendors "earn the right" to sell upstairs, they have nothing to sell to a customer manager who opens by asking,

"What have you got for me?" The vendor's typical response is a valueless value proposition that cannot price the investment because it cannot value the return.

NCR offers a valueless value proposition when it says, "NCR is your knowledgeable, safe, and innovative partner with proven experience." What is the value to a customer of NCR's "unmatched knowledge and expertise"? What is the added value of making "the safe choice"? NCR does not say.

Digital Equipment was typical of valueless proposers when it put forward characteristics of itself that may enable value but contribute no quantifiable value in themselves:

- "Proven track record"
- "Reliability and confidence"
- "Considerable expertise"
- "Diverse set of capabilities"
- "Customized approaches to addressing needs"
- "Commitment to implementation"

A single number—the most likely improvement in a customer operation's contribution to profits—would be worth all these words. In addition, it would be a true value proposition.

There are three steps to take before you can propose profit improvement:

1. Analyze a customer's business position.
2. Position penetration strategies.
3. Pinpoint penetration opportunities.

Analyzing a Customer's Business Position

A customer's business position determines your sales strategy. Each position presents a different penetration challenge.

1. *Penetrating a growing customer.* A growing customer is sales-driven. If you want to affect the sales function, you must increase its productivity so that it can generate more profits per sale or yield added profits from incremental sales. If you cannot

affect sales but you can only reduce costs, the savings you achieve for a customer must be valued for their ability to support more sales. Your entire penetration strategy must focus on improving the customer's profit by increasing sales.

2. *Penetrating a mature customer.* A mature customer is driven from two directions at once. Sales must be increased, but not if this requires increased costs. If projected sales fail to result, the customer's stability can be threatened. Costs must be reduced, but not if this will reduce sales or market share. If sales fall, the customer's stability can be threatened. Your penetration strategy can focus on improving profit through sales increases or cost decreases, but it must avoid the unaffordable risk of increasing costs or decreasing sales in the process.

Positioning Penetration Strategies

The purpose of analyzing a customer's business position is to be able to custom-tailor your sales penetration. If a customer is growing or stable, you must present yourself as an improver of profit on sales. If the customer is declining, you must present yourself as a reducer of costs.

Unless your sales position coincides with the customer's business position, you will never be able to create a partnership in profit improvement. The customer will not understand where you are coming from in your proposals. You, in turn, lacking a sense of your customer's objectives, will not know where the customer is going. As two unknowns, you will be talking past each other; you will be proposing to yourself.

To ensure that your sales positioning is in gear with how your customer is positioned, your penetration strategy should be preceded by a positioning statement. Here is a model statement:

> In our penetration of the manufacturing functions of the ABC Company's XYZ Division, a stable business, we will position ourselves as the manufacturing vice president's partner in profit improvement primarily by means of the reductions in cost we can deliver through our quality control system. We will also show how enhanced

product quality can help improve profit through incremental sales.

Pinpointing Penetration Opportunities

A customer's inability to bring down a cost, or his need to increase profitable sales volume, are business problems. Accordingly, they can be your sales penetration opportunities. In order to find out, you will have to identify them and then put dollar values on them and on the most cost-effective solutions.

Opportunities to penetrate a key account have a special genesis. A penetration opportunity does not automatically come into being simply because a customer has a problem and you happen to have a solution for it. Discovery is not opportunity. To determine whether a penetration opportunity exists, you must first analyze three specific dollar values.

1. *The dollar value of the customer's problem.* How significant is it? Is it making a significant negative contribution to customer profit? Does it justify a significant expenditure for solution?
2. *The dollar values of the profits from your solution* that will accrue both to you and to your customer. How significant are they? When will they begin to flow? How long before their total amount finally accrues?
3. *The dollar values of the costs of your solution* that will be incurred both by you and by your customer. How significant are they? Are they all up front or can they be paid for progressively out of the solution's improved profits?

Penetration opportunities are entry points. You should regard them as windows. An opportunity window opens for you when the following conditions are met:

1. The dollar value of the profits from your solution exceed the dollar value of the customer's problem.
2. The dollar value of the profits from your solution exceed the dollar value of the costs of your solution.

3. The dollar value of the profits from your solution exceed the dollar value of the profits from competitive solutions.

The first condition ensures that a customer problem is worth solving; that is, it is beneficial to solve. The second condition ensures that a problem is profitable to solve. The third condition ensures that your solution will be the preferred solution. All three conditions place the burden of proof squarely where it belongs—on your ability to create the most profitable solutions to customer problems in the business functions you can affect. This is the supreme standard of performance for Consultative Selling.

Prescribing Solution Systems

A consultant's solutions improve customer profit in proportion to the consultant's skill in prescribing added value.

The ability to prescribe the right solution system the first time is a result of three factors. One is the consultant's experience. The second is expertise. The third factor is skill in solving customer business problems and helping capitalize on opportunities: in other words, helping a customer improve profit.

A system's combined advantage is expressed as a single benefit: profit improvement of the customer's business operations in which the solution is installed. This benefit is a partial function of system price. It is also a function of the system's return on investment. The ability of a system to yield a return on investment that exceeds price endows it with premium-price capability.

Prescribing a system and pricing it for high customer return are the two most demanding tasks of Consultative Selling. Together they determine the customer's value and the profit from the solution. Because they have such a direct effect on both value and profit, the acts of prescription and pricing are keystones of the consultant's selling proficiency.

The standard of performance for prescribing and pricing a solution is met when its system's premium price is accepted as a cost-effective investment in added value to meet customer objectives.

When a consultant prescribes a profit-improvement package,

he must follow the rule of "necessity and sufficiency." Components should be sufficient, but only those that are necessary to solve the customer's problem should be prescribed. This guideline helps protect consultants against underengineering or overengineering a system. If a system is overengineered, it may have to be overpriced; if it is underengineered, it may contribute to customer dissatisfaction and invite competitive inroads.

To avoid underengineering, you may have to incorporate equipment or service components from other manufacturers to round out some systems. At times, it will be possible to market these components under your company's own brand name. This is the preferred way. But even if they cannot be branded, they should nonetheless be integrated into your systems if they are necessary to realize value objectives.

To be of maximum benefit to your customer and deliver maximum profit to you, a system should have turnover built into it—that is, one or more of its components should be consumable. This allows you to generate an ongoing razor-and-blades type of market for product-related services and consumable supplies by providing continuing sources of income for your business and continuing participation in your customers' businesses.

A basic rule of system prescription can be stated in this way: *To maximize profit, standardize the hardware and customize the services and consumables.* When services and consumables are customized, a system's premium price is justified. When frequent turnover of consumables is multiplied by premium price, maximum profits can result.

Deciding Which System to Propose

The return-on-investment approach is the most helpful tool for determining which of two or more systems to propose to a customer as well as how to price them. Two competitive systems illustrate how a choice is made.

1. *System A* is forecast to improve customer sales by $200,000 and yield a profit on sales of 10 percent, or

   $20,000. The investment required from the customer is $100,000.
2. *System B* is forecast to improve customer sales by $300,000 and yield a profit on sales of 10 percent, or $30,000. The same $100,000 of customer investment will be required.

These two systems appear equally worthwhile in terms of their 10 percent profit yield on sales. But in terms of the return each system can achieve on the amount of customer capital it employs, System B is superior. With System B, $100,000 of capital can produce a $30,000 profit—a 30 percent return. System A also requires $100,000 of capital but can produce only $20,000 in profit, for a 20 percent return.

The difference between the two is the relationship of the improved sales volume to the capital employed. System A allows its capital to appreciate at the rate of 200 percent. With System B, however, the appreciation is 300 percent: It turns inventories into cash faster.

There is a shorthand formula you can use to determine ROI:

$$\frac{\text{profit}}{\text{sales}} \times \frac{\text{sales}}{\text{capital employed}} = \%\text{ return on investment (ROI)}$$

In the case of System A:

$$\frac{20{,}000}{200{,}000} \times \frac{200{,}000}{100{,}000} = 20\%\text{ ROI}$$

In the case of System B:

$$\frac{30{,}000}{300{,}000} \times \frac{300{,}000}{100{,}000} = 30\%\text{ ROI}$$

In this simplified approach, the first fraction calculates the percentage of profit on sales; the second fraction calculates the turnover rate. When the two are multiplied, the result is return on investment. Any improvement in the circulation of funds invested in a system's total assets, working assets, or any component part of an individual asset will have a multiplying effect on profits.

A system's marketability lies in its competitive advantage: the value added by improving customer profit. This customer advantage becomes the system advantage in the minds of customers, who evaluate systems both individually and competitively. A system does more than offer a customer advantage; the system comes to "own" the advantage as its single most crucial selling point. This is *preemption,* a system's ability to seize an advantage uniquely to itself.

The competitive advantage of a system acts as its market selecting mechanism. It selects customers in two ways. First, it seeks out and qualifies the segment of a market that has the greatest need for the system's advantage. Second, it comes to represent the system by acting as a shorthand way of describing its incremental contribution. The customer advantage determines the market and documents the system's capabilities.

A system's customer advantage must conform to three requirements:

1. It must confer a superior added value over competitive systems, as well as over the option of doing nothing, in at least one important respect.
2. It must be at least equal to competitive systems in all other respects.
3. It must not be inferior to competitive systems in any important respect.

A competitive advantage can be an attribute of the system, or it can come from the way it is implemented, maintained, migrated, or marketed. The question of how much quality to build into a system therefore merits a minimal answer. Enough quality to deliver the customer advantage is enough quality. A maximum quality system as determined by the aggregate quality of its components may not be perceived as offering the maximum customer advantage. Minimal systems from the consultant's perspective are often preemptive systems from the customer's perspective.

The concept of competitive advantage is not just an argument against overengineering, overpackaging, or overcosting, although it speaks powerfully against all three. It is essentially an argument in favor of prescribing systems from a customer orientation. And it provides the direction for establishing a system's branding: the capture of customer preference because the *customer's profit is being improved best,* not because the *consultant's system is constructed best.*

Customers who use EVA, the Economic Value Added to their operations. as a criterion for what to acquire or apply to their operations are ready-made partners for consultative sellers whose value propositions are additive to the customer's EVA.

EVA is the sum of two components, the second of which is subtracted from the first to get the added value:

1. NOPAT, Net Operating Profits After Taxes, which is calculated by adding the cost of products manufactured to GS&A expenses (general, sales, and administrative) and subtracting the result from sales revenues. In order to improve the contribution of NOPAT to EVA, a consultative seller's PIPs must improve sales revenues or reduce either GS&A or the manufactured costs of products.
2. Cost of Capital, which is the sum of outstanding receivables plus inventories. In order to reduce the contribution of a customer's capital costs to EVA, a consultative seller's PIPs must reduce receivables or inventory.

In addition to increasing the contribution of sales revenues to NOPAT and decreasing the contributions of receivables and inventory to the customer's cost of capital, PIPs can also improve EVA by speeding up new product development, improving production scheduling, reducing scrap and rework, and cutting down on warranty expenses.

DEFENDING AGAINST DESYSTEMIZING

A consultant's prescription for improved customer profit is always threatened by desystemizing. You should not fear the process. It plays the vital role of confirming the value of your prescriptive expertise and your ability to apply it to a customer's problems.

The essential consultative value is the ability to apply. This is what a prescription really is—an application of the consultant's expertise to a customer's business.

To this extent, you are an applications consultant. All the professional expertise in the world is valueless unless you can apply it to a customer's business. By protecting a system against customer attempts to desystemize it, you learn the competitiveness of your prescriptive and applications skills.

Challenges to desystemize a system are actually a customer's attempt to test the worth of your applications expertise, which is the trump card that justifies premium price. Desystemizing is a price reduction strategy. Since premium price lies at the heart of Consultative Selling strategy, the system must be protected if premium price is to be maintained.

A system is only as good as its consultant's applications ability. Unless the consultant's expertise can be *branded*—that is, accepted as providing a value that exceeds its price and that cannot be obtained elsewhere—a system cannot be protected from customer attempts to desystemize it.

You can always be certain of two facts about a system. For one, no matter how novel the hardware components may be initially, they are prospective commodities. For this reason, you cannot allow customers to regard hardware as the core of your systems. Second, the only component that can be branded against commodity status is the "software" represented by your own prescriptive and applications expertise. Every consultant must educate customers to accept this basic truth from the very beginning of each relationship: The compelling reason to do business with you is your *intellectual capital*, not the physical capital represented by your products and services. This is your only sustainable offering because it is the only one that is brandable—that is, your sole source of high margins.

If you bring a vendor heritage with you into Consultative Selling, the physical capital components of Profit Improvement Proposing will seem to be the causes of its benefits. You will assume that, just as in vending, customer managers at the Box Two level will send your PIPs out to bid in an attempt to buy the same value at a lower price. Why not? you will think. A lower price permits a smaller total investment, which would appear to yield a higher return and a more closable proposal.

There are two reasons why you will be wrong, in addition to the fact that Box Two managers are not buyers and do not go out for bids in the manner of Box Three.

- In order to make a significant impact on a proposed return, a competitive price would have to be significantly lower. By the time a request for proposal could be sent out and bids collected, evaluated, and a winner selected—if, indeed, a significantly lower price could be found—the opportunity cost of delaying the onset of your proposed benefits could exceed the value of a price difference. Therefore, going out for bids incurs what can turn out to be an unaffordable cost.
- Even if the same physical capital components can be obtained at a significantly lower price without incurring unaffordable opportunity cost, it is the intellectual capital component of your PIP—your own personal brainpower—that has the power to maximize its value. The physical capital itself, whether it consists of hardware equipment, software, or systems, does not predict the muchness, soonness, or sureness of a PIP's benefits. These are the results of application skills rather than performance features. This must be your key selling point—that no one has better norms than you do for the outcomes of applying commodity physical capital.

If you fear that a lower priced competitor can out-PIP you on the basis of price of physical capital alone, it means that you calculate zero value for the application of your intellectual capital to the conception, implementation, and evaluation of profit improvement projects. If so, you are a vendor.

Part III

Consultative Partnering Strategies

7

How to Set Partnerable Objectives

In order to grow a customer's business, you must get inside it. *Unless you know it, you cannot grow it.* No business can be grown from the outside. By being an insider, you can be *in business* together with your customer instead of just *doing business* as an outside supplier. The opportunities to be in business together are found in the customer operations where you can affect outcomes, which is where growth can take place if you are able to improve them.

Contributing to customer results shows up in one survey after another as one of the top three critical success factors in customer satisfaction. Few customers say that they need better products. Many products actually exceed customer needs, such as Digital Equipment's "fastest-on-earth" Alpha microprocessor, whose price has to be cut back periodically to compete with the lower-priced, slower systems of Hewlett-Packard and Sun, whose performance is "good enough." What comes across is customer needs for supplier performance—not product performance—in three categories: more knowledge of customer operations, more understanding of customer competitive situations and more strategic ways to deal with them, and more proactive contributions to customer profit improvement that are made without having to be asked for.

Customers are the genesis of your business. For this reason, the two of you must be in the same business. This means that the customer must come first, by making customer profitability your combined prime objective and managing your business as being *of* your customers, *by* your customers, and *for* your customers.

Every business has natural partners. Who are yours? They are other businesses whose growth is dependent on you. Selecting your growth partners is the single most important act of Consultative Selling.

Good partners meet five criteria:

1. They want to grow.
2. They want you to grow them.
3. The growth they want from you is within your norms.
4. They can grow you in return.
5. Their growth by you will convert additional good partners.

If you know who your natural partners are and what they need from you in order to grow, you can dedicate your Profit Improvement Proposals (PIPs) to them from the outset. Your business positioning can be a natural response to theirs. Also, your system capabilities can be exactly receptive to their needs. Furthermore, your database can contain knowledge of their growth problems and opportunities. Your entire business can be the reciprocal of the businesses of your partners.

You have two types of natural growth partners. One is composed of businesses that are currently growing because of you. The other is composed of businesses that you could grow but are not currently growing.

CHOOSING PARTNERABLE CUSTOMERS

There are four questions to answer about your current customers in order to determine which of them you should partner with.

1. *Whom are you growing right now?* Some of your growth partners will be customers you are already growing. You may not be aware of your contribution to their growth. You may think you

are merely selling to them. But they are actually partners without portfolio. In order to determine whether any one of them should be selected as your partner, you will have to answer three more questions.

2. *How much more can you grow them?* Growth takes place in the future. What is the most likely projected rate of improved profits you can plan for in the growth of their business over the next three years? If the projected rate of growth is static or in decline, you may not have a true growth partner. Instead, you may have a mature customer to whom you can continue to vend products at competitive prices, whom you should sell to and profit from but not partner.

3. *How much are they growing you?* You may be unable to know the full extent to which you are bringing growth to a current customer. But you can much more easily calculate the profits by which you are growing as a result of the customer's business with you. There are four standards by which you should measure profits: their absolute value, their comparative value ranked against your customer list as a whole, their rate of growth, and the trend of their growth rate over the past three years.

4. *How much more can they grow you?* Because growth partnerships must be reciprocal, you must evaluate the most likely projected rate of your own profit growth over the next three years to see whether it is increasing, becoming static, or entering decline. If the projected incremental rates of growth are increasing for both your customer's and your own business, you have the ideal basis for growth partnering.

There are three questions to answer about prospective partners in order to determine which of them you should partner with:

1. *Whom else can you grow?* Growable businesses that you are not currently growing are your source of consultative expansion. In order to qualify as a growable customer, a business must meet two criteria. Its business function problems must be susceptible to significant cost reduction by the application of your expertise. In addition, your expertise must be able to increase the customer's own profitable sales opportunities.

2. *How can you grow them?* For each growable customer that you determine is potentially partnerable, you must plan a growth strategy. The strategy will set forth the precise means by which you will add new profits to the customer's business. You will need to specify how much profit will accrue from reducing business function costs, how soon its flow will begin, and how long it will continue. You will also have to specify the amount and flow of profit from new sales opportunities that you can make available and the markets they can be expected to come from.

3. *How much will they grow you?* A business that you can grow must be able to grow you in return if it is to be partnerable. Its contribution to your profit volume and its projected three-year rate of growth must meet or exceed your company's minimum growth requirements.

When it comes to gainsharing, all partnerships are not created equally conducive. Gainsharing represents the essence of partnering, where rewards are shared in proportion to risk and contribution. Relationships that, for one reason or another, stop short of profit sharing are stopping short of full partnering.

"Full Monty" partnerships of total comity meet selective criteria. These criteria allow partnerships to be assessed with a good deal of predictability. Some criteria are personal to the customer partner: Is he a natural sharer by personality or a self-aggrandizing nongiver? Is he predisposed to think in terms of benefits or their costs? Is he a dealmaker or a traditionalist about price being the sole basis for transactions?

"Know your customer" means to know these things. Over and above them are situational factors that may modify or nullify personal criteria. They include the following:

- A business that wants or needs to be first to apply a new technology, either because it is a leader and wants to stay that way or because it must get closer to the leader.
- A business that is cash-poor and cannot pay for the benefits it needs.
- A young business that must conserve cash for growth but needs every accelerant to growth that it can get its hands on.

- A business whose industry is in an economic downturn and can use gainsharing as a form of barter to trade present uplift for a future payment.
- A business in a highly competitive industry that cannot risk a negative impact on its stock price from a major cash outlay on its balance sheet.

For businesses in any of these situations, selectively used gainsharing can be an incremental growth strategy. Depending on a customer's position in its industry, its market, or its life cycle, partnerability may be more dependent on the speed with which gain can be created than by its total amount. Fast gain can make fast partners. It can also predispose negotiations to yield a favorable share for the consultative seller.

DESPERATELY SEEKING PIPPABILITY

A customer manager is constantly under Box One pressure to maximize his contribution to profitability. He is always in a state of dynamic tension. There is no steady state in which profit contribution can be maximized once and for all. Cost creep continually challenges control. Shifting demand, competitive campaigns, and margin slippages challenge earnings. Managers are reminded every day that the only constant is change.

The art of managing a business function or a business line is a perpetual tinkering process of adjusting the mix of the resources that go into it and the returns that come out of it. The manager's quest is to learn how few resources need to be invested to produce maximum return. The ideal answer is: The fewer the better. But, in practice, managers are always in disequilibrium from the ideal. Investments turn out to be not as productive as they promise. Returns turn out to be not as great or as quick or as certain. The productivity of each dollar never seems to be maximized.

A manager who is desperately seeking maximum profitability is "eminently PIPpable" with Profit Improvement Proposals. As a result, a consultative seller's most partnerable position is to be desperately seeking PIPpability, the ability of the consultant to improve a manager's profits. The most PIPpable managers make the best partners. It is not that they are poorer managers and therefore have the most costs and smaller or more sporadic cash flows. Quite the contrary, the most eminently PIPpable managers are the best managers, alert to every prospect for a competitive advantage, filled with a sense of urgency to achieve it, and bold enough to sell the consultant's PIPs internally to their Box One funders.

Good managers have the same problems and opportunities that poor managers have. Good managers do something about them with a heightened aggressiveness, a foreshortened time drive, and a greater receptivity to partners who can help ensure their success.

The seller's search for PIPpability in a customer manager is the search for good managers with whom to partner. Poor managers may seem to need a consultative partnership. But only good managers are prepared to accept its offers and implement them with the skill and concentration they require. A good manager would still be a good manager without the seller's partnership. With it, however, he can be even better. This edge can be his competitive advantage, the value added by the seller.

The value-adding process takes a customer manager through three steps:

Step 1 samples the partnership's MO: its method of operation. This is a zero-risk step. It involves teaching and learning PIPping so that the partners can standardize it as their method of doing business.

Step 2 prototypes the partners' method in the form of a closable PIP.

Step 3 realizes the PIP's proposed outcome and shares its reward.

CYCLING CONTINUOUS IMPROVEMENT

How can you tell if a customer manager is a partner? If he gives you leads by telling you where he hurts or what unrealized opportunities he fantasizes about, he is your partner. If he keeps asking you, what next? or, what else can you do for me? or, where do we go from here? after each successful PIP project, he is your partner. If he sells for you by going upstairs with you to help get funds for your PIPs, he is your partner.

Figure 7-1 shows a continuous improvement cycle composed of consecutive PIPs. Each successive PIP is initiated while the preceding PIP is no more than halfway into its projected life. As soon as PIP #1 produces profits, a share of its gains can be allocated to fund a part or all of the investment required by PIP #2, and so on.

As PIP self-funding proceeds, a "partners' pool of funds" is created for you to draw on. This is the ultimate outcome of your partnering—a partnership that capitalizes itself to achieve financial autonomy, free from the need for third-party sponsorship of its investments in continuous profit improvement.

A business partnership is legitimized only when a partners' pool of funds is created. Up to that point, it is merely a relationship. Once a pool of funds is capitalized by the partners, they can dip into it at their discretion as if they were a miniature business. The customer manager ceases to be a customer and becomes a *client*. The consultative seller ceases to be a seller and becomes a *co-manager*.

Partnering requires two choices. One choice is your selection of the customers you will grow. The second choice is made by your customers: Why should they partner with you? There are three reasons:

1. *You are an important source of their growth profits*. The contribution of new profits that you can make to a customer must be significant. Only then will your partnership be important enough to both of you to merit top-of-the-mind attention, both his and yours.

To be an important source of growth for a customer means that you must account for worthwhile incremental profits. You must also be able to deliver them in a timely fashion, recognizing the time value that money has for him. In this, you must be dependable. He must be able to count on you to improve his profits when you say you will and by the amounts you promise. Your importance to him will be in direct proportion to your reliability.

Figure 7-1. Continuous improvement cycle.

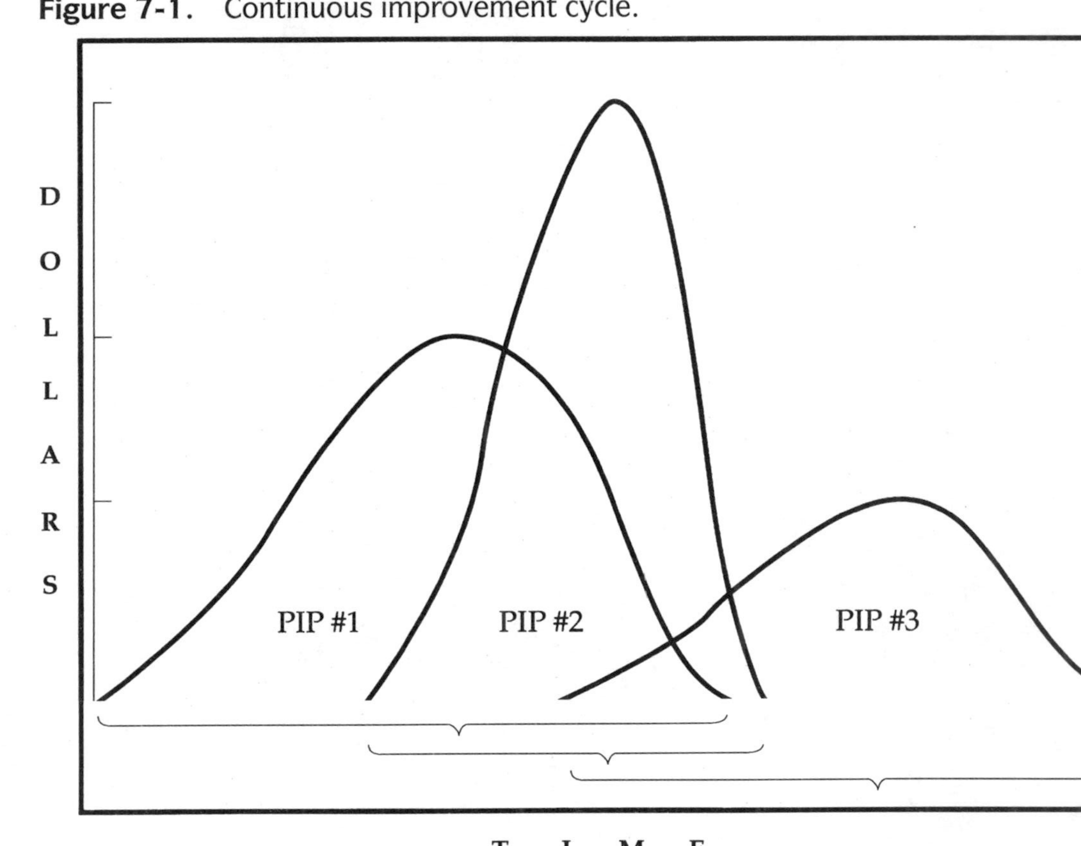

2. *You are one of their best investments in continuous profit growth.* When a partner does business with you, he must perceive the price he pays to be an investment rather than a cost. The distinction is vital because only an investment yields a return. He must understand that he is not investing in your products or services or systems, not even in your solutions. He will be investing in new profits. The return he receives from his investment with you must be among the best yields he can make.

Just how high does a customer's return on investing with you have to be? You must compare yourself with his options. Normally a customer will invest in his own business in order to make profits. He has a "hurdle rate" that sets his minimum return. As his partner, you must offer him a better choice. You must make it more profitable for him to invest in your business. Either the investment he is required to make will be smaller yet yield a similar or faster return, or the return he receives from you will be larger even though the investment may also be correspondingly larger.

3. *You both have the same competitors.* When you sell products or services, positioning yourself as one of a customer's several alternate vendors, you are concerned only with defeating your own competitors—rival vendors. To be a business partner means that you must concentrate on defeating your *customer's competitors.* Unless you have the same objective, you cannot be partners.

A customer's competitors are the constraints on his growth. He has two of them. One is his current costs, against which he competes every day and which he must reduce if he is to improve his profits. You must help him. His second source of competition is in the area of sales opportunities. He competes for them every day too, trying to win customers against his competition. If he is going to improve his profits, he must increase his profitable market penetration. You must help him.

As your partners, your customers will grow you if you can make three transformations in your relationships with them.

You must first transform yourself from a supplier of products and services to a supplier of profits. You must change from a manufacturing or service business into a supplier whose product is profits.

You must transform yourself from representing an added cost to representing continuous added value. You must change your basis for doing business from selling performance values at a price to returning dollar values on an investment.

GROWING CUSTOMER MANAGERS

A consultative seller's partner is a customer manager who will sell their joint PIPs internally. That is the acid test of partnership—not simply giving the seller access to himself or information about his business, not coaching and counseling the seller on how to penetrate his business, and not passively going along with the seller's penetration initiatives. A customer manager must be a seller to be a partner.

Consultative Selling partnership strategies are designed to give customer managers the mix of comfort and urgency they require in order for them to share in preparing and presenting a PIP to their Box One managers and in supporting it and implementing it for its full realization. This means that your proposals must become "our proposals," jointly prepared, presented, and achieved. Until this takes place, would-be consultants will be running up against one of the basic truths about all businesses: No one from the outside can get a hand on a customer's funds. Only the customer's own people are fundable, because only they are accountable for their payback and positive return. Without an internal seller as a client, a consultant has no one to sell to and no one to sell for him.

Box Two managers who make the best partners conform to a handful of characteristics:

1. They want to grow their business operations.
2. If you grow them, they can grow you.
3. You can grow them, as proved by your norms for expanding markets like theirs or cutting their significant costs.
4. They will partner with you to come closer to your norms by sharing data with you, contributing a team to work

with you and your team, and acting as a testifier and reference site for you.
5. They can be an important influence on other customers in their industry, with prestige and a reputation that induce emulation.

Growability must be your key partnering objective. Only by growing can your partner ensure a fast turnover of your sales and their prolonged continuance. This requires a high turnover in the sales your customer makes to his own customers. If they become stable, turnover will stagnate. For this reason, stable customers—especially those with large shares of market that cannot be grown—are to be avoided. They make good customers, but they are poor partners.

If you have a choice among growable customers—customers who meet your primary objective—what fine-tuning criteria should you apply to select among them? You should look for three attributes:

1. *Nascent opportunity.* You should seek the maximum opportunity to grow and be grown. Change is the mother of opportunity. A growable customer that is undergoing reorganization or restructuring to provide for further expansion offers enhanced partnership prospects. Change at the top tier is an added enhancement. Whenever major change is taking place, you have the chance to create a new role for yourself, meet new or newly perceived needs in new ways, and form relationships with new managers who can benefit significantly from your expertise.

2. *Positive attitude.* You should prefer to partner with customers who prefer to partner. Their receptivity to your overtures will be greater. So will their awareness of and concern for growth. At the minimum, you should expect them to be willing to share data with you and to create a correlate profit-improvement team to work with yours.

3. *Industry repute.* You should understand that the most sophisticated customers make the best partners. They will have the highest standards of performance. That will push you. They will

have the most intelligent managers in their industry. That will pull you. Your contribution to them will most likely be maximized; they will take what you give them and run with it. Your odds for a successful track record will increase, as will your ability to draw on them for references that will attract other sophisticated customers to you.

PRACTICING COMMON PARTNERING DENOMINATORS

All partnering is based on a few common denominators:

- Partners have a *common objective.* Each partner wants to improve profit.
- Partners have *common strategies* for achieving their objective. Their methods are based on mutual need-seeking and mutual need-fulfillment. In both cases, needs are arrived at through negotiation.
- Partners are at *common risk.* Each partner has something of value to gain or lose.
- Partners have a *common defense* against all others who are not included in the partnership. Each party deals as an equal. Outsiders range from being less equal to being perceived as competitors.

Cooperative negotiation strategies enable partners to treat each other as equals. This is the principal rule of partnerships. There are ten additional rules that can help in partnering:

1. *Add value to each other.* Teach each other new ways to improve personal achievement and professional productivity so that both partners profit by the relationship.
2. *Be supportive of each other, not competitive.* Form a staunch team.
3. *Avoid surprises.* Plan work together and work according to plan.
4. *Be open and aboveboard.* Always level with each other.
5. *Enter into each other's frame of reference.* Learn each

other's perceptions in order to see things from the other's point of view. Learn each other's assumptions to understand the other's expectations of the partnership.

6. *Be reliable.* Partners must be there for each other when they are needed.
7. *Anticipate opportunities and capitalize on them.* Forecast problems and steer the partnership around them. Keep the partnership out of trouble. If trouble is unavoidable, give the partnership a head start in solving it.
8. *Do homework.* Know what's happening. Know what may happen.
9. *Treat each other as people, not just as functionaries.* Be willing to provide the personal "little extras" that make a partnership a humane as well as a mighty force.
10. *Enjoy the relationship and make it enjoyable.* Both partners should prefer to work within the partnership rather than within any other relationship because it is one of the most rewarding associations either of them has ever had.

The customer decision makers who must be partnered as clients are multimotivated. They rarely act on the basis of one motive alone. Status, money, autonomy, and self-realization propel them. Of all their drives, three are likely to be major: power, achievement, and affiliation.

Client Need Set

In Figure 7-2, three aspects of client needs are illustrated in typical proportion. They contrast with the proportions shown in Figure 7-3 for the consultant's need set. The major difference lies in the relative significance of self-actualization income and psychic income. For the consultant, self-actualization must always take precedence over the psychic rewards of power, prestige, and promotion. For the client, however, you should assume that power and promotion—which represent realizable objectives for a client—supersede self-fulfillment. By remembering the primacy of power and promotion when you negotiate, you will be able to keep your client's perspective in mind. You will also be able to

Figure 7-2. Client need set.

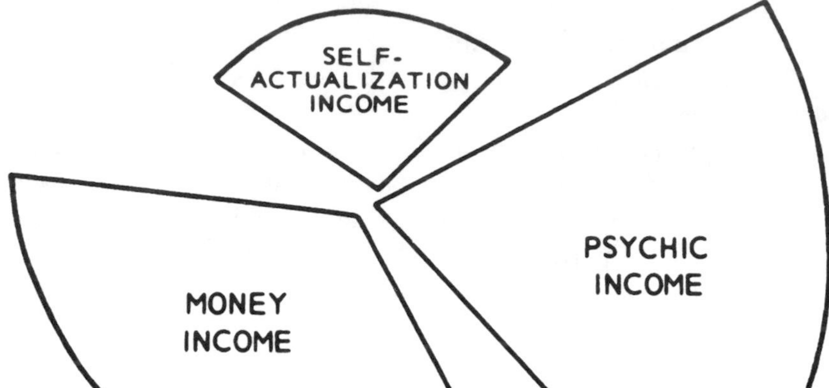

visualize your role fairly accurately in the way the client will see it: to help the client obtain increased power income and maximize money income as well.

Consultant Need Set

There are three aspects of consultant needs. Each represents a certain type of income: *money income; psychic income,* representing such rewards as power, prestige, and promotion; and *self-actualization income,* including self-fulfillment, competence, and the realization of talent potential.

These needs are present in every consultant's motivation set. Yet they vary widely from one consultant to another. To negotiate effectively, your need set must be proportioned something like Figure 7-3. The money drive you have should be significant. But your use of it to give you power, especially the power to dictate solutions or appropriate a client's leadership, should be small. Although you may enjoy great prestige, you will always be required to work through your client to accomplish your purposes. You

Figure 7-3. Consultant need set.

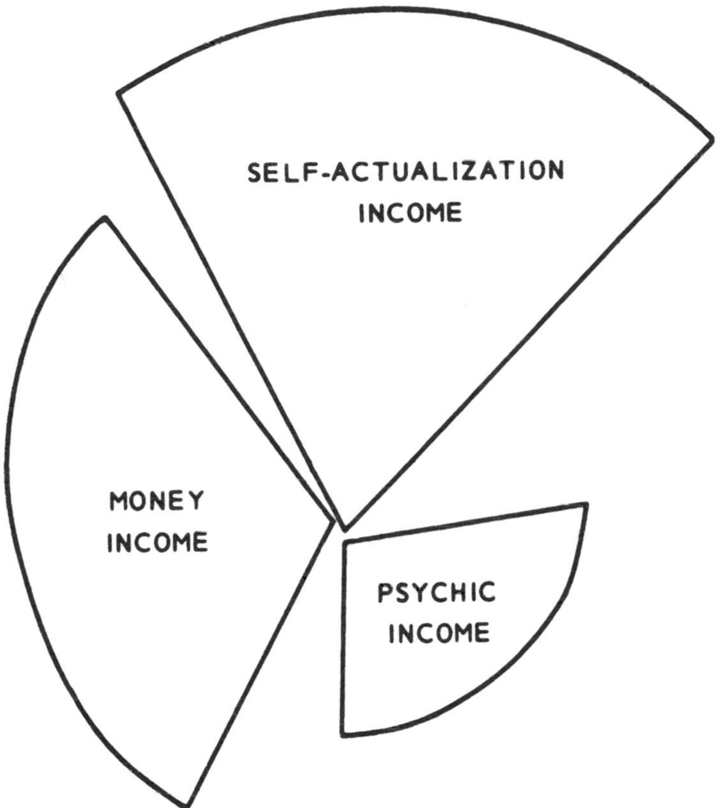

can help a client achieve power and promotion and thereby share vicariously in them. But you will often work unheralded, usually anonymously.

On the other hand, consultants must have an unusually large amount of self-actualization in their need set. This aspect is the key to success. You must have, and be driven by, a need to realize your own fullest growth and development by growing and developing your client partners. You must want to utilize all of yourself in your client's behalf, engaging your full complement of skills and expressing your widest range of knowledge. You must need to translate these qualities into unique profit projects that only he and he alone should ever know have originated with you.

OBSESSING ON CONTROL

The Box Two mindset is obsessed with *control.* Every manager knows that costs must be controlled. So must sales, since too much demand that cannot be met can overwhelm manufacturing, inventory, and distribution just as seriously as too little demand can underwhelm them. If shipments get out of control, a manager gets into trouble. An uncontrolled rate of scrap or mean-time between downtime or repair and replacement under warranty, or market share that deviates from plan, is an ominous sign that a manager is going to be off budget and off plan. This will bring him to the attention of Box One.

In most customer companies, deviations from plan call for Box One to "manage by exception"—to apply supervisory management practices and procedures to correct the exceptions and either get the manager back on plan or find a new manager who will be unexceptional. Box One's philosophy is often expressed like this: "When a manager goes off plan, I invite him to lunch. No one gets invited to lunch twice."

When a customer manager partners with you, his or her purpose is to reduce the risk of being invited to a "box lunch" by Box One. That is why you must be sure that you can help him achieve the new contributions to profits, either by cost reductions or revenue increases, that you have proposed to him and that he can achieve them within the time you propose. Otherwise you will expose him to catastrophic risk.

To be "in control" means that a manager is on plan—on budget, on time, attaining each milestone on schedule—so that payback of Box One's investment can be made on or before its due date and so that the manager's return on investment reaches its projected rate. This is the way that your Box Two partner builds his track record as a good manager. As a good manager, he will again be favored to manage the next cycle of investment and you will again be favored to be his partner in replicating your mutual success. Together, you will become a reliable team.

All business is based on reliability. Customers prize reliability over every other attribute; they prize it in their people, their products and services, their operations, and their reputations for their own customers' satisfaction. To be out of control is to be unreliable, which means that the profit contribution you and your partner have proposed cannot be *counted on* any longer. You should take these words literally. The expression "counted on" is a quantitative measure of your value, and it says very clearly that you and your customer-partner will come in with new profits as scheduled or you and your partner may be out.

Making PIPs that can be counted on is your transcendent task. It is the basis for your partnered positioning. Take that away and you have what the computer industry calls vaporware and the food industry calls empty calories—promise without performance, the essence of unreliability.

In order to be an acceptable partner for a customer's Box Two manager, you must share his obsession with control. In consultative terms, control means two things: controlling a client's costs to help him maintain low-cost production, and controlling the flow of his revenues to help him maintain high margins or high market share.

To be admitted into a major client partnership depends on a single compelling requirement: Can you bring more money to the client's party than any other candidate for partnership?

If you "make partner," you can achieve control of the contributions to costs, revenues, and earnings in the client's business functions and lines of business that you affect. He will place responsibility for controlling these contributions in your hands, either as a dedicated supplier or a facility manager of his operations. As his partner, he will count on you—counting dollar by dollar, in the most literal sense—to deliver your contributions "on the money" and on time.

By controlling your contributions according to the proposals you make to your clients, you control the continuity of your business with them. If your contributions slow or falter, your partnerships will be in trouble. Every time you deliver a proposed contribution, you earn the right to propose again. If you lose control of your ability to improve a client's profits dependably, you will lose your client.

So what is it that you can actually control? It is not the client, nor is it the client's business. You can control only the contributions you make to it.

As a result, PIP control becomes essential for partnering. Your PIPs must be reliable contributors to customer profits. The best way to ensure this is to set up a three-phase process of PIP control:

1. *PIP previews.* These will enable each client-consultant team to preview the potential proposals in each account's penetration plan, rank them in priority order of their perceived sureness in dollar value and timeliness, and then certify their value before presentation.
2. *PIP reviews.* These will enable each team to review each proposal after its acceptance to warrant its deliverability, and to schedule its monitoring and measurement milestones to make certain that its full proposed value is progressively delivered.
3. *PIP overviews.* These will enable each team to agree on each PIP's contribution, to log it in their joint database, and to seek follow-on enhancements for it and natural migration opportunities in the near-term future. At each overview, the partnership's norms for improved customer profits can be updated to keep them current.

Accounts that get out of control are caused by PIP management processes that become uncontrollable. Through PIP management, you can always know where you stand in account control by asking questions like these:

- Are we making the profit contributions we are proposing?
- Are we measuring and monitoring them with our customers?
- Are we keeping up enough "PIP flow" to earn our partnership all over again every day?
- Are we maintaining our contributions above the level of the industry standard?
- Are we generating a steady state of future leads from each completed proposal?

- Are we making our competitors *beat us* in our norms or *beat it?*

MAINTAINING PROFESSIONAL ACCOUNTABILITY

Partnership is a no-nonsense, no-surprises alliance. You must embrace your client partner's objectives and be incremental to their achievement. You must supplement or complement your partner's strategies so that the two of you pull together, culturally and operationally. You must protect your partner against the risks of failing to achieve your incremental contribution to his objectives or failing to achieve them on time. In short, you must be accountable for your partner's success.

Once your partner agrees on your solution, he shoulders the major share of risk. He is on the line with his top managers, who are his lenders—in other words, your funders. He works with them in a partnership similar to your own with him. It is based on no nonsense and no surprises. Once he has signed off on the loan he receives from his internal bankers, he is mortgaged to them. It is unthinkable to believe that he will not pay them back. It would be a shocking surprise if he did not earn the return on their investment on which he has signed off. Once he partners with you, there is no place for either of you to hide. He is responsible for making your proposal work. You are accountable to him for making sure it does.

Vendors are accountable for making their products work successfully. They can afford to ask only, What can I *sell?* As a consultative seller, you are accountable for making your client successful. You must ask different questions: What can I *do for* my partner? What can I *do with* my partner that will ensure his success?

Partnering with you should be like taking out an insurance policy. Your partner must be protected by you, enhanced in his ability to make a superior contribution by the added assets you represent. He must be stronger as a lower cost producer, or he must be stronger as a market leader. He must know what you are insuring him against—unnecessary costs—and what you are insuring him for—higher volume sales or increased profits on sales. This is how he will measure your contribution.

In vending, you are in the middleman position between your customer and your competitors. From both sides you are subject to margin pressure in the form of greater discounts, bigger deals, and free services. When you sell as a consultant, however, your client partner is in the middle between his supervisory manager, who is his lender and to whom he is responsible, and you, on whom he is dependent to fulfill his responsibility. If you fail him by turning out to be a liability instead of an asset, you put him at risk in his partnership with his own managers. For him, this is the ultimate risk. It is not just your project that is endangered; it is his career.

Your partner has no alternative except to count on you—in other words, to hold you accountable. As a professional consultative seller, you have no choice either. You must perform; you must deliver; you must be prepared to pay the price of success if you want to collect its rewards. Are you there for your partner? He can never be too sure. Accordingly, you can never provide too much reassurance.

You assure your partner of your accountability by being there, working with him and his people in high-profile visibility. You assure him by measuring and monitoring your joint progress toward his objectives and taking prompt remedial action if your evaluations indicate you are in danger of going off plan. You assure him by taking advantage of new opportunities as soon as they arise and being prepared for them with an inventory of PIPs based on multiple what-ifs.

You cannot reassure your partner by telling him not to worry; he is paid to worry. Your assurance must come in the form of setting up an early-warning system to head off worrisome events, having remedies on hand for problems so you can nip them in the bud, and keeping your finger, along with his, on the pulse of your joint projects.

MEASURING ADDED VALUE

Your need to be accountable is dictated by your Box Two partner's need to be consistent. The single most admired trait that

Box One managers covet in the men and women who report to them is the consistency of their contributions to profits. Quarter after quarter, year after year, the managers who demonstrate consistency in their ability to "make plan" are the managers who get the chance to do it again, to do it with greater budgets and even more responsibility, and, finally, to manage others who will do it for them.

Box One has limited patience. Top managers believe that a manager who is going to be consistent is consistent from the start. Flashes in the pan get weeded out early as "brilliant but erratic"—in other words, undependable. From Box One's perspective, Box Two managers must serve an apprenticeship that proves they can maintain a consistent level of performance. During this time, which can take up to 80 percent of a manager's career, he is developing his personal norms. Over the remaining 20 percent of career time, all the manager must do is to hold on to his norms and manage others to equal or exceed them.

You must manage your own norms as well. This means that you must know the value you add as a partner. If you remain ignorant of your value as a consistent profit improver, the only other contribution you make that your partners will be able to quantify will be your added cost.

Whatever business you are in, you must enter into a second and parallel business in order to measure your partnered value. You must become a tester of your value as well as an implementer and applier of it. To do this, you will need to develop a standardized test and measurement system to assess your value and to install it simultaneously with each major sale. Then you and your partner can measure its results at regular, periodic intervals.

You must know what to test for, how often and how to test for it, and how to interpret and apply your findings. There are three rules that should govern your assessment strategy:

1. Never install a product and service system without installing a measurement system to assess it.
2. Sell only the values you can measure.
3. Always measure the values you sell.

Selling and measuring are two parts of a single sale. Unless you measure your value, the bases of your partnerships will be ephemeral. They will be based on how much of a "good guy" you are, which is an implicit invitation to your competitors to devalue you.

If you are forced to undergo a devaluation or reevaluation by a partner, you will learn the hard way what partnership is all about. It is not about faith and trust. It is not about charity. Partnership is about proven value. Only when value cannot be measured and offered as proof does charity come into play.

Your value as a partner is nothing to get starry-eyed about. It is measured in cold, hard cash: how much of it you contribute, how soon you contribute it, and how sure your partner is that you will contribute it consistently. The worst case is not failing to do these things. It is being able to do them, yet not being able to prove what you can do. When that happens, you cannot sell yourself as a partner because you will not be able to put a value on your contribution. You will be unmarketable on the partner market.

8

How to Agree on Partnerable Strategies

A consultant's job can be defined in three ways: Bring back sales, bring back customer information that can lead to sales, and leave behind alliances with top-tier decision makers.

Sometimes a sale will build an alliance. More often, alliances help build sales.

There are four levels on which alliances must be structured in a key customer account. Three of them are in the upper management tier: top managers, financial managers, and operating managers. The fourth is the purchasing level, where the traditional adversary relationship must be converted into a more partnerable affiliation.

The objectives of all key account alliances are similar, regardless of the level at which they are to be achieved. Their overriding goal is to ensure customer continuity. Unless key account relationships are continuous, there will be no way to maximize the profit opportunity that a major customer represents. Unless you can keep your key customers, everything else is academic.

Making Mutually Profitable Alliances

Three strategies will help you build lasting alliances: Collaborate, educate, and negotiate.

1. *Collaborate.* In key account situations, it takes two to make every sale. An unpartnered consultant cannot sell within a

customer's company. There will be no one to sell *to*. There will be no one to sell *with*. There will be no one to *help sell*. For consultant and collaborator, there must be the same dedication, the same commitment, and the same conviction that a sale will add genuine value to both parties. When a sale is finally made, it should be impossible to tell who made it. This is the test of a true collaboration: The sale is the thing, not the seller.

2. *Educate.* You and your key customers must do more than buy and sell if your relationships are to be continuous. Along with making new dollars, you should both be making new information available to the people on each side who will be collaborating on proposing sales. Not only must you both *earn* as a result of your relationships, you must both *learn* as well. Professional growth and personal growth should attend profit growth.

3. *Negotiate.* The main subject area of the mutual education between collaborators is how to improve profits. This requires continuing back-and-forth dialogue. The flow of input must be unimpeded. The ideal environment will be rich in options but sparse in negative thinking, put-downs, editorializing, or defensiveness against anything that is "not invented here." Free-swinging relationships where there is a high degree of give-and-take allow you and your customers to avoid losing out on important opportunities. They also allow you to cash in fully on solving the problems that come off the top of the customer's head.

Alliances With Top Managers

By selling as a consultant, you can obtain access up and down the entire vertical chain of a customer's organization, including the chief operating officer, who is usually the president. If you sell to a division or subsidiary of a large customer company, your top ally may be its COO. Selling to several divisions or to the corporate management itself will require you to partner at the top company level as well as at top divisional levels.

Alliances With Middle Managers

For the most part, your alliances will be at Box Two midlevels.

At the profit center level, you will be partnering with two different types of profit center managers: those who run *margin businesses* and others who run *turnover businesses*. Each type requires its own partnership strategy. You will also be partnering with cost center managers.

1. *Partnering with margin business managers.* A margin business makes money on high profit per unit of sale. Most margin businesses are brand businesses, smaller rather than larger, and serve niche markets. A small improvement in volume for a margin business can yield a large increase in profits. When you PIP a margin business manager, propose to increase his sales revenues without raising his variable costs or propose to reduce his variable costs without having an adverse effect on his revenues.

2. *Partnering with turnover business managers.* A turnover business makes money on high volume. Most turnover businesses are commodity businesses, larger rather than smaller, and serve mass markets. A large improvement in volume for a turnover business is required to yield significantly improved profits. When you PIP a turnover business manager, propose to increase his sales revenues while keeping operating funds requirements constant or reducing them. Alternatively, you can propose to reduce operating funds requirements, as long as you do not reduce revenues. Operating funds requirements can be reduced by cutting down on current variable costs or by displacing some of them by leasing or outsourcing assets instead of purchasing them.

Improving cycle times of a turnover business, such as its time to market or its order fulfillment rate, are the most cost-effective strategies to improve its manager's performance. By speeding up cycle times, you can increase the amount of goods shipped and billed. This speeds up cash flow without having to increase sales volume by increasing the speed of collecting accounts payable. Accelerating the order fulfillment cycle also reduces inventory costs by cutting down on the amount of funds that are tied up in working assets. Accelerating collections cuts down further on the same funds. Each operating cycle that you speed up improves productivity by reducing a manager's unit costs of labor and materials.

3. *Partnering with cost center managers.* A cost center manager is preoccupied with running an operation in the most cost-effective manner based on best practices, TQM (Total Quality Management), continuous innovation, and JIT (Just-In-Time) inventory. Cost center managers in R&D, manufacturing, engineering, marketing, information systems, and human resources are always being measured by their contributions to cost. As a result, work flows and cycle times are key indicators of performance for them. Wasted materials, wasted time, and wasted money are constant targets for improvement.

AGREEING THROUGH NEGOTIATION

Negotiation is the agreement style that partners use. It is designed to make sure that each partner wins something and that neither partner loses everything. If one of the partners comes away without a win, he has not been negotiated with; he has been commandeered. He has been mastered, not partnered.

What is it that each partner in a partnered negotiation must win? Each must win new, improved profits. The customer partner must have his profits improved by coming away with a lowered cost or higher revenues or earnings. The supplier partner must have his profits improved by coming away with a lowered cost of sale and a higher margin.

In vendor selling, negotiation centers on price. As soon as a price is proposed, discounting begins. Vendors often mistake this process for negotiation. They call it "negotiating price" when they really mean "discounting price." Discounting price is not negotiation because the supplier cannot win. He can only limit his loss. If his margins are not directly attacked, he will be subjected to other forms of price pressure such as requests for free goods and services, advertising or promotion allowances, free carrying of inventory, and so on.

Because price does not exist in Consultative Selling, partners do not include it in their dialogues. Instead, they negotiate about the yield from the consultative substitute for price: investment. *How much* can it earn? *How soon* can it start to flow? *How sure* can we be—how can we be even surer—that we will receive the muchness we have planned as soon as we have planned for it?

These are the three subjects of partnered negotiation. Both partners want to maximize the sureness of their deals together. Without sureness, everything else is fanciful; Profit Improvement Proposals will be fiction, like a midsummer night's dream. Within the constraints that sureness imposes on the partners, how much return can they manage from their investments, and how soon can they hold it in their hands?

In your role as a consultative seller, you must always be ready to propose more muchness or soonness. The way you do this is by constant what-ifing: What if we add this positive value to our proposal: What effect will we have on return? What if we subtract this negative value from our proposal: What effect will we have on return? With PIPWARE, each option takes only a minute to answer.

The best partnerships consistently earn the highest returns from their investments. They realize that each of them is making an investment of money, time, and resources, and that each must maximize its payoff. As a result, it is not just the consultative partner who proposes and the customer partner who disposes. Both propose to add the maximum value to their mutual proposals. Both what-if each other so that their proposals are true joint ventures. Joint proposals, in which each partner is invested both personally and professionally, are the outcomes of partnered negotiation.

If you are asked how you know you are practicing partnered negotiation, a joint Profit Improvement Proposal is not only your best answer; it is your only answer.

Separating Partners From Nonpartners

Every decision maker can be considered as a fraction. The denominator is always the same: common needs and aspirations. Every numerator, though, is exceptional; numerators are composed of individual differences. In order to penetrate a customer organization, you have to analyze what is individual as well as what is common. This can be done by answering two questions: Who are the decision makers I can partner with? Who are the decision makers I will have difficulty partnering with?

Decision Makers Who Make Good Partners

There are six types of decision makers who have high partnering potential. Figure 8-1 summarizes their principal characteristics and most probable negotiating modes.

Decision Makers Who Make Difficult Partners

There are six types of decision makers who have low partnering potential. Figure 8-2 summarizes their principal characteristics and most probable negotiating modes.

Consultative Selling enables sustainable commercial relationships. As long as a customer manager's profit contribution is being improved by a consultative seller, they can continue to grow each other as "partners in profits."

Consultative sellers do not make calls. They make projects that can migrate from one profit contribution to the next so that the seller's initial cost of sale is amortized over infinity. Nor do consultative sellers transact business through finite, sporadic engagements. Instead, they become partners in perpetuity. As long as a manager has a line of business or a business function to run, his or her profit contribution will always be susceptible to improvement, just as his or her KPIs will always be made more stringent and less readily achievable.

The traditional product vendor skills of maximizing the number of calls per day in order to sell something to everybody have no place in Consultative Selling. The same is true for the service vendor skills of selling finite engagements whose termination, no matter how successful, more often than not leaves their vendors back where they were: on the street to start all over again.

The selling in Consultative Selling should take place once, at the beginning of each partnership, when PIP number one must be agreed on. From then on, the principle of capital turnover should act as the flywheel of each relationship so that its cash flow never stops. The benefits of continuity of turnover—PIP turnover, customer capital turnover, and the seller's turnover of customer investments—compose the added values of partnering. Once a partnership gets up to speed, the seller's cost of sales and sales cycle time should approximate zero. So should the customer partner's cost of acquiring new profit opportunities from the seller.

Partners who are brought together by Consultative Selling gain new money together. But that is not all. They also gain in the time value of their new cash flows. Funds can be earned or saved faster. They can be reinvested faster. There are more funds to reinvest each period because they become available sooner. This is where the payoff of Consultative Selling comes from.

Figure 8-1. High-partnering decision makers.

Manager Type	*Characteristics*	*Negotiation Modes*
Bureaucrat	Rational, formal, impersonal, disciplined, jealous of rights and prerogatives of office, well-versed in organizational politics.	Follows rules; stickler for compliance; more concerned with tasks than with people; logical strategist (but can be a nitpicker); predictable negotiator.
Zealot	Competent loner, impatient, outspoken, a nuisance to bureaucrats, insensitive to others, minimal political skills.	Devoted to good of organization; aggressive and domineering negotiator; blunt and direct; totally task-oriented.
Executive	Dominant but not domineering, directive but permits freedom, consultative but not participative, sizes up people well but relates only on a surface level, cordial but at arm's length.	Organization-oriented; high task concentration; assertive negotiator; adroit strategist; flexible and resourceful.

Integrator	Egalitarian, supportive, participative, excellent interpersonal skills, a born team builder, a catalyst who is adept at unifying conflicting values.	Shares leadership; permits freedom of decisions and delegates authority; welcomes ideas; open and honest negotiator who seeks win-win relationships.
Gamesman	Fast-moving, flexible, upward-moving, impersonal, risk taker, one convinced that winning is everything, innovative, opportunistic but ethical, plays the game fairly but will give nothing away.	Wants to win every negotiation; enjoys competition of ideas, jockeying for position, and maneuvers of the mind; sharp, skilled, and tough negotiator; can be a win-win strategist.
Autocrat	Paternalistic, patronizing, closed to new ideas that are not invented here, not consultative or participative, but partnerable on own terms.	Binds people emotionally; rules from position of authority; makes pronouncements of policy; a sharp trader who negotiates on a tit-for-tat basis.

Figure 8-2. Low-partnering decision makers.

Manager Type	*Characteristics*	*Negotiation Modes*
Machiavellian	Self-oriented, shrewd, devious, and calculating, insightful into weaknesses of others, opportunistic, suave and charismatic, can turn in an instant from collaboration to aggression.	An exploiter of people; cooperates only for selfish interests; totally impersonal negotiator, unmoved by human appeals; will win as inexpensively as possible, but will win at all costs.
Missionary	Smoother of conflict, blender of ideas, must be liked, identifies harmony with acceptance, highly subjective and personal.	A seeker of compromise and leveler of ideas to lowest common denominator; negotiates emotionally with personal appeals to agree for his sake.
Exploiter	Arrogant, what's-in-it-for-me attitude, coercive, domineering, rigid, prejudiced, takes advantage of weakness, makes snap judgments, unswayed by evidence.	Exerts constrictive personal control over negotiation; makes others vulnerable by using pressure and fear to get own way; demands subservience; sees others as obstacles to be overcome.

Climber	Striving, driving, smooth and polished demeanor that masks aggression, opportunistic, without loyalty to others, goes with flow.	Excellent politician; uses self-propelling change to call attention to herself; always thinking ahead; self-serving negotiator based on what-will-this-do-for-me?
Conserver	Defends status quo, resists change, favors evolutionary improvement, uses the system skillfully to safeguard personal position and prerogatives.	Imposes own sense of order and nonimmediacy on negotiation; slows everything down; preaches traditional values; defensively blocks innovation and undermines agreements before implementation.
Glad-hander	Superficially friendly to new ideas but essentially a nondoer, effusive, socially skilled and politically skillful, superior survival instincts.	Overreactive and overstimulated by everything, but impressed by little; promises support but then fades away; endorses only sure things that can do some personal good; never takes risks.

9

How to Ensure Partnerable Rewards

You and your support staff are the essential partnering agents in Consultative Selling. Together, you compose a profit-improvement team for each of your customers. You, the consultant, are the leader of the team. You will partner with the customer business function managers whose costs you can reduce and with the managers of the customer's lines of business whose sales can be increased. The minimal resources you need as team leader, and their relationship to you, are shown in Figure 9-1.

Three types of support from within your company will be essential: financial, data, and technical. All supportive team members will play two roles. Internally, within the team, they will coach and counsel you in preparing and presenting Profit Improvement Proposals, as well as implementing them. Externally, they will create partnerships with their correlates in the customer's business—finance to finance, data to data, technical to technical.

Your first act as consultant should be to form your profit-improvement teams on a customer-by-customer basis. Your second act is to consult with your clients on the organization of companion teams composed of their own staff resources. As Figure 9-2 shows, a client team is built around the decision makers who will be your partners. By melding the two teams, you create your partnership.

In Figure 9-1 you must be able to see yourself in the box marked "Consultant Co-manager." This will enable you to be the partner in charge of your team. As such, you will be a playing

Figure 9-1. Supplier profit-improvement team.

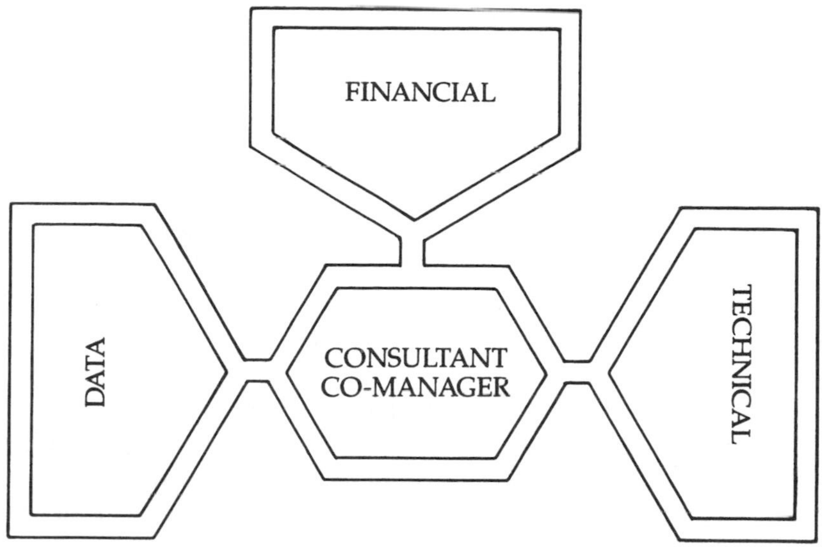

Figure 9-2. Client profit-improvement team.

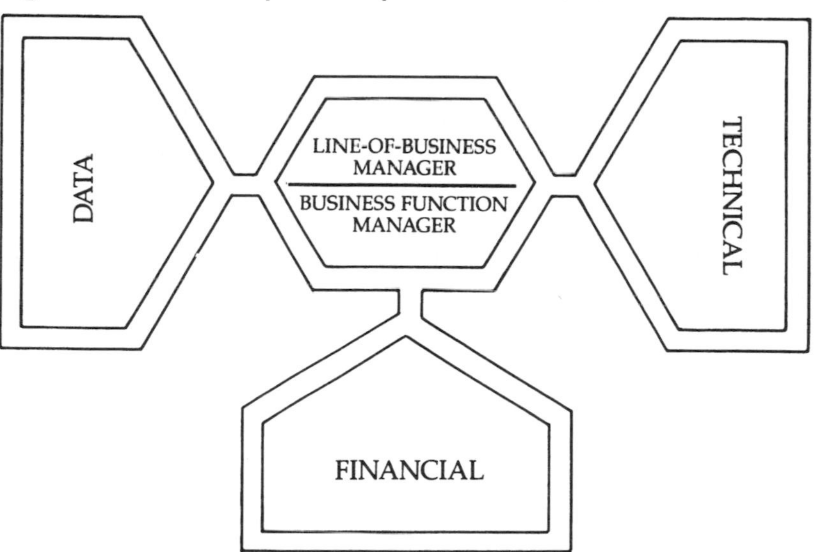

coach, a manager who also plays a position, charged with setting each profit project's objectives and the most cost-effective strategy for achieving them.

PREDICTING PARTNERABILITY

Before admitting you into partnership, a customer manager screens you through a checklist like this:

- What is the *reward*—can he produce what he proposes within the time he has proposed it?
- How much will it *cost* to educate him in my operation?
- How much *disruption* will it cause if I bring him in? What is the most likely interruption to my people's productivity?
- What is the *risk* of sharing my priorities and proprietary objectives with him?

You can predict your own partnerability by evaluating yourself against a profile of the critical success factors of partnerable consultative sellers:

- Gains rewards by rewarding others, credits others for his contributions, likes to mentor others and leave them improved.
- Negotiates by presenting options for the single best solution. Asks "What if?" rather than tells "What-to."
- Enjoys collaboration. Acts as a co-leader and co-manager. Demonstrates acute people-sensitivity.
- Displays high frustration tolerance. Enters unstructured situations and shapes them according to his or her model.
- Lives a consultative lifestyle. Partners at work or play.
- Stands up to being evaluated.

Customer satisfaction for clients is not a prescription from Dr. Feelgood. It is a pairing of two quantifiable outcomes that come together to form the standards of minimally satisfactory partner performance:

- *Zero cost,* which requires that all significant discretionary expenditures must be investments, not costs, and as such they must earn a positive return.
- *Zero risk,* which requires 100 percent certainty of achieving each proposed profit improvement.

These are the "hurdle rates" for satisfying clients. That means they get you in the door, but they do not compel a customer to invite you to sit down and partner. They serve to put a floor under your performance. You provide the ceiling, consisting of the height of the profits you can contribute and the frequency rate with which you can repeat your contributions. These are the measurements that determine how high your customers' satisfaction with you can be.

Departnering occurs when two conditions are met. An alliance that is incomplete or unfulfilled within itself is vulnerable. When a more promising partner appears, it succumbs. Many troubled partnerships linger on because both partners temporarily subscribe to the belief that "You know what you've got, but you don't know what you're going to get." As soon as one partner believes that what he or she is going to get is better, the partnership will end. In Consultative Selling, this means that the client will also be lost.

Because markets are tight communities, the loss of one client inevitably raises doubts, creates assumptions, and fosters anxieties that threaten the stability of other client relations. A domino effect can follow. The loss of one key account opens the door to competitors who, even if they have not been a cause of departnering, will be anxious to take advantage of its effects.

What leaves a partnership incomplete or causes it to be unfulfilled? There are two major factors that predispose to eventual departnering: divergence of objective and inequality of risk.

1. *Divergent objective.* Partnerships rest on a common objective. Both partners must have the same result in mind before they partner, see the same result as being achieved while they are partnering, and be able to look back at the accomplishment of their result as a consequence of the partnership.

Consultative partnerships are known by the objective the partners have in common. The eternal question of what partners see in each other is easily answered: They want to achieve the same objective, and they perceive the partnership as the optimal means of reaching it. This is their hidden agenda.

A consultative partnership is not a one-on-one situation. More accurately, it is a two-for-one relationship. Both partners share one objective—to improve the client's profit. Unless this is accomplished, the consultant's objective of improving profit on sales will be impossible. For this reason, the client's objective must come first for both of them. It is not philanthropy but enlightened self-interest that makes it so.

When objectives diverge, or simply appear to be going off in different directions or losing conviction, alliances atomize. A client partner may acquire the belief that the consultant is more interested in self-promotion to the client's top tier than in merchandising the partnership. The client partner may feel used, demeaned, and taken unfair advantage of by helping the consultant develop business elsewhere, either inside or outside the organization. The consultant, on the other hand, may believe many of the same things about the client partner. Whether such perceptions are true or not, they will have an erosive effect on the partnership.

Restating objectives and recommitting to them are essential elements in keeping partnerships on track. Objectives should be brought up for discussion at frequent intervals; this should be at the consultant's initiative. A good time to introduce them is when progress is being measured against them. At some of these checkpoints, the original objective may have to be downgraded. Perhaps it can be increased. In either event, keeping objectives current will perpetuate the values that both partners are working for.

2. *Unequal risk.* Partnerships are a means of reducing risk. Two parties can share the load, divide the responsibility, and parcel out the components of the risk that would otherwise be borne by one or left undone. Although risk can be reduced, it can never be eliminated. It must be shared as equally as possible if the partnership is to be preserved. Otherwise, one partner may accuse the other of "putting your hand out farther than your neck."

No matter how hard consultants try to bring into balance the risks inherent in improving customer profits, clients will always be left with the major exposure. They are exposed on their own behalf. They are exposed on their recommendation of the consultant. And they are exposed to their topmost tier of management. In any business situation, there can be no riskier combination of exposures.

Once clients commit themselves to work with a consultant to improve their profit, they must be successful. It is no wonder that they will be ultrasensitive to their own inherent risk and to the support they receive from you. They have a lot to lose.

Because clients bear the major share of partnership risk, you must take on the major share of reducing the risk and providing the reassurance that it has been reduced. There is no way you can have the same degree of risk as your clients incur, but you can provide a greater degree of risk calculation and limitation. This must be your equalizer.

ENSURING NO SURPRISES

In Consultative Selling, you have several equalizing tools at your disposal. One is to be thorough in your fact-finding and in putting together your database on client problems and opportunities. Another is to be diligent in obtaining feedback from your clients about their needs. A third is to manage your progress review sessions with care so that deviations from objectives are caught early and corrected, so that strategies can be revised to meet changed conditions, so that opportunities can be capitalized when they are still fully available, and so there are no surprises. A fourth is to guarantee your profit improvements.

If you fail to keep a partnership's objective unified or its risks from being equalized, the result is fairly easy to forecast. Your client will seek a new partner who meets two qualifications: a lowered risk and a more advantageous objective. In the process, the client may find a partner who can deliver improved objectives from greater profits or from a quicker flow of profits, with new monies coming on stream sooner or existing costs being reduced faster.

When objectives fall out of harmony, and the inequality of risk becomes uncomfortably oppressive, the emergence of a new partner is inevitable. It is invariably a lengthy process for clients to decide to open up a search, evaluate candidates, and make a selection. But it always seems sudden to the consultants on whom the boom is lowered. Their lack of awareness is proof of how far the partners have drifted apart.

The history of terminated partnerships is filled with surprised consultants. "Why, it was only yesterday," they say, "that he was telling me what a great guy I was—how much we had been through together, and how he would always be indebted to me." If it was not "only yesterday," it was "only last week" or "last month." The epitaph is generally the same: how great it *was*. Meanwhile, for the new partner, the benediction is how great it is *going to be*.

Appendix A

How Customer Managers Budget Capital Expenditures

When a capital expenditure is proposed, the project must be evaluated and the economic consequences of the commitment of funds determined before referring it to a budget committee for review or to management for approval. How are the economic consequences described best? This is done in two steps:

First, set up the project in a standard economic model that can be used for all projects, no matter how dissimilar to each other they may be.

Benefits − costs = cash flow

To describe the formula in accounting terminology:

Benefits:	*Projected cash revenue from sales and other sources*
Costs:	*Nonrecurring cash outlays for assets, plus recurring operating expenses*
Cash flow:	*Net income after taxes plus noncash charges for such items as depreciation*

Thus, if the model were stated in a conventional accounting form, it would appear as:

Add:	*Cash revenues projected (benefits)*
Less:	*Cash investment outlay and cash expenses (costs)*
Total:	*Cash flow*

The "benefits less costs" model is usually developed within the framework of the company's accounts and supported with prescribed supplementary schedules that show the basis of the projection.

COMPARING COSTS AND BENEFITS

It should be apparent that in setting up an economic model, the conventional accrual accounting concept, net income after taxes, has been abandoned. The established criterion is cash flow—net income after tax plus noncash charges.

The second step is to adjust the cash flow into relevant financial terms. The cash flow projected for each year over the life of the proposal has to be translated into financial terms that are valid; that is, the annual dollar cash flows must be translated into a common dollar value in a base year. This concept must not be confused with attempts to adjust for changes in the purchasing power of the dollar.

The calculations assume no significant erosion in the purchasing power of the dollar. Should this occur, the time-adjusted common dollar concept may require adjustments for the diminished real value (purchasing power) of future dollar payments. The common dollar value concept used in capital budgeting adjusts for time value only. This is achieved through the development of the concept of discounting and present value that will be examined in the next section. An examination of how a simple two-step model is developed will illustrate the rationale of this approach.

In the first step, we set up the economic model: Benefits minus costs equals cash flow. To complete this model, we need to identify in detail all economic benefits and costs associated with the project. Benefits typically take the form of sales revenues and other income. Costs normally include nonrecurring outlays for fixed assets, investments in working capital, and recurring outlays for payrolls, materials, and expenses.

For each element of benefits and costs that the project involves, we forecast the amount of change for each year. How far ahead do we forecast? For as long as the expenditure decision will continue to have effects: that is, for as long as they generate costs and significant benefits. Forecasts are made for each year of the project's life; we call the year of decision "year 0," the next year "year 1," and so on. When the decision's effects extend so far into the future that estimates are very conjectural, the model stops forecasting at a planning horizon (ten to fifteen years), far enough in the future to establish clearly whether the basis for the decision is a correct one.

We apply a single economic concept in forecasting costs: opportunity cost. The opportunity cost of a resource (asset) is what the company loses from not using it in an alternative way or exchanging it for another asset. For example, if cash has earning power of 15 percent after taxes, we speak of the cash as having an opportunity cost of 15 percent. Whenever an asset is acquired for a cash payment, the opportunity cost is, of course, the cash given up to acquire it. It is harder to establish the opportunity cost of committing assets already owned or controlled. If owned land committed to a project would otherwise be sold, the opportunity cost is the aftertax proceeds from the sale. The opportunity cost of using productive equipment, transportation vehicles, or plant facilities is the incremental profit lost because these resources are unavailable for other purposes. If the alternative to using owned facilities is idleness, the opportunity cost is zero. Although opportunity costs are difficult to identify and measure, they must be considered if we are to describe the economic consequences of a decision as accurately as possible. An understanding of this concept of opportunity cost is probably the most critical to this economic analysis and is generally quite foreign to the manager.

At the end of the first step, we have an economic model for the project's life showing forecast cash flows for each year. In the second step, we convert the results into financial terms that are meaningful for decision making. We must take into account the one measurable financial effect of an investment decision left out in step 1: time. Dollars shown in different years of the model cannot be compared since time makes them of dissimilar value. We clearly recognize that if we have an opportunity to invest funds and earn 15 percent a year and we have a choice of receiving $1,000 today or a year from now, we will take the $1,000 today, so that it can be invested and earn \$150. On this basis, \$1,000 available a year from now is worth less than \$1,000 today. It is this adjustment for time that is required to make cash flows in different years comparable; that is, discounting.

This time value of funds available for investment is known as the opportunity cost of capital. This should not be confused with the cost of raising capital—debt or equity—or with the company's average earnings rate. Like the opportunity cost of any resource, the opportunity cost of capital is what it will cost the company to use capital for an investment project in terms of what this capital could earn elsewhere.

The opportunity cost of capital is alternatively referred to as the minimum acceptable rate of interest, the marginal rate of interest, the minimum rate of return, the marginal rate of return, and the cost of capital. Whatever the term used, and they are used loosely and interchangeably, it reflects the rate the corporation decides it can be reasonably sure of getting by using the money in another way. It is developed through the joint efforts of management, which identifies relevant opportunities, and the controller, who translates management's judgment into a marginal rate.

Another simple economic concept must be introduced: incremental cost, sometimes called differential cost or marginal cost. By definition, it is the change in cost (or revenue) that results from a decision to expand or contract an operation. It is the difference in total cost. In performing the capital budgeting analysis, we deal with incremental costs (revenues) only. Sunk or existing costs are not relevant to the evaluation and decision.

DETERMINING PRESENT VALUE

Discounting is a technique used to find the value today or "present value" of money paid or received in the future. This value is found using the following formula:

Future dollar amount × discount factor = present value

The discount factor depends on the opportunity cost of capital expressed as an interest rate and a time period. Figure A-1 illustrates how discount factors are usually displayed. The discount factors are grouped according to the annual interest rate, expressed as the present value of $1.00, and then listed according to the year the amount comes due. The table should be read this way: When a dollar earns 10 percent per year uniformly over time, a dollar received at the end of the second year is equivalent to (worth) about 86 cents today.

To adjust the model's results for the time element, we discount both the positive and negative cash flow forecasts for each period at the company's marginal rate of return to determine their present value. This discounting process makes the forecasts equivalent in time. We can now add the present values of these cash flow forecasts to derive the net present value (NPV). The NPV is a meaningful measure of the economic consequences of an investment decision since it measures all benefits and all costs, including the opportunity cost of capital.

When the NPV of a proposed investment is determined, we are ready to decide whether it should be accepted. This is done by comparing it to the economic consequences of doing nothing or of accepting an alternative. The general rule followed in comparing alternative projects is to choose the course of action that results in the highest NPV.

Figure A-2 illustrates the cash flow forecasts and time-value calculations for a typical proposal to invest in a new project when the alternative is to do nothing, that is, to maintain liquidity rather than invest. A discount rate of 10 percent is assumed as the company's marginal rate.

Figure A-1. Present value of $1 at 10 percent.

Year	*Present Value (Today's Value)*
0–1	$0.9516
1–2	0.8611
2–3	0.7791
3–4	0.7050
4–5	0.6379

Figure A-2. Arithmetic of determining net present value (NPV).

Year	*Benefits*	*Costs*	*Cash Flow*	*PV of $1 @ 10%*	*Discounted Cash Flow*
0	$ 0	$ (500)	$(500)	1.000	$(500)
0–1	425	(200)	225	.952	214
1–2	425	(200)	225	.861	194
2–3	350	(200)	150	.779	117
3–4	250	(200)	50	.705	35
TOTAL	$1,450	$(1,300)	$ 150		$ 60 NPV

The proposed project will cost $500 in year 0, and cash operating expenses thereafter will be $200 per year for four years. Assume the cash benefits will be positive but decline over the four years and total $1,450. The cash flow is negative in the year of investment but positive in the succeeding years, and there is a net positive cash flow over the life of the project of $150 before discounting. When the cash flow forecasts are made equivalent in time by multiplying each annual cash flow by the present value of the dollar for each period, the time-adjusted cash flow is determined, and the NPV is found to be $60. The proposed investment is better than doing nothing because all costs are covered, the 10 percent opportunity cost of the corporation's funds is realized, and in addition, the project will yield an additional $60 return.

Figure A-2 indicates an NPV of $60. Depending on the cash flow and/or the discount rate, the NPV could be negative or zero. If the NPV were zero, the company would have projected earnings exactly equal to its marginal rate of 10 percent. If there were no alternative projects, and the only alternative were to do nothing, the project with the NPV of zero would be accepted because the company would earn its marginal rate of return. (As explained later, the NPV of zero would yield the discounted cash flow rate of return, that is, 10 percent.) If the NPV were negative because of an inadequate cash flow, assuming the same 10 percent marginal rate required by management, it would mean the project would earn less than 10 percent, and it would be rejected.

A number of evaluation methods are employed in capital budgeting; however, after critical examination of all methods, only the arithmetic developed in this simple model will be used to examine three methods used in evaluating capital budget proposals: (1) cash payback, (2) net present value, and (3) discounted cash flow rate of return (DCF-ROR)—sometimes referred to as the "internal rate of return."

Cash payback is commonly used by business managers evaluating investment opportunities, but it does not measure rate of return. It measures only the length of time it takes to recover the cash outlay for the investment. It indicates cash at risk. In our model there are costs of $500 committed in year 0. To determine payback, we merely add the unadjusted cash flow for each year and determine how many years it takes to get the outlay back. In the first two years $450 is recovered, and by the end of the third year $600 is recovered. By interpolation we find cash recovery to be approximately 2.3 years. It is obvious that the rational manager does not commit a large sum of money just to recover it. He expects a rate of return commensurate with the risks and his alternative use of his funds in alternative investments (opportunity cost). In our example, the calculation of payback reveals a relatively short exposure of funds and cash flow continuing beyond the payback period. It is interesting information in overall project evaluation, but it is not conclusive. Our model will automatically throw off payback as a by-product as we calculate the crucial time-adjusted NPV of the investment and DCF-ROR.

A version of cash payback is the cash bailout method. This approach takes into account not only the annual cash flow as shown in Figure A-2 but also the estimated liquidation value of the assets at the end of each year. If the liquidation value of a highly specialized project is zero, then cash payback and cash bailout are the same. But if it is assumed in our example that the liquidation value of the investment at the end of year 1 will be $275, the cash bailout would be one year (cash flow $225 plus liquidation value $275 = $500 original cash commitment).

We consider NPV as described a valid basis for determining the economic consequence of an investment decision. Many business economists use it as their sole criterion for the go–no-go decision for investment. We recognize this method as paramount throughout our analysis but prefer using it in conjunction with other measures rather than as the sole criterion.

CALCULATING RATE OF RETURN

We are now ready to examine the concept of DCF-ROR. It is completely different from the return on investment (ROI) commonly used in business. The conventional ROI is computed for an accounting period, generally on the accrual book figure; investment is taken at original cost, although it is sometimes taken at half original cost; no adjustment is made for time value when looked at in the long run.

We are talking about a very different ROR on investment: The DCF-ROR is the interest rate that discounts a project's net cash flow to zero present value. Let us expand Figure A-2, which shows a $60 NPV when a discount factor of 10 percent is used, to Figure A-3, which adds a discount factor of 18 percent and yields a $0 NPV.

The DCF-ROR is 18 percent. By definition, the DCF-ROR is the rate of return on the project determined by finding the interest rate at which the sum of the stream of aftertax cash flows, discounted to present worth, equals the cost of the project. Or, stated

Figure A-3. Arithmetic of determining DCF rate of return.

Year	*Cash Flow*	*PV of $1 @ 10%*	*Discounted Cash Flow*	*PV of $1 @ 18%*	*Discounted Cash Flow*
0	$(500)	1.000	$(500)	1.000	$(500)
0–1	225	.952	214	.915	206
1–2	225	.861	194	.764	172
2–3	150	.779	117	.639	96
3–4	50	.705	35	.533	26
TOTAL	$ 150		$ 60 NPV		$ 0 NPV

another way, the ROR is the maximum constant rate of interest the project could pay on the investment and break even. How was the 18 percent determined? By trial and error.

Many analysts use the NPV method exclusively; some use the DCF-ROR; others use the two methods to complement each other. Using NPV, positive or negative dollar values are determined with the cost of capital as the benchmark. Excess dollar PV is evaluated and a judgment is made. The DCF-ROR approach ignores the cost of capital in the calculation and determines what the ROR is on the total cash flow. The result of this approach on our example is to convert the $60 NPV into a percentage. It works out to 8 percent on top of the 10 percent that had been calculated for the NPV. Many businesspeople prefer working with the single figure of 18 percent for evaluating a project against a known cost of capital, instead of describing a project as having an NPV of $60 over the cost of capital. The two methods complement each other, and under certain circumstances one may give a better picture than the other.

Let us reexamine this special DCF-ROR to see what distinguishes it from the conventional ROR. It is time-adjusted to base year 0, so that all dollars are on a common denominator basis; it is calculated absolutely on a cash flow basis; the investment is a definite time-adjusted value; the ROR is determined at a single average rate over the total life of the investment. Certain implications of this statement require explanation.

The DCF-ROR is calculated over the full life of the project, and the accountant's yearly ROI cannot be used to test the success/failure of the new investment. If the planned life of a project is ten years, and if it can be segregated from other facets of the operation, the DCF-ROR has meaning only when the full economic life of the project is completed. However, in this case it is possible to monitor results on a year-to-year basis by examining the actual dollar cash flow and comparing it with the projected cash flow.

The one thing that disturbs business managers most with the DCF-ROR concept is the underlying mathematical assumption that all cash flows are reinvested immediately and constantly at the same rate as that which yields an NPV of 0. In our example in Figure A-3, 18 percent was used as the discount factor as a constant. Another case could just as easily have indicated a 35 percent ROR, with the implicit assumption that the cash flow was reinvested at 35 percent. But if the earning experience indicates a cost of capital of 10 percent, how can we reconcile the assumption that we can continue to earn 35 percent on the incremental flow?

Even though a company's average earnings reflect a cost of capital of 10 percent, the demands on incremental new investment may well have to be 18 to 35 percent to compensate for investments that fail to realize projected earnings. Opportunities to invest at 18 percent or 35 percent are not inconsistent with the average earnings of 10 percent. However, if it is felt that a projected rate of return of 18 percent, in our example, is a once-in-a-lifetime windfall and no new opportunities can be found to exceed the average 10 percent rate, then we are in trouble with our DCF-ROR concept. The reinvestment rate will not stand up. In this situation we have to combine both NPV and ROR to explain the situation in this way: The 10 percent ROR of this project covers the opportunity cost of money and throws off an additional $60 cash flow. If other projects of the same magnitude can be found so that the total cash flow generated can be reinvested at the same rate, there would actually be an ROR on the project of 18 percent (the DCF-ROR). The lack of other good investment opportunities is a constraint on the full earning capacity of the project.

We have examined three methods of evaluating investment opportunities. Cash payback evaluates money at risk. Present value measures the ability to cover the opportunity cost of an investment on a time-adjusted basis of money and indicates by an NPV whether the project under consideration will yield a "profit" or a "loss." The DCF-ROR is an extension of the NPV concept and translates it into a single ROR that, when compared with the opportunity cost of capital, gives a valid basis for evaluation.

Since NPV and DCF-ROR concepts take into account the opportunity cost of capital through the discounting technique, it may be stated as a principle that all projects under consideration where this opportunity cost is covered should be accepted. This proposition is both theoretically and practically sound, but three factors need to be considered: How do you determine the minimum acceptable ROR (the opportunity cost of capital) to select the proper discounting factor? How can you assume no constraints on the supply of capital so that all worthwhile projects can be accepted? How do you take risk into account when examining indicated results? These questions are examined in the next three sections.

USING COST-OF-CAPITAL GUIDELINES

How do you determine the minimum acceptable ROR (cost of capital) used in discounting? The cost of capital concept used here is not the same as the cost of borrowing. This is probably the most critical factor in the evaluation process. It is a unique and personal rate to each company. There is no guide to look to in other companies. Two companies looking at a potential investment, say an acquisition, may place two completely different values on it. To Company A, with a minimum required ROR of 10 percent, the investment could be attractive, while to Company B, with a required ROR of 25 percent, the investment would be totally unacceptable. The difference is centered in the cost of capital to each company, its opportunity ROR—the rate that can be expected on alternative investments having similar risk characteristics. An example of the arithmetic involved in reaching this conclusion can be seen when we modify Figure A-2 to include both a 10 percent and 25 percent discount factor and assume that both Companies A and B are the sole potential bidders for an investment with an asked price of $500 and a net cash flow of $150 (see Figure A-4).

The investment is very attractive to Company A but completely unacceptable to Company B—it would realize less than its objective of 25 percent. If Company A were in a position to know the cost of capital of Company B, it would know that Company B would not bid at all for this investment. Company A would know that it would be the sole bidder.

If a company has successfully earned 25 percent on the capital employed in it, an investment opportunity, to be attractive, would have to yield at least that rate. The 25 percent represents the cost of capital to that company, and an investment opportunity offering only 15 percent would be rejected. A second company with a

Figure A-4. Comparison of NPV using 10 percent and 25 percent discount factors.

		(A)		(B)	
Year	*Cash Flow*	*PV of $1 @ 10%*	*Discounted Cash Flow*	*PV of $1 @ 25%*	*Discounted Cash Flow*
0	$(500)	1.000	$(500)	1.000	$(500)
1	225	.952	214	.885	199
2	225	.861	194	.689	155
3	150	.779	117	.537	81
4	50	.705	35	.418	21
TOTAL	$ 150		$ 60 NPV		$ (44) NPV

10 percent cost of capital would find the same 15 percent potential attractive and accept it. Thus the same 15 percent opportunity investment is attractive to one and unattractive to the other. Both companies analyzing the identical situation reach different logical conclusions.

Cost of capital is *always* considered to be the combined cost of equity capital and permanent debt. We evaluate economic success/failure of a project without regard to how it is financed. Yet we know that money available for investment is basically derived from two sources: debt, with its built-in tax saving so that its cost is half the market price for money (assuming a 50 percent tax rate), and equity, which has as its cost the opportunity cost of capital of the owners.

It is necessary at times to break down the combined cost of capital into its components of cost of debt capital and cost of equity capital to put it in terms understandable to the businessperson who commonly measures results in terms of return on equity. To illustrate this cost of capital concept, we will assume that a corporation is owned by a single individual whose investment objectives are clearly defined. The total capitalization of the company is $100, made up of $30 permanent debt capital and $70 owner's equity capital. If preferred stock was outstanding at a fixed cost, it would be treated the same as debt. The aftertax interest rate of the debt money is 2.75 percent. The aftertax dollar return on the combined debt and equity capital of $100 under various operations would appear as shown in Figure A-5.

To restate these dollars as rates of return on the investment of $100, $30 debt, and $70 equity, the percentage return on capital would be as shown in Figure A-6.

If the company has been earning an average of $10 on the total investment of $100, and the cost of debt is $.825, the earning on owner's equity is $9.175. Stated as a rate of return, the $10 earned on $100 is 10 percent return on the total investment (combined cost of capital), and because of the leverage built into the capital structure with long-term debt, the $9.175 earning on equity yields a return on equity of 13.11 percent (cost of equity capital). When there is a 30 percent debt structure and the average cost of debt is 2.75 percent after taxes, we can readily convert return

Figure A-5. Aftertax dollar income on investment of $100.

Income on Total Investment (Before Interest)	*$30 Debt × 2.75% Cost of Debt Capital*	*$70 Equity Income on Owner's Equity*
$ 8.00	$0.825	$ 7.175
9.00	0.825	8.175
10.00	0.825	9.175
11.00	0.825	10.175
12.00	0.825	11.175

Figure A-6. Aftertax rate of return on investment of $100.

Rate of Return	*Cost of Debt Capital*	*Rate of Return on Owner's Equity*
8%	2.75% ($0.825 ÷ $30)	10.25% ($7.175 ÷ $70)
9	2.75	11.68
10	2.75	13.11
11	2.75	14.54
12	2.75	15.96

on total investment into return on equity by reading our table. It is quite simple to create similar tables for each company and its debt/equity ratio (e.g., with a 50/50 ratio and debt cost of 2.75 percent, a 10 percent return on total investment yields a 17.45 percent return on equity capital). If there is the opportunity to invest the company funds in alternative situations or reinvest the funds in the business and continue to earn at least 10 percent on the combined debt/equity funds, we would describe this as the opportunity cost of capital. This is the critical rate used in discounting: The discount rate used to determine NPV and the benchmark for comparing DCS-ROR are based solely on the combined cost of capital. The ROR to the stockholders can be derived and compared with their opportunity cost, that is, the ability to invest their funds elsewhere and earn at least the same rate.

EVALUATING PROFIT PROJECTS

Evaluating components of an investment program for a company is complex at any time. There are many categories of investment: (1) revenue-producing projects, (2) supporting facilities projects, (3) supporting services projects, (4) cost-savings projects, and (5) investments required to comply with public authority that will yield no return. Each must be evaluated to determine its incremental consequence.

When a project is isolated from the rest of the operation, evaluation is relatively clear. But sometimes a planned major investment embraces several auxiliary projects which, evaluated by themselves, are not very meaningful. When this occurs, it is necessary to construct a master model that includes all of the projects. Some of the auxiliary projects may not come into being for several years after the main investment is made, and may or may not produce a new positive cash flow. The master model in simple form may take on the appearance shown in Figure A-7 if individual projects of the types (a), (b), and (c) above are assumed (the figures do not add up—only format is demonstrated).

If the three projects are interrelated, they should be projected

Figure A-7. Master project.

Project	*NPV*	*0*	*1*	*2*	*3*	*4*	*5*	...	*15*
(a)	100	(30)	(2)	14	14	13	13		40
(b)	40	—	—	(15)	5	5	5		20
(c)	(26)	—	(2)	(2)	(4)	(4)	(4)		(10)
TOTAL	114	(30)	(4)	(3)	15	14	14		(50)

as a single entity. In our example, (a) is assumed to be a major facility that to be successful needs (b) added in three years as supporting facilities; (b) would have no basis for existence if (a) were not created. Project (c) may possibly be identified as a new computer/information system that will produce only costs, but would not exist if (a) and (b) were not created. All costs and all benefits for all corollary investments need to be projected as far into the future as possible to get a true evaluation. Investment evaluations that are made of a project with all the certainty of a DCF percentage can be grossly misleading if the supporting investment of satellites is not taken into account. Actually, these are not separate investments. There is only one—Project abc. The evaluation has to be of the new single entity. The postaudit can be of only the conglomerate single entity (abc).

Projects of the cost-savings category are generally easiest to identify and evaluate. There are relatively clear-cut choices: Invest $40,000 today for new labor-saving machines that will reduce labor costs $12,000 per year; the machines will last eight years, and quality of performance will be unchanged. Determine the NPV and/or DCF-ROR and accept/reject. Such investment opportunities constantly arise, but it is almost impossible to project them as part of a master project. As a result, such investments are evaluated as isolated investment opportunities that may occur in three years, or eight years, or never. When they occur, if of major proportions, they affect the potential return on the total investment.

A cost-incurring project, such as spend $100,000 to prevent air pollution or be closed up, is one of the few black-and-white decisions a manager faces. Ideally it would be expensed. It may have to be capitalized and written off and in addition have annual related operating expenses. This nondiscretionary investment falls into the same general category as a support project. The cash flow is always negative and must be included as an integral part of the master investment. A large enough commitment may sharply reduce the original projection, and a revision may be necessary.

On the basis of the techniques for evaluating planned capital investment, it is now possible to move to the methods of selecting among projects. As noted previously, in theory, selecting among projects is easy. Invest in anything that, when discounted at the appropriate marginal rate, will yield a positive NPV. Practically, for many reasons, there are constraints on capital in the minds of most managers. Let us look at the project selection problems that are involved for projects under consideration in a particular risk category when there is a limit on capital.

We have selected the NPV method as the best approach to analyze proposed projects of varying lives. Comparing projects under the DCF-ROR method can be misleading because of the different life factor and the reinvestment factor inherent in each ROR. Excess NPV avoids this difficulty. When the various projects are converted into a profitability index, selection is further facilitated. The profitability index is the ratio of the NPV to investment. For example:

$$\frac{\text{Present value of expected benefits}}{\text{Investment}} = \frac{\$132{,}000}{\$100{,}000} = 1.32$$

In selecting projects when a limit is imposed upon the amount available for investment, we look for the combination that will maximize combined NPV without exceeding the imposed limit. We know that we have reached this goal when we can no longer increase the combined NPV by substituting one project for another and still satisfy the constraint.

A way to achieve a satisfactory combination of projects is through trial and error. As a guide, we can use the profitability index (see Figure A-8). However, such ratios are not foolproof. This is illustrated where there are three possible projects requiring a total of $1,500 in initial outlays, but where $1,000 is the imposed limit.

Figure A-8. Profitability index.

Project	Net Present Value	[÷]	Investment: Cash Outlay	[=]	Profit-ability Index
A	$1,000		$600		1.67
B	700		500		1.40
C	500		400		1.25

The choice is between investment in A + C (cash outlay $1,000) or investment in B + C (cash outlay $900). Since A + C have a combined greater NPV than B + C ($1,500 vs. $1,200), A + C should be selected even though C's ratio (1.25) is less than B's ratio (1.40). Such differences are common. The profitability index must always be used judiciously. When there are numerous projects to choose among, the combining process becomes more difficult.

Appendix B

How Customer Managers Make Lease-vs.-Buy Decisions

Ownership may be effected through outright purchase without indebtedness, through financed purchase, or, for all practical purposes, through a long-term lease. In an outright purchase, the buyer has full rights of ownership. Where the buyer obtains financing (before or after the purchase), his ownership is diminished by the limitations on his control of the asset. For example, in an installment purchase, the buyer's right to sell may be restricted by the lender's lien. In a long-term lease, the lessee lacks not only the right to sell but also all of the asset's residual rights, except for any purchase options available.

Short-term leasing is an alternative to the above forms of ownership. Here, the lessee is freed of almost all the risks of ownership, including obsolescence and maintenance, but the amount of the rental naturally reflects these advantages. In choosing between some form of ownership (as described above) on the one hand and short-term leasing on the other, management is faced with such *operational* considerations as maintenance, risk of obsolescence, and the degree of control desired. If ownership is selected, a further decision—this one involving essentially *financial* considerations—is necessary with regard to the form of ownership. It is with this second, basically more complex, decision that this appendix is concerned. The focus will be specifically on the choice between outright purchase and long-term lease as a form of ownership.

CHOOSING OUTRIGHT PURCHASE VS. LONG-TERM LEASE

The decision to buy or lease can be made only after a systematic evaluation of the relevant factors. The evaluation must be carried out in two stages: First, the advantages and disadvantages of purchase or lease must be considered, and second, the cash flows under both alternatives must be compared.

Figure B-1 shows the principal advantages and disadvantages of leasing from both the lessor's and lessee's standpoint. This listing is only a guide. For both parties, the relative significance of the advantages and disadvantages depends on many factors. Major determinants are a company's size, financial position, and tax status. For example, to a heavily leveraged public company, the disadvantage of having to record additional debt may be considerable, even critical; the disadvantage may be insignificant to a privately held concern.

ANALYZING CASH FLOWS

A cash-flow analysis enables the potential lessee to contrast his cash position under both buying and leasing. This is essentially a capital budgeting procedure, and the method of developing and comparing cash flows should conform to the company's capital budgeting policies and practices. There are several comparison criteria in current use, among which the three most common are rate of return, discounted cash flow, and net cash position.

1. *Outright purchase.* The cash outflows in an outright purchase are the initial purchase price or, assuming the asset is purchased with borrowed funds, as is almost always the case, the subsequent principal and interest on the loan. There will also be operating expenses, such as maintenance and insurance, but these

Figure B-1. Leasing advantages and disadvantages.

Lessee Advantages

• *One hundred percent financing of the cost of the property (the lease is based on the full cost) on terms that may be individually tailored to the lessee.*

• *Possible avoidance of existing loan indenture restrictions on new debt financing.* Free of these restrictions, the lessee may be able to increase his base, as lease obligations are generally not reflected on the balance sheet, although the lease obligation will probably require footnote disclosure in the financial statements. (It should be noted, however, that a number of the more recent loan indentures restrict lease commitments.)

• *General allowability of rental deductions for the term of the lease, without problems or disputes about the property's depreciable life.*

• *Possibly higher net book income during the earlier years of the basic lease term than under outright ownership.* Rental payments in the lease's earlier years are generally lower than the combined interest expense and depreciation (even on the straight-line method) that a corporate property owner would otherwise have charged in the income statement.

• *Potential reduction in state and city franchise and income taxes.* The property factor, which is generally one of the three factors in the allocation formula, is reduced.

• *Full deductibility of rent payment.* This is true notwithstanding the fact that the rent is partially based on the cost of the land.

Lessee Disadvantages

• *Loss of residual rights to the property upon the lease's termination.* When the lessee has full residual rights, the transaction cannot be a true lease; instead, it is a form of financing. In a true lease, the lessee may have the right to purchase or renew, but the exercise of these options requires payments to the lessor after the full cost of the property has been amortized.

• *Rentals greater than comparable debt service.* Since the

(continues)

Figure B-1. (Continued)

lessor generally borrows funds with which to buy the asset to be leased, the rent is based on the lessor's debt service plus a profit factor. This amount may exceed the debt service that the lessee would have had to pay had he purchased the property.

• *Loss of operating and financing flexibility.* If an asset were owned outright and a new, improved model became available, the owner could sell or exchange the old model for the new one. This may not be possible under a lease. Moreover, if interest rates decreased, the lessee would have to continue paying at the old rate, whereas the owner of the asset could refinance his debt at a lower rate.

• *Loss of tax benefits from accelerated depreciation and high interest reductions in early years.* These benefits would produce a temporary cash saving if the property were purchased instead of leased.

Lessor Advantages

• *Higher rate of return than on investment in straight debt.* To compensate for risk and lack of marketability, the lessor can charge the lessee a higher effective rate—particularly after considering the lessor's tax benefits—than the lessor could obtain by lending the cost of the property at the market rate.

• *The lessor has the leased asset as security.* Should the lessee have financial trouble, the lessor can reclaim a specific asset instead of having to take his place with the general creditors.

• *Retention of the property's residual value upon the lease's termination.* The asset's cost is amortized over the basic lease term. If, upon the lease's expiration, the lessee abandons the property, the lessor can sell it. If the lessee renews or purchases, the proceeds to the lessor represent substantially all profit.

Lessor Disadvantages

• *Dependence upon lessee's ability to maintain payments on a timely basis.*

• *Vulnerability to unpredictable changes in the tax law that*

(1) reduce tax benefits and related cash flow or (2) significantly extend depreciable life. The latter measure would lessen the projected return upon which the lessor based his investment.

• *Probable negative after-tax cash flow in later years.* As the lease progresses, an increasing percentage of the rent goes toward nondeductible amortization of the principal. Both the interest and depreciation deductions (under the accelerated method) decline as the lease progresses.

• *Potentially large tax on disposition of asset imposed by the Internal Revenue Code's depreciation recapture provisions.*

---

items are excluded from the comparison because they will be the same under both purchase and leasing, assuming a net lease. The charge for depreciation is a noncash item. Cash inflows are the amount of the loan, the tax benefit from the yearly interest and depreciation, and the salvage value, if any.

2. *Leasing.* The lessee's cash flows are easier to define than the buyer's. The lessee pays a yearly rental, which is fully deductible. The lessee will thus have level annual outflows offset by the related tax benefit over the lease period. Salvage or residual value does not enter the picture because the lessee generally has no right of ownership in the asset. Figure B-2 is a comparison of cash flows developed under both buying and leasing.

3. *Comparing the cash flows.* Once the annual cash flows from outright purchase and leasing have been developed, the next step is to contrast the flows by an accepted method (such as discounted cash flow) to determine which alternative gives the greater cash benefit or yield. In so doing, some consideration must be given to the effects of changes in the assumptions adopted. Examples could include a lengthening by the IRS of the depreciation period or a change in interest rates. In this manner, a series of contingencies could be introduced into the analysis, as follows: Assume a ten-year life and a borrowing at 10 percent. If outright purchase is better by x dollars, then:

- A two-year increase in depreciable life reduces the benefit of outright purchase to $(x-y)$ dollars.

Figure B-2. Buying vs. leasing: a comparison of cash flows.

	Buy								Lease			
Period	Debt Service[a]	Principal Repayment	Interest Payment	Depreciation[b]	Interest Plus Depreciation	Tax Benefit at 50 Percent	Aftertax Cash Cost	Cumulative Aftertax Cash Cost	Rental[c]	Tax Benefit at 50 Percent	Aftertax Cash Cost	Cumulative Aftertax Cash Cost
1	$ 11,507	$ 3,614	$ 7,893	$ 12,500	$ 20,393	$10,197	$ 1,310	$ 1,310	$ 10,990	$ 5,495	$ 5,495	$ 5,495
2	11,507	3,912	7,595	11,667	19,262	9,631	1,876	3,186	10,990	5,495	5,495	10,990
3	11,507	4,234	7,273	10,833	18,106	9,053	2,454	5,640	10,990	5,495	5,595	16,485
4	11,507	4,583	6,924	10,000	16,924	8,462	3,045	8,685	10,990	5,495	5,495	21,980
5	11,507	4,961	6,546	9,167	15,713	7,856	3,651	12,336	10,990	5,495	5,495	27,475
6	11,507	5,370	6,137	8,333	14,470	7,235	4,272	16,608	10,990	5,495	5,495	32,970
7	11,507	5,813	5,694	7,500	13,194	6,597	4,910	21,518	10,990	5,495	5,495	38,465
8	11,507	6,292	5,215	6,667	11,882	5,941	5,566	27,084	10,990	5,495	5,494	43,960
9	11,507	6,810	4,697	5,833	10,530	5,265	5,242	33,326	10,990	5,495	5,495	49,455
10	11,507	7,372	4,135	5,000	9,135	4,567	6,940	40,266	10,990	5,495	5,495	54,950
11	11,507	7,979	3,528	4,167	7,695	3,848	7,659	47,925	10,990	5,495	5,495	60,445
12	11,507	8,637	2,870	3,333	6,203	3,101	8,406	56,331	10,990	5,495	5,495	65,940
13	11,507	9,349	2,158	2,500	4,658	2,329	9,178	65,509	10,990	5,495	5,495	71,435
14	11,507	10,120	1,387	1,667	3,054	1,527	9,980	75,489	10,990	5,495	5,495	76,930
15	11,507	10,954	553	833	1,386	693	10,814	86,303	10,990	5,495	5,495	82,425
	$172,605	$100,000	$72,605	$100,000	$172,605	$86,302[d]	$86,303		$164,850	$82,425	$82,425[e]	

Notes

(a) $100,000 of debt borrowed at 8%. The debt service, payable quarterly in arrears, will be sufficient to amortize the loan fully over 15 years. (b) Asset cost of $100,000 will be depreciated over 15 years using the sum-of-the-years method. It was assumed that the asset had no salvage value. (c) Rental on a 15-year lease will be payable quarterly in arrears. The rental was based on an interest factor of 7¼%. It was assumed that the lessee's credit would require 8% interest. Since the lessor retains the depreciation benefits of the asset, he can charge a rent based on 7¼% even though he has financed the acquisition at 8%. (d) Present worth of $86,302 cost of buying, at 8%, is $41,198. (e) Present worth of $82,425 cost of leasing, at 8%, is $47,034.

Comment on notes (d) and (e). When comparing the cumulative aftertax cash costs, buying is the more expensive alternative by about $4,000. However, present valuing the annual outflows results in buying's being the most economical alternative by approximately $6,000.

- An upward change in interest rate reduces the benefit of outright purchase to $(x - z)$ dollars.

Probabilities could be assigned to the contingencies; for example, that the depreciable life could be extended by two years, 30 percent; or that interest rates could rise by one half a percentage point, 10 percent. Once the contingencies have been quantified, an overall probability of achieving the expected saving can then be calculated.

It must be stressed that the rate of return—the product of the cash-flow analysis—is not the exclusive or even, in some cases, the main determinant in deciding whether to buy or lease. Such factors as impact on financial statements, desire for operational flexibility, and loan restrictions, as well as other accounting, tax, economic, and financial considerations, may be collectively at least as important. These aspects are essentially nonquantitative, but they can be evaluated with a satisfactory degree of accuracy by weighing the advantages and disadvantages.

CONSIDERING TAXES

There are two ways in which a lease can be treated for tax purposes: as a true lease or as a form of financing. If the lease is viewed as a true lease, the lessee is entitled to a deduction, in the appropriate period, for his annual rental expenses. (Normally, the appropriate period is the period in which the liability for rent is incurred, in accordance with the terms of the lease, granted that the timing of the liability is not unreasonable.) If the lease is viewed as a form of financing, the lessee is deemed the property's equitable owner and is thus permitted to deduct the depreciation and interest expense.

The test the IRS applies to determine whether a lease is a true lease or a form of financing is basically an evaluation of the purchase options. If the lessee can purchase the property for less than the fair market value or for an amount approximately equal to what the debt balance would have been had the asset been bought outright, the transaction is viewed as a financing agreement. If the lessee has a purchase option in an amount substantially exceeding the probable fair market value or the debt balance, the transaction would probably be recognized as a lease.

PROTECTING THE BUSINESS RELATIONSHIP

A final aspect of the lease-buy decision relates to the lessor-lessee relationship. If the lessor encounters financial difficulties, under certain circumstances the prospective lessee can be adversely affected. That is, depending upon the terms of the lease and the lessor's financing arrangements, a lender might look to the property to satisfy a default by the lessor. Although careful wording of the agreement can afford a measure of protection, it is essential that the lessee look into the prospective lessor's financial condition, business reputation, and client relationships. If the findings are favorable, negotiations may be carried out with a minimum of delay and expense. If the findings are unfavorable, the prospective lessee might still wish to proceed, relying on the protective clauses in the agreement, or he might abandon the lease (at least with that party) entirely.

INDEX